Belonging Through a Psychoanalytic Lens

Watching people protest, one hypothesis is that underlying these actions for specific justifiable causes is a sense of wishing to belong, of wishing not to be alone. Recent knowledge from patients and empirical research shows the importance of belonging to groups to both psychological and physical well-being. The problems of many students, minority group members, immigrants, terrorists, and lonely people are linked to an insufficient sense of belonging. Whereas psychoanalytic theory has focused on the need for a secure attachment to a primary caretaker, it has failed to note the importance of a sense of belonging to the family group, a friendship group, a community, a religious group, a nation-state, etc.

This book demonstrates the difficulties faced by those who immigrate, those who never feel a sense of their true selves as belonging in a family or a cohesive professional group, and the difficulties of psychoanalysts themselves in knowing where they belong in patients' lives. The problems of breaking up marital and professional relationships as well as our relationship with the Earth are also discussed.

Freudian theory rejected the idea of a sense of "oneness" with humanity as being infantile. Recent developments regarding the similarities between meditational practices and psychoanalysis have questioned Freud's idea. This book shows the importance of an interpersonal/relational psychoanalysis focusing on real relationships and not simply one that examines inner conflicts. It will be useful to psychologists, other mental health practitioners, social scientists, and anyone with normal struggles in life.

Rebecca Coleman Curtis, PhD, is Professor Emerita of Psychology, Adelphi University, and Faculty, White Institute in New York. She is the author of *Desire, Self, Mind, and the Psychotherapies: Unifying Psychological Science and Psychoanalysis*, editor or co-editor of eight books, and has published numerous articles and given over 100 presentations around the world.

Belonging Through a Psychoanalytic Lens

Edited by
Rebecca Coleman Curtis

Routledge
Taylor & Francis Group

LONDON AND NEW YORK

First published 2021
by Routledge
2 Park Square, Milton Park, Abingdon, Oxon OX14 4RN

and by Routledge
52 Vanderbilt Avenue, New York, NY 10017

Routledge is an imprint of the Taylor & Francis Group, an informa business

British Library Cataloguing-in-Publication Data
A catalogue record for this book is available from the British Library

Library of Congress Cataloging-in-Publication Data
Names: Coleman Curtis, Rebecca, editor.
Title: Belonging through a psychoanalytic lens / edited by Rebecca Coleman Curtis.
Description: Milton Park, Abingdon, Oxon; New York, NY: Routledge, 2021. |
Includes bibliographical references and index. |
Identifiers: LCCN 2020037510 (print) | LCCN 2020037511 (ebook) |
ISBN 9780367671983 (hardback) | ISBN 9780367671969 (paperback) |
ISBN 9781003130192 (ebook)
Subjects: LCSH: Belonging (Social psychology) | Social isolation.
Classification: LCC HM1111 .B45 2021 (print) |
LCC HM1111 (ebook) | DDC 302.5/45–dc23
LC record available at https://lccn.loc.gov/2020037510
LC ebook record available at https://lccn.loc.gov/2020037511

ISBN: 978-0-367-67198-3 (hbk)
ISBN: 978-0-367-67196-9 (pbk)
ISBN: 978-1-003-13019-2 (ebk)

Typeset in Times
by Newgen Publishing UK

Contents

Contributors

Elizabeth Allured, PsyD, is on the teaching faculty at Adelphi University's post-graduate training programmes in Psychoanalysis and Psychotherapy and at the Suffolk Institute for Psychoanalysis and Psychotherapy. She has published articles on the environmental crisis from a psychoanalytic perspective and has been presenting her ideas about this issue at international psychoanalytic conferences since 2007. Dr Allured is the co-president of Climate Psychology Alliance North America and has a clinical practice in Port Washington, New York.

Ehud E. Avitzur, PhD, is a clinical psychologist in private practice and an adjunct professor in the psychology department at York University, Toronto, Canada. Before devoting his time to clinical psychology, he took part in research teams in the fields of children of schizophrenic mothers (the Danish longitudinal study led by Melnik and Schulzinger), war-related PTSD (Israel, led by Zehava Solomon), and attachment (with Dr Mario Mikulincer). His academic work has been presented in various international conferences and published in well- known journals such as the *Journal of Personality and Social Psychology*.

Emad El-Din Aysha is an academic and English-language journalist currently residing in Cairo, Egypt. He was born in the United Kingdom to Arab parents and attained his MA (1997) and PhD (2001) in International Studies at the University of Sheffield. He has taught a variety of topics, including Arab society and history, at the American University in Cairo, the British University in Egypt, and Heliopolis University for Sustainable Development. He has also written on Middle Eastern politics, business, economics, and arts and literature for the *Egyptian Gazette*, *Daily News Egypt*, *Egypt Oil & Gas*, *Mada Masr*, *Cairo Scene*, and *The Levant* (a publication of the Beirut Center for Middle East Studies). He has published on Samuel Huntington's Clash of Civilizations thesis, with other articles following on topics as varied as Michel Foucault and the Iranian revolution, the psychoanalysis of Erich Fromm, and Islamist suicide terrorism. Apart from terrorism and political violence, he is currently researching the Arab Spring and its aftermath from a media ecology perspective and topics related to Orientalism and indigenous literature.

Daniel Berry, RN, MHA, has practised as a Registered Nurse in New York City since 1987. He worked for almost two decades in community-based programmes and private care for HIV/AIDS and substance abuse populations. He is currently the Assistant Director of Nursing for Risk Management at a public hospital serving homeless and undocumented victims of street violence, drug addiction, and severe traumatic injuries. He is co-author with Mark Borg and Grant Brenner of *Relationship Sanity: Creating and Maintaining Healthy Relationships* and is a co-author with Drs Borg and Brenner of chapters on the costs and benefits of bad relationships.

Robert Besner, PsyD, is a psychologist and graduate of the Toronto Institute of Contemporary Psychoanalysis. He is a longtime student and practitioner of Buddhism and has a longstanding interest in exploring the relationship of western psychology and Buddhist meditation. Recently he has written on integrating both of these systems with our experience of our bodies. His focus is on the psychological and sacred aspects of our lives and on integrating scientific knowledge with traditional wisdom.

Mark B. Borg, Jr., PhD, is a community psychologist and psychoanalyst, founding partner of the Community Consulting Group and Irrelationship Group, and a supervisor of psychotherapy at the William Alanson White Institute. He has written extensively about the intersection of psychoanalysis and community crisis intervention. He has been in private practice in New York City since 1998. He is the author of *Don't Be A Dick: Change Yourself, Change Your World* (2019) and *Community Psychoanalysis: Developing a Model of Psychoanalytically-Informed Community Crisis Intervention* (in press).

Arthur Caspary, PhD, is in private practice in Toronto and is faculty at the Toronto Institute for Contemporary Psychoanalysis and the Toronto Institute for Child and Adolescent Psychoanalytic Psychotherapy, adjunct faculty at the University of Toronto, Department of Psychiatry, and does teaching and clinical supervision at the Hospital for Sick Children. He is a member of the International Psychoanalytical Association, the Canadian Psychoanalytic Association, the Toronto Psychoanalytic Association, and the Toronto Society for Contemporary Psychoanalysis and Fellow in Psychoanalysis at the Canadian Psychology Association. His publications include articles on therapeutic action and psychoanalytic perspectives on film.

Nina E. Cerfolio, MD, Assistant Clinical Professor of the Icahn School of Medicine at Mount Sinai Hospital in New York City, is an award-winning internationally recognized board certified psychiatrist and psychoanalyst practising in New York City. In practice for over thirty years, Dr Nina Cerfolio's approach integrates traditional psychiatric training with her decades of spiritual training. She is a champion of fitness for greater mental health and an active writer and speaker advocating mindful psychiatry to help others transcend emotional suffering and adversity to find healing, happiness, and fulfilment.

Renée Cherow-O'Leary, PhD, is President of Education for the 21st Century, a consulting group in New York and Los Angeles that develops curriculum and conducts research on issues related to media, education, literacy, literature, and social change. She is a professor in the Arts, Culture and Media Program at Rutgers University, Newark Campus, and teaches the Senior Colloquium on the topics of "Imagery, Identity and Culture" and "The Human-Machine Connection". Dr Cherow-O'Leary co-chaired the Interfaith Committee at Congregation B'nai Jeshurun in New York City for five years and is currently on the board of Lab Shul in New York, an artist-driven, progressive congregation that is "everybody friendly", where she is a leader of GENERATE, a year-long experience for older adults involving text study, new ritual development, and the building of community. She is the author of many academic articles and several psychoanalytic papers presented at international conferences, as well as an article on older women to be published in the journal *Psychoanalytic Inquiry*.

Rebecca Coleman Curtis, PhD, is Professor Emerita of Psychology, Adelphi University, and Faculty and Supervisor, William Alanson White Institute. She is the author of *Desire, Self, Mind, and the Psychotherapies: Unifying Psychological Science and Psychoanalysis* (2009) as well as the editor of *Self-Defeating Behaviors* (1989) and *The Relational Self* (1991) and co-editor of *Taboo or Not Taboo in Psychoanalysis and Psychotherapy: Forbidden Thoughts, Forbidden Acts* (2009), *How People Change* (1991), *On Deaths and Endings: Psychoanalysts' Reflections on Finality, Transformations, and New Beginnings* (Gradiva Award Winner 2008), *On Loneliness and Longing* (2011), and *Understanding and Coping with Failure* (2013). Dr Curtis has published over 50 articles, chapters, and reviews; given over 100 presentations in North and South America, Africa, Asia, and Europe; and appeared on 8 television shows. Dr Curtis works on the integration of clinical psychology, psychoanalysis, and scientific psychology.

Joy A. Dryer, PhD, wears three hats as a psychologist/psychoanalyst in private practice in New York City and Poughkeepsie, NY. First, as a clinician, she works with individuals, families, and couples using PACT – Psychobiologic Approach to Couples Therapy. Second, as a divorce mediator and collaborative divorce coach, she helps couples decide whether to separate and what their next steps are. Third, as an educator and former adjunct associate professor, she continues to supervise graduate students and speaks nationally and internationally. In her writings she applies psychodynamic principles to applied clinical areas such as couples' therapy and divorce. She wrote a monthly blog at HuffPost/JoyADryerPhD, and her last chapter was "Secure Uncoupling: Healthy Divorce through Three Neuroscience Principles" in anthology *The Divorce Puzzle: Connecting the Pieces Collaboratively* (2017).

Michelle Flax, PhD, CPsych, is Supervising Psychoanalyst and Faculty, Toronto Institute for Contemporary Psychoanalysis; Executive and Faculty, Advanced

Training Program in Psychoanalytic Psychotherapy, Toronto Psychoanalytic Society; and works in private practice. She has multiple publications in books of past Joint International Conferences and has refereed journal articles in *Psychoanalytic Quarterly*, *Gender and Psychoanalysis*, and the *Canadian Journal of Psychoanalysis*.

Jenny Kahn Kaufmann, PhD, is Faculty, Training and Supervising Analyst at the William Alanson White Institute and is on the editorial board of the Institute's journal, *Contemporary Psychoanalysis*. Early in her career she ran groups for patients and clinicians who had experienced suicides. Her focus on the topic and more generally upon very early loss, trauma, and mourning is reflected in her teaching, writing, and clinical work. Recently she has co-presented a series of papers with Peter Kaufmann on "Emerging from the Shadows of Parental Narcissism". Their most recent paper, given at the White Institute in September 2019, was "The Costs of Emerging from the Shadows of Narcissism: We Have Met the Enemy and It Is Us!"

Robert Langan, PhD, is Supervising and Training Analyst, Faculty, and Fellow at the William Alanson White Institute in New York City, where he maintains a private practice. He lectures nationally and internationally and has published widely in professional journals. His ongoing interest in Buddhism and psychoanalysis led to *Minding What Matters: Psychotherapy and the Buddha Within* (Boston: Wisdom, 2006).

Dayi Lian graduated from the New York University Global MSW programme and received her psychoanalytic training from the William Alanson White Institute of psychiatry, psychoanalysis, and psychology. She has abundant clinical experience working with patients from various racial, ethnic, and social backgrounds in both China and the United States. She is a member of the American Psychoanalytic Association and the China-American Psychoanalytic Alliance. She also teaches psychodynamic psychotherapy and supervises in this orientation.

John V. O'Leary, PhD, is Faculty and Supervisor at the William Alanson White Institute and Staff Psychologist at the Columbia Presbyterian Hospital in New York City.

Alison Ross, MPH, PhD, graduated with a BA from Stanford University with Honors and Academic Distinction and received a master's degree in public health from Yale University's School of Medicine. She received her PhD in psychology from the Graduate Center at the City College of New York and her certificate in psychoanalysis from New York University's Program in Psychotherapy and Psychoanalysis. She currently has a full-time private practice in New York City and is an adjunct associate professor at the clinical psychology programme at City College. She has been quoted on topics such as depression, anxiety, and psychotherapy in numerous popular online periodicals such as *World News & Report*, *Women's Health*, and *SELF Magazine*. She has given presentations on the topic of "home" in New York, Florida, California, and Israel. She is currently a member of the American Psychological Association and the International Association for Relational Psychoanalysis and Psychotherapy.

John Sloane, MD, is a psychiatrist and psychoanalyst in private practice in Toronto. He is an Assistant Professor in the Department of Psychiatry, University of Toronto, and a supervisor at the Toronto Institute for Contemporary Psychoanalysis (TICP) and the Institute for the Advancement of Self Psychology (IASP). He is a long-time participant in the TICP Relational Study Group as well as a theological discussion group called "Challenging Christianity". He has published articles on psychotherapy supervision (*Progress in Self Psychology*); the interface between psychoanalysis and Christianity (*Free Associations*); sleep, death, and rebirth in the countertransference (*Contemporary Psychoanalysis*); the loneliness of the analyst; the failure to become a training analyst; and wounded healer/healing wounder.

Sara L. Weber, PhD, is a clinical psychologist-psychoanalyst, Adjunct Assistant Professor and Clinical Consultant at the New York University Postdoctoral Program in Psychotherapy and Psychoanalysis, and faculty of the William A. White Child and Adolescent Psychotherapy Training Program. In 2006 she founded the Contemplative Studies Project, in which she teaches study groups and serves as the chair. She has lectured internationally and published papers on the interpenetration of Buddhism and psychoanalysis, some of which appear in *Psychoanalysis and Buddhism: An Unfolding Dialogue* and in *Freud and the Buddha: The Couch and the Cushion*. Her private practice is in Brooklyn, New York.

J. Gail White, PhD, is Supervising Psychoanalyst and Faculty, Toronto Institute for Contemporary Psychoanalysis, and works in private practice. She is a former lecturer at the University of Toronto and York University. She has multiple publications in books of past Joint International Conferences and has published in *Gender and Psychoanalysis*.

Brent Willock, PhD (Clinical Psychology, University of Michigan), spent several years in the Department of Psychiatry at the University of Michigan, after which he relocated to Toronto to become Chief Psychologist at the C. M. Hincks Treatment Center; Adjunct Faculty, York University; Associate Faculty Member, University of Toronto; President, Toronto Institute and Society for Contemporary Psychoanalysis; board member, the Canadian Institute for Child and Adolescent Psychoanalytic Psychotherapy; Faculty, Institute for the Advancement of Self Psychology; and a member of the advisory board, International Association for Relational Psychoanalysis and Psychotherapy. He is on the editorial board of the *Journal of Infant, Child, and Adolescent Psychotherapy*, Rodopi Press's Contemporary Psychoanalytic Book Series, and Rowman & Littlefield's Psychoanalytic Studies: Clinical, Social, and Cultural Studies book series; he is also associate editor of *Psychoanalytic*

Dialogues. Dr Willock is the author of *Comparative-Integrative Psychoanalysis and the Wrongful Conviction of Oscar Pistorius: Science Transforms Our Comprehension of Reeva Steenkamp's Shocking Death*. He is the author of chapters in books published by Routledge and Karnac and articles in journals such as the *Journal of Contemporary Psychotherapy*, *Psychoanalytic Psychology*, the *International Journal of Psychoanalysis*, the *Journal of Personality Assessment*, the *Canadian Journal of Psychoanalysis*, and *Psychoanalytic Dialogues*. His contributions have been honoured with awards from the Ontario Psychological Association, the American Psychological Association (Div. 39), the Canadian Psychological Association, the National Association for the Advancement of Psychoanalysis, the Sonia Shankman Orthogenic School, the University of Chicago, and the Child Analytic Program of the Chicago Institute for Psychoanalysis; International Federation for Psychoanalytic Education.

Zvi Steve Yadin, PhD, PhD, PMHNP, is in private practice in psychiatry and psychoanalysis on Long Island, New York. He holds doctorates in clinical psychology and Hebrew literature. He was an adjunct professor at Adelphi University and Long Island University and a clinical instructor in the Department of Psychiatry at Stony Brook University, New York.

Laura C. Young, PhD, is a clinical psychologist in private practice in Ottawa, Ontario, Canada. She works with adults, adolescents, and children, primarily providing psychotherapy. She is also a psychoanalytic candidate currently completing the final stages of psychoanalytic training through the Toronto Institute for Contemporary Psychoanalysis.

Acknowledgements

Many of the chapters in this volume are based on papers presented at a conference on Belonging held in Halifax, Nova Scotia in August 2018 organized by Ionas Sapountzis, Lori Bohm, Rebecca Curtis, Brad Peters, Michael Stern, and Rhonda Sternberg. The event was sponsored by the Adelphi Society for Psychoanalysis and Psychotherapy, the Psychoanalytic Clinicians of Nova Scotia, the Psychoanalytic Society of the New York University Postdoctoral Program, the Toronto Society for Contemporary Psychoanalysis, and the William Alanson White Psychoanalytic Society. At Routledge, Kate Hawes and her associates such as Hannah Wright facilitated the creation of this volume.

1   Introduction

You are not alone

Rebecca Coleman Curtis

> No man is an island.
> John Donne

As I write these words, I find myself thinking of Tom Hanks all alone on an uninhabited island in *Cast Away*, his FedEx plane having crashed in a storm. He speaks to the volleyball that also washed ashore, calling it "Wilson." For four years he spoke with and argued with Wilson until he constructed a raft and they sailed away. At one point Wilson becomes untethered, and although Tom, playing a character called Chuck, swims after him, he is unable to retrieve him. Returning to his raft, he breaks down in tears. I heard from someone else that everyone in his movie theater cried then, too. And to a lonely patient who had seen the film, I suggested that she talk to Wilson. She did, and this became a joke between us over time.

Many people on our planet speak to God. But religion is declining in the West these days (September 5, 2016, https://blogs.lse.ac.uk), so to whom do we speak? As a child I sang the song, "I come to the garden alone, when the dew is still on the roses. And he walks with me and he talks with me, and tells me I am his own." Although I have plenty of people with whom to speak, this song is still with me as I walk out to my pond and talk to the anolis … and to the universe … and to you.

Gregory Walton and colleagues (Walton & Cohen, 2007) have shown that when people shift blame for negative events from "It's just me" to "I'm not alone, and there are others going through it," the 45-minute intervention in his research study leaves participants feeling happier, improves their health and leads to less activation of negative stereotypes. The intervention has a dramatic effect on achievement, especially for minority students and women. In the experiments, upper-class students at Stanford believed they were writing for freshmen about their own struggles and how they got through them.

Isolation, loneliness and low social status can harm a person's subjective sense of well-being, as well as his or her intellectual achievement, immune function and health. Research shows that even a single instance of exclusion can undermine well-being (Bernstein & Claypool, 2012), IQ test performance and self-regulation

(Baumeister, Twenge, & Nuss, 2002; DeWall, 2013; Stillman & Baumeister, 2013), although the effects can be complicated.

"We don't have a word for the opposite of loneliness, but if we did, I could say that's what I want in life," stated Marina Keegan (2014, p. 1) in *The Opposite of Loneliness*. This was Marina's final message to her college classmates, distributed in a special edition of the *Yale Daily News* at the 2012 Commencement exercises. After her death in a car accident five days after she graduated, her words of inspiration resounded around the globe to 1.4 million viewers in 98 countries.

Wondering why students on many college campuses were name-calling and engaging in other undesirable behaviors, Annie Murphy Paul, a psychology journalist, questioned whether a lack of discipline explained these students' actions. What are these students really asking for? Why are they protesting? she asked (2015). Reflecting on her experiences at Yale and trying to understand what was going on elsewhere as well, she concluded that what these students really wanted was a "sense of belonging."

There are other books on the topic of belonging from political, sociological and social psychological perspectives. In research psychology, there even exists a measure for "The Sense of Belonging" (Bavely, 1995). The subject is so important that there are also measures for social belonging, school belonging, group belonging, academic belonging, sport belonging, community belonging and belonging in the congregation! The current volume examines the topic—not from empirical research, however, but from experiences in psychoanalysis and from psychoanalysts' own points of view. Writing about the process of assimilation experienced by immigrants, Boulanger (2004) previously criticized this as an impossible task, saying, "Assimilation is a construct belonging to a world of discrete categories and forced choices; you belong to one culture or another, you are an insider or an outsider, a member or an 'other'" (p. 289). Two special issues of the *International Journal of Psychoanalytic Self Psychology* were dedicated to the theme of one of their recent conferences, "Where do I feel at home? Belonging and Not Belonging." The first of these special issues relates considerably to the Arab-Israeli socio-political-ethnic context of belonging, as their conference was held in Jerusalem. There are articles including topics such as the interplay between "house" and "home," language, literature and of a single self belonging to two enemy cultures. The second issue has articles that are autobiographical narratives and articles dealing with the issue of bilingual patients with monolingual analysts, religion in psychoanalytic sessions, bullying, differences in appearance between parent and child, and being gay in a psychoanalytic community. They are all quite stimulating.

After such a feast you may worry that there is nothing left for psychoanalysts to address. Don't despair! The articles briefly described above were written by psychoanalysts in the tradition of Heinz Kohut, whereas the chapters in the current volume are written by interpersonal-relational psychoanalysts whose theories derive more from the early ideas of Harry Stack Sullivan and Erich Fromm, among others, and more recently from Stephen Mitchell, Jay Greenberg, Donnel Stern, Philip Bromberg, Lou Aron and Jessica Benjamin, among many (cf. Curtis, 2019; Willock, 2007).

The current volume is separated into six parts. In the first section are three chapters dealing with the timely topic of immigration. This is fitting, as most were based on presentations at a conference held in Halifax, a city that houses an immigration museum portraying many experiences of immigrants who arrived at that port, many getting on the railroad right across the street to populate remoter areas of Canada.

Alison Ross, after reflecting on the meaning of "home" in various literary works, describes her work with two immigrants: one who was traumatized in Russia but had never spoken about it, and another who become panicked at the thought of moving to another country without realizing how disturbing her move to the United States without knowing English had been as a child. Adoption can result in many issues if a person believes they were not wanted by their own parents. Ehud Avitzur writes about a patient who was adopted whom he saw after he himself immigrated to Canada. His own issues and those of the patient converged. This is also the case in the next chapter by Dayi Lian. An immigrant from China to the United States, she was conducting psychotherapy with many immigrants to the US from various countries. Sometimes her appearance helped her patients to feel a sense of safety; sometimes it led to devaluation.

Belonging and loneliness is the subject of the next three chapters. Emad El-Din Aysha attributes Islamic terrorism simply to the failure of the nation-state in the Arab world. But he states that the crisis of Isis is really a crisis of belonging. Citing Erich Fromm's ideas about defenses against the insecurity of modernity, he states that the sheer brutality of the movement enables one to inflate oneself psychologically so that the "world outside becomes small in comparison." Nina E. Cerfolio then attempts to understand the issue of terrorism, specifically in the case of Chechen nationals and the Tsarnaev brothers who carried out the Boston bombing. Citing Hannah Arendt, she notes that loneliness and humiliation are often at the root of terrorism. The loneliness of the travelers in the film *Lost in Translation* is discussed by Arthur Caspary. These individuals manage to connect in a meaningful way after meeting in a Japanese bar. Many of us can relate to the sense of loneliness one feels in a foreign country where no one even speaks our language.

The next section is about groups, culture and the environment. The unity of a group of boys at a scout camp is the topic of the chapter by Robert Langan. The fictionalized interchange among the group provides for the triadic interplay of modes of being: "self as subject, self as object, and a self as an interbeing." He does this in the context of Freud's (1919/1961) experiential distinction between the *heimlich* and the *unheimlich*, the comfortably homey and the disconcertingly uncanny. Next, Zvi Yadin describes the early feelings of belonging in a kibbutz and how, with time and other changes, the atmosphere has regrettably, from his perspective, deteriorated. The original culture of "we" was reinforced by the common efforts to bring forth fruit from land that was often barren, as well as the fight for survival against attacks by neighboring Arab militias. Cultural and economic changes led to the slow erosion of the "we" as Israel transformed into a more capitalist and individualist society. This paper analyzes vignettes of modern Hebrew literature related to the kibbutz as it follows the transformation from members' sense of belonging, with total commitment to the collective, to the privatization of their property and a radical shift in social and economic values, focusing on the psychological aspects of these changes. It is always difficult to part from a primary identity group or tribe, as Renée Cherow-O'Leary discusses in her chapter on an interfaith marriage, a practice becoming much more common for Jews, a group that she was born into. Her marriage to a Jewish man did not last, but she found herself welcomed into her second husband's Catholic family. Joy Dryer discusses how couples can uncouple well and poorly. She includes relevant information from neuroscience regarding safety, attachment, and emotional regulation to support her ideas. Elizabeth Allured, a psychoanalyst in a private practice, documents her experiences getting involved in a climate change group that was willing to take on this issue and what they have done to try to make a difference. With her fervent interest in this topic, she felt rather isolated in the psychoanalytic community. Fortunately, she found others who shared her deep concerns and has been educating psychoanalysts and their readers ever since.

The following two chapters concern belonging and mindfulness. Robert Besner explores the relationship between Buddhism and psychoanalysis and how both practices intend to increase conscious awareness, with mindfulness therapies growing in popularity and leading people to expand their sense of belonging with others and the universe. Sara Weber in the next chapter describes the glee she experienced as a child writing her name and address, starting with her street, town, state, US, and eventually Earth and universe. Embedded in a Buddhist perspective, she explains that the Buddhist word *shunyata* is composed of *shunya*, which means "empty," and *ta*, which means "belonging to," although it frequently gets translated misleadingly as "emptiness."

The next section concerns self-organization and how it relates to a sense of belonging. Mark Borg and Daniel Berry describe the sort of belonging and not belonging that can occur in groups and how it can lead to confusion about one's identity. This chapter follows the experience of five psychoanalytic professionals who become involved serially in a project to write a book jointly—an experience that brought to light the themes of anxiety around closeness and trust, which were finally resolved through mutual exposure of vulnerability and a willingness to contain conflict rather than to act it out in ways that would have been destructive to their ongoing collaboration. The difficulties of a patient leading a pseudo-life are described by Laura Young. The patient had taken care of her mother instead of herself and later tried to belong in high school by behaving as someone she did not really feel was herself. In psychoanalysis she was becoming clearer about who she wished to be, but her continued use of marijuana, although less than previously, still often left her in a fog. Jenny Kahn Kaufmann then describes two patients: one who controls others by spilling—saying too much—the other who gave up her life for her narcissistic mother. With a mother who was inattentive, a patient struggled to find her place in the world and a sense of belonging by saying more than what was appropriate. The other became very private, had to hide, and felt terror about being seen. Kaufmann puts these cases into the context of a movement from belonging *to* a mother and belonging *with* a mother developmentally. She describes finding the courage to hold back in herself and not say everything that she wanted to—in spite of group pressures—as a developmental achievement.

The psychoanalytic process itself and its institutions are the subjects of the final part. Michelle Flax and Gail White describe the paradoxical position of psychoanalysts in terms of belonging in the patient's life. They describe as an example a psychoanalyst attending the funeral of a patient. John O'Leary discusses the issue of class in psychoanalysis. Because most psychoanalysts are either middle or upper-middle class, the poor may have a defensive feeling with analysts. He discusses his feelings in one case where the patient was of low income, hording and stalking, and had experienced bed bugs. He discusses reasons why some analysts may not wish to work with the poor, even though his own institute has services for low-income people. He thinks the issue of class has been largely ignored in psychoanalysis.

Noting the partisan politics that occur within psychoanalytic institutes, the issue of some people belonging to their institute and others not can be as intense there as in the rest of social-political life. Brent Willock claims that the divisions within psychoanalysis are hampering it as a discipline and the intellectual functioning of its adherents. He argues for a comparative-integrative psychoanalysis. John Sloane discusses his decision to leave his psychoanalytic institute. He did not believe he was sufficiently respected and found himself more respected elsewhere. This was a very hard decision, but he felt liberated afterwards.

The groups to which we feel we most belong will probably always be of major concern for people. Today, at the same time as the prominence of identity politics, we have others who simply say that they are "citizens of the world." Some humans are including more and more in their basic identity groups, with animals even being included for many. With these issues in mind, we invite you to read what some psychoanalysts have to say as they add their voices to the topic of belonging and not belonging.

As Chaundry (2019) noted in her book *Haunting Paris*, death doesn't end our thirst for a human touch. As death beckons, we still long to belong with others.

References

Baumeister, R. F., Twenge, J. M., & Nuss, C. K. (2002). Effects of social exclusion on cognitive process: anticipated aloneness reduces intelligent thought. Journal of Personality and Social Psychology, 83, 817–827.

Bavely, T. (1995). Sense of belonging scale. doi:10.1037/t03562-000. Retrieved October 28, 2019.

Benjamin, J. (2004). Beyond doer and done to: an intersubjective view of thirdness. *Psychoanalytic Quarterly, 73*(1), 5–46.

Bernstein, M. J., & Claypool, H. M. (2012). Not all social exclusions are created equal: emotional distress following social exclusion is moderated by exclusion paradigm. *Social Influence, 7,* 113–130.

Boulanger, G. (2004). Lot's wife, Cary Grant, and the American dream: psychoanalysis with immigrants. *Contemporary Psychoanalysis*, *40*, 353–372.

Boulanger, G. (2015). Seeing double, being double: longing, belonging, recognition, and evasion in psychodynamic work with immigrants. *American Journal of Psychoanalysis*, *75*, 287–303.

Chaundry. M. (2019). *Haunting Paris*. New York: Doubleday.

Curtis, R. C. (2019). Relational psychoanalytic psychotherapy. In S. B. Messer & N. Kaslow (Eds.), *Essential psychotherapies* (pp. 71–108). New York: Guilford Press.

DeWall, C. N. (Ed.). (2013). *The Oxford handbook of social exclusion* (pp. xvi, 31–42). New York: Oxford University Press.

Donne, J. (1839). Meditation XVII. In H. Alford (Ed.), *The works of John Donne* (Vol. 3, pp. 574–575). London: John W. Parker.

Freud, S. (1961). The uncanny. In J. Strachey (Ed. & Trans.), *The standard edition of the complete psychological works of Sigmund Freud* (Vol. 17, *An infantile neurosis and other works*, pp. 217–256). London: Hogarth Press. Originally published 1919.

Keegan, M. (2014). *The opposite of loneliness*. New York: Scribner.

Murphy Paul, A. (2015, November 11). The Yale controversy is really about belonging. Time Magazine. Retrieved from https://Time.com/yale-controversy-belonging

Stillman, T. F., & Baumeister, R. F. (2013). Social rejection reduces intelligent thought and self-regulation. In C. N. Dewall (Ed.), *Oxford handbook of social exclusion* (pp. 132–139). New York: Oxford University Press.

Walton, G., & Cohen, G. L. (2007). A question of belonging: race, social fit, and achievement. *Journal of Personality and Social Psychology*, *92*(1), 82–96. doi:10.1037/0022-3514.92.1.82

Willock, B. (2007). *Comparative-integrative psychoanalysis: a relational perspective for the discipline's second century*. New York: Taylor & Francis.

Part 1
Belonging and immigration

2   Two immigrants' search to find home

Discovering authentic ways of being and belonging

Alison Ross

There's no place that resonates more deeply or meaningfully within us than the place we call home. From the moment we're born, the longing for home is ever present inside us (Winnicott, Shepherd, & Davies, 1986). When we're young children and throughout our lives, our experiences of home—and the sense of belonging and connection that underlies them—shape fundamental aspects of our inner emotional world (Seiden, 2009). Ideally, home is a place that anchors us, literally and emotionally. But because the world today is fast paced and ever changing, transient and increasingly anonymous, the comfort, safety and stability that home can provide has never been harder to find or hold onto (Turkle, 2011). The many things that home can be—a point of reference, a familiar presence, a place of reunion and return—are no longer constants we can rely on (Iyer, 2000).

In speaking of home I'm referring to the actual physical spaces we inhabit as well as the thoughts and feelings, memories and meanings that we associate with these places. If I were to ask you what home means to you, you might think of the house you're currently living in or the childhood home you grew up in, the city or town where you were raised, the country you're originally from or the country you have emigrated to where you've settled down and established roots.

Our thoughts and feelings about home include an amalgam of experiences—tangible and intangible, conscious and unconscious—that we carry inside us and that become a core part of who we are. I call these internalized experiences the *Home Within*. The *Home Within* is the prism through which we see ourselves and others and make sense of the world around us. It's the inner touchstone that defines us and guides us as we journey through life. The household we're raised in as a child lays the foundation for the fundamental conflicts, relational constructs and psychological dynamics in our *Home Within*, and all of its facets impact on every aspect of our lives. It influences the decisions we make, the personal and professional paths we take, and the ways we navigate the changes and challenges we face.

"Home is where we start from," the title of Winnicott's book (1986) tells us—a quotation the editors of the book appropriated from a work by T. S. Eliot (1940) because it affirms the premise that unifies this psychoanalyst's unique intrapsychic concepts about childhood and home. "Home is where we start from" is a profound universal truth and, at the same time, takes into account the diversity of experiences of home that each of us has and the impact they have on us as children as well as the adults we eventually become. This observation is no less true today than when it was first written, yet I want to include an addendum: "Home is where we start from," but the places many of us end up calling home are likely to be very different and far from the places where we were originally born. I say this because these days more people than ever before are leaving their country of origin in the hope of establishing a new home in a new homeland (Iyer, 2017). At last count, 232 million people—3 percent of the entire world's population—are living in countries other than the ones they're originally from (Cilluffo & Cohn, 2018). In this chapter, I will describe how my psychotherapeutic work with two immigrants made it possible for them to establish a new inner sense of home and, as a result, discover more authentic ways of being and belonging.

Pico Iyer, an essayist and novelist, has given a great deal of thought to these transglobal migrations and their impact on the meaning of home. He himself embodies the multiplicity of meanings that home can have: the son of parents of Indian ancestry, he was born and raised in England, moved to America in his early twenties, where he obtained his US citizenship, yet where he currently lives and the place he thinks of as home is a small village in the countryside of Japan. Iyer states in a 2017 Ted Talk about home:

> I am not rooted in a place, I think, so much as in certain values and affiliations and friendships that I carry everywhere I go; my home is both invisible and portable.
>
> (Iyer, 2017)

To my way of thinking, Iyer is speaking of the *Home Within* and the ways in which our experiences of home—inside ourselves and in the external world—contribute to how connected we feel to ourselves, to others and to the world around us.

Thoughts about home are often on the minds of immigrants, whether they've recently immigrated to a foreign country or have been living there a long time (Grinberg & Grinberg, 1989). Questions that get at issues of belonging and connection are often at the heart of the day to day as well as the overarching issues they wrestle with. The kinds of experiences that immigrants have involve a complex interweaving of intrapsychic and external factors (Akhtar, 1999). While the actual circumstances of their new environment count for a lot—does the person have an affordable, safe place to live? Can they find work to support themselves and their family? Are they welcomed or shunned in the country they've emigrated to?—fundamental characteristics of their *Home Within*—its stability, integrity and emotional accessibility—play a key role in determining how well they manage the losses, absences and feelings of dislocation and disconnection that are an inevitable part of relocating from one country to another.

André Aciman, an Egyptian-born novelist who is the author of *Call Me by Your Name* (2017) and *Out of Egypt* (2007), came to the US as a teenager. He describes his efforts to lessen his feelings of homesickness in this way:

> I had come here, an exile from Alexandria, doing what all exiles do on impulse, which is to look for their homeland abroad, to bridge the things here to things there, to write about the present so as not to write off the past.
>
> (Aciman, 1997, p. 37)

My work with two immigrants, Miriam and Dmitri, illustrates how understanding a person's experiences of home—in the past and in the present—allows for the recognition and integration of painful experiences that have previously been disavowed.

Miriam was a Polish American immigrant who sought therapy because she had begun having panic attacks. She was thirty-nine years old, a successful book editor and the happily married mother of two young sons. "A few days ago, I was giving a presentation at work and all of a sudden, I could feel my heart racing, my hands shaking, I could barely think straight," she told me. "Recently I've been on edge all of the time worrying that at any moment a catastrophe is going to happen; that everything in my life is going to fall apart."

Miriam told me that she was born in Warsaw and lived there until she was eight years old, when her parents decided to immigrate to New York City, where she'd lived ever since. Becoming a US citizen at the age of eighteen solidified her sense of herself as an American and New York City as her home. Miriam said that she was baffled by the panic attacks she'd been having, since as far as she could tell, everything in her life was going well. When I asked her if anything new or unexpected had recently happened, she told me that her husband, Aaron, had been offered a job heading up his firm's business offices in Barcelona, Spain. But she didn't think her panic attacks were connected to that, since she and Aaron had spent a number of years traveling abroad before deciding to settle down to raise a family. It didn't make sense, she said, that the idea of relocating would be causing her to feel so upset, but then as an afterthought she added:

> But the truth is I don't want to move. I love the home that Aaron and I have built for ourselves and the life we've created for our children here. Leaving everything that's stable and familiar feels overwhelming. Moving to Barcelona means I'd have to live the life of an immigrant all over again.

Miriam's words "live the life of an immigrant all over again" stayed with me, and in the next session I asked her to tell me more about the experiences she'd had as a child immigrating to the US. In the months that followed, what became apparent in our sessions was how traumatic her experiences as a child immigrant had been. When Miriam and her parents arrived in the US, they stayed with distant relatives they barely knew in a tiny, overcrowded apartment in a desolate, run-down neighborhood in Brooklyn. Miriam didn't understand what the English-speaking people around her were saying. She was surrounded by strangers and spending time in places that were entirely unfamiliar to her. Her parents—single-mindedly focused on their own struggles adjusting to a new life—barely registered her distress and paid little attention to her emotional needs. She felt overwhelmed, confused and scared a lot of the time. Her parents' decision to enroll her in an elite Yeshiva worsened her feelings of disconnection and isolation, since many of her classmates were from well-to-do families—Miriam's parents were struggling and could hardly make ends meet—and many of the classes were conducted in Hebrew, a language she wasn't fluent in. She felt like an outsider who didn't fit in or belong anywhere.

Aspects of Miriam's home life compounded these feelings. Her mother was a demanding, highly critical person whose exacting standards she never seemed to meet. "My mother was on this relentless campaign to make me into the kind of daughter she wanted me to be," Miriam explained. "In her eyes, I was never thin enough, beautiful enough, or devoted enough to her needs to warrant her approval or praise."

Miriam dealt with the situation she found herself in by investing all of her energies into being an excellent student. When she was accepted at her top choice university after graduating from the Yeshiva, she left home to live on campus. She did well in her classes, made a few close friends and during her sophomore year started dating Aaron.

While there were times through the years when Miriam wrestled with feelings of insecurity, anxiety and self-doubt, it was only recently that these feelings had become overwhelming and ultimately unmanageable. What Miriam and I came to understand over the course of our many sessions together was that the acute sense of fear and foreboding she felt was connected to her early childhood years as an immigrant, which had been resurrected in response to Aaron's job offer. The prospect of leaving home and moving someplace new stirred up painful feelings— of fear, loneliness and abandonment—that until then dissociation had rendered inaccessible (Bromberg, 1998).

Revisiting this time in Miriam's life made it possible for her to become aware of this long-buried aspect of her *Home Within*, which had been the prism through which she had been viewing the prospective move. As we worked on this in her therapy sessions, Miriam came to understand that she was viewing this experience from the perspective of a young child whose sense of home was so precarious and ambiguous that it left her feeling ill-equipped to handle this life-changing event. Recognizing this enabled her to access the inner and external resources she, in fact, had. That is, that she was a smart, capable, resilient adult who would be making this move with a supportive, loving spouse. What Miriam also recognized was that being a mother herself with two young sons had added to the complicated mixture of feelings she was wrestling with. She saw herself in her sons and feared for their well-being. She didn't want them to be subjected to the traumatic experiences that she'd had.

Becoming aware of these dynamics and understanding how her childhood experiences of home were impacting her as an adult lessened the hold that they had on her. That is to say, reconfiguring her *Home Within* by allowing into consciousness the extent to which her childhood experiences of home were coloring her view of herself and her expectations of the move to Barcelona enabled Miriam to see Aaron's job offer in a much more positive light. In one of our last sessions, I asked her how she felt about her and Aaron's decision to leave New York City and move to Barcelona.

"It no longer feels like the end of the world, but as an exciting opportunity," Miriam responded. "I'm still a little nervous and uncertain about it, but what I've come to understand is that it doesn't matter where you are, home is what you make of it."

What I learned about Dmitri the first time we met was that he was a 22-year-old gay man who had left Russia the previous year after graduating from the Moscow Institute of Physics and Technology. Since coming to America he'd been earning a living waiting tables at a Russian restaurant in midtown Manhattan. He had friends he felt close to and a boyfriend he'd been seeing for the past several months. He explained that his reason for seeking therapy was because "a horrible thing" had happened to him in Russia; it was the reason why he had decided to immigrate to America and leave a country and a family he loved. "One night," Dmitri told me, haltingly and with tears in his eyes,

> I was coming out of the Metro when three guys jumped me and started punching and kicking me. One of them was screaming that he was going to kill me because I was gay. Someone saw the fight and called the police. I was sent to the hospital and while I was there one of the policemen who'd shown up that night came to my bedside and told me that if he'd known I was gay he never would have stopped the beating. When he said this, I realized that no place in Russia could be home for me.

In moving to the US, Dmitri had hoped that time and distance would help him get past the assault, but to his great dismay that hadn't happened. Instead, the symptoms of Post-Traumatic Stress Disorder (PTSD) he was struggling with persisted. He continued having nightmares about the assault, disorienting flashbacks and pervasive fears that caused him to feel unsafe when he was out in the world, especially at night (Herman, 1992).

In the sessions that followed, Dmitri spoke about his having grown up in a religiously conservative, working-class town. He was an excellent student, especially in math and science, yet growing up, he'd been ridiculed and bullied by his teachers and classmates for being "too girly." Even his parents—who he felt loved and appreciated him, and with whom he frequently texted and Skyped since moving to New York City—did not object when the school administrators insisted that he endure years of a grueling acrobatics training program in the hope that it would turn him into a "more normal, masculine boy." Dmitri had dreamed of the day when he would leave his small town and go to college in Moscow, where he could blend in and no longer be targeted for being gay. The assault shattered him physically and it also shattered his dreams of there being a place in his homeland where he could feel accepted and safe.

Sharing the assault with me—something he'd kept entirely secret from his parents and friends—was, in and of itself, healing as Dmitri and I processed the traumatic experience he'd undergone. But what emerged in his therapy sessions revealed that more work needed to be done for him to truly put the past behind him. As we talked in greater detail about his home life growing up, it came as a surprise to him to realize that he'd never actually spoken to his parents about being gay. "They never asked, and I never told them," he explained matter-of-factly. Understanding the meaning of their shared yet unacknowledged agreement to never speak of his sexuality at home was pivotal in Dmitri's understanding that his parents' silence had instilled in his *Home Within*—without his realizing it—feelings of guilt and shame about his homosexuality.

His country's and church's denunciation of his sexuality had fostered in him a determination to stand his ground about an essential part of his identity. Yet hidden underneath were disavowed feelings of shame and guilt that he hadn't known were there. He realized that the tight-knit, loving household his parents had provided for him had also conveyed an implicit message that he had taken to heart, which was that there must be something wrong with his being gay if no one in his family ever spoke of it. Dmitri was surprised to realize that because of this assumption about his parents' silence, some part of him had believed he deserved the assault, and it was this realization that helped lessen its far-reaching aftereffects.

With my encouragement, months into Dmitri's therapy he spoke to his parents about this aspect of his home life with them. Both parents, open and forthcoming in their responses, assured Dmitri that their silence was born out of fear and a wish to protect him, and not because they didn't love, respect and accept him for who he was: a smart, brave young gay man who was pursuing his own life on his own terms.

This conversation with his parents and then in the following months with other important people in Dmitri's life (e.g., acknowledging his homosexuality in a conversation with his boss at the restaurant rather than allowing it to remain unspoken yet understood) helped him feel more at home with himself and in the world at large. In time, the lingering effects of the beating he'd suffered began to diminish until eventually the nightmares and flashbacks disappeared.

> Everyone back home believes that being gay is a shameful thing. I didn't realize how much of that message I'd taken in. But now that I know about it, I can choose to reject it because I don't believe that's right. I want to be the kind of man who embraces who he is. I don't want to live a life where I'm hiding from myself or from anyone else.

Dmitri's realization that his parents' silence was not a condemnation of his sexuality but a loving effort to protect him, to keep secret in their strict, punitive community information they knew was dangerous for others to know, was transformative in altering an aspect of his *Home Within*; the internalized homophobia he had been living with all his life (Adams, Bell, & Griffin, 2007).

Focusing on the meaning of home in my work with Miriam and Dmitri enabled them to connect the present with the past and in doing so to uncover and understand unacknowledged aspects of their *Home Within* and its inner emotional world. Their work in therapy enabled them to bridge things here with things there *à la* André Aciman. What we all know as psychoanalysts and what was a revelation for both Dmitri and Miriam was that a person can leave behind his or her actual home and original homeland, yet their experiences of home stay with them; no matter how many miles they travel or oceans of water they cross, their *Home Within* serves as the conduit linking "what was" with "what is." Traumatic experiences from the past can have far-reaching implications. It is the work we engage in with our patients that can free them from these constraints so that they feel a greater sense of connection and belonging inside themselves and in the world at large and, as a result, live lives that are immeasurably more authentic, satisfying and joyful.

References

Aciman, A. (1997). Shadow cities. *The New York Review of Books*, 35–37.

Aciman, A. (2007). *Out of Egypt*. New York: Picador.

Aciman, A. (2017). *Call me by your name*. New York: Picador.

Adams, M., Bell, L. A., & Griffin, P. (Eds.). (2007). *Teaching for diversity and social justice* (2nd ed.). New York: Routledge/Taylor and Francis.

Akhtar, S. (1999). *Immigration and identity: turmoil, treatment and transformation*. New York: Jason Aronson.

Bromberg, P. M. (1998). *Standing in the spaces*. Hillsdale: Analytic Press.

Cilluffo, A., & Cohn, D. (2018, April 25). *7 demographic trends shaping the US and the world in 2018*. Fact Tank News in the Numbers (online). Washington, DC: Pew Research Center.

Edugyan, E. (2014). *Dreaming of elsewhere: observations of home*. Henry Kriesel Lecture Series. Alberta: University of Alberta Press.

Eliot, T. S. (1940). *Four quartets: Quartet 1, Section V. East Coker*. London: Faber and Faber.

Fairbairn, W. R. D. (1952). *Psychoanalytic studies of the personalities*. New York: Routledge.

Grinberg, L., & Grinberg, R. (1989). *Psychoanalytic perspectives on migration and exile*. New Haven: Yale University Press.

Herman, J. L. (1992). *Trauma and recovery*. New York: Basic Books.

Iyer, P. (2000). *The global soul: jet lag, shopping malls, and the search for home*. New York: Vintage Books.

Iyer, P. (2017, August). *Where is home?* TED Talk. Retrieved from www.ted.com/talks / where_is_home

Kaufman, G. (1995). *Coming out of shame*. New York: Doubleday.

Murthy, V. H. (2017, September). Work and the loneliness epidemic. *Harvard Business Review*. Retrieved from HBR.org. Reprint BG1705, 3–7.

Seiden, H. M. (2009). On the longing for home. *Psychoanalytic Psychology*, 26(2), 191–205.

Turkle, S. (2011). *Alone together: why we expect more from technology and less from each other*. New York: Basic Books.

Winnicott, C., Shepherd, R., & Davis, M. (Eds.) (1986). *Home is where we start from: essays by a psychoanalyst*. New York: W. W. Norton.

3 Self-fragmentation in relation to the need for belonging in the context of adoption and immigration

Ehud E. Avitzur

Psychoanalytically informed treatment of patients who were adopted in infancy emphasizes an important theme of abandonment: an early disruption of the continuity of maternal holding, which can have severe long-term ramifications. Brinich (1990) articulates it exquisitely: '… adoption implies losses and demands mourning of those losses. The adopted child loses the precious fantasy that he is and always has been wanted …' (p. 61).

When the disruption occurs in infancy, this potentially traumatic experience cannot be formulated (Freud, 1961; Stern, 2003). As such, that disruption and its emotional derivatives may impact the person from the depths of the unconscious. Because this is difficult to access at a conscious level, it is extremely resistant to psychotherapeutic work and difficult to work through. Treating an adopted patient, therefore, is expected to involve a slow unfolding of this primal motif of abandonment and unwantedness. Although we cannot directly observe the trauma, its shadows are often expressed in the relationship between the patient and their objects. The task of adoptive parents and of psychotherapists of adoptees isn't easy: 'to change an unwanted child into a wanted child' (Brinich, 1990, p. 61).

Psychoanalytic literature (e.g., Kirschner, 2007) suggests that a typical symptomatic behaviour among adoptees is their way of dealing with the primal abandonment by acting it out in the context of close relationships. The literature suggests a myriad of difficult-to-contain behaviours among adoptees, especially during adolescence. These behaviours imply deep doubts about oneself. As a vicissitude of feeling unwanted, the adoptee may believe that the reason for giving them up for adoption is a fundamental flaw in them. 'I am really a difficult case. This is the reason that my biological mother couldn't care for me.' Vis-à-vis the adoptive parent, the adoptee may exhibit a provocative position by challenging their acceptance: 'You'll end up regretting the adoption and break up ties with me too!' At an even deeper layer, the adoptee is yearning to be proven wrong, to be loved and cared for and to break the cycle of feeling unwanted and expecting abandonment or rejection. Adoptive parents are advised to contain the storm while securing the bonds with their child. Easier said than practised.

Therapists of adoptees often face a similar dynamic within the transference. Understanding this dynamic and working through it is an important foundation for psychoanalytic therapy with adoptees. Due to the tendency to act out this theme of abandonment, too often adoptees are oversimply regarded as having a border-line personality disorder. This is a crucial matter, as it carries implications for the conduct of treatment.

So far I have mentioned the externalizing, acting-out adoptees, who through repetition make compulsive attempts to test the boundaries of acceptance and love. But there is another way of dealing with the trauma of abandonment: by being a 'good child' who behaves extremely well within the adoptive family. These are seemingly perfect children, and their parents may feel as if they won the jackpot of the adoption lottery. Echoing other authors (such as Weider, 1977), I would like to suggest that this perfection is misleading. The struggles of these 'perfect' adoptees are just as impacted by the feeling of being unwanted and the fear of abandonment, and by a desperate need to belong, as those of the externalizing adoptees.

My patient, 'Shelagh', is a prime example of that. But first, I would like to make a detour and share with you some of my own experiences while struggling to find my place in my adopted country, Canada.

Although a well-established clinical psychologist and professor of psychology in my homeland, Israel, when I moved to Canada, I went through a stressful period of doubts about my own sense of belonging. I moved to Canada with my wife and three young children, holding in my hands a financially meagre contract to teach Introduction to Psychology at a university in Toronto. Simultaneously, as I wanted to be licensed to practice clinical psychology in Ontario, I had to go through the ordeal of formal registration. Throughout my first years in Canada, I had the feeling that this opportunity must work out – or else …

Standing in front of 600 students who spoke better English than I did was nerve-racking. Every week, I prepared a slide show on a chapter in psychology; I learned to pronounce difficult words and was looking forward to the moment during class when I could stop lecturing and show the students a video – and breathe. Disturbing thoughts bothered me: I need the students to like me. I need them to write good course evaluations; most importantly, I need to be hired next year – or else …

While going through the supervised practice (as a part of the registration process in Ontario), I kept my records defensively: detailed accounts, written in easy-to-read handwriting so as to be able to present them to the regulating body when going through an audit. I needed to make a good impression; I needed to find my place within the professional community – or else …

During the first years of my immigration, I felt that my need to belong pushed me to conform to perceived social demands to an extent that I would not have done when feeling secure in my homeland. This need to belong recruited in me a kind of conformism that I do not recall ever experiencing before. One of the losses I experienced through immigration was my Israeli peer study group on adoption. For years, we had met every month, discussing adoption through readings and cases from a psychoanalytic perspective.

This brings me back to Shelagh.

A forty-year-old paediatrician was referred to me to treat her bulimia. The trigger for seeking therapy was a separation from her boyfriend. In the first session, she told me with great shame about her struggles with food. She described her childhood as 'perfect', with loving parents. At the very end of that session, she added, 'By the way, my parents adopted me when I was six months old.'

Like when one meets an old friend unexpectedly in a foreign city, I was surprised by the serendipity of this. 'Why are you smiling?' she asked suspiciously. 'Back in Israel,' I told her, in a burst of unplanned self-disclosure, 'I was specialized in the field of adoption, and I believe that that knowledge is very important while working with adoptees. So I am glad that you were, by mere chance, referred to me.' She replied critically and somewhat angrily, 'I don't see any relevance of that detail! As I told you, my childhood and my family are wonderful. Nothing about my history of adoption, which I do not remember anything about, could be connected with my symptoms.'

I wasn't sure that Shelagh would continue therapy with me. But she did.

Soon, I learned that her adoption papers included details about her biological parents. Her mother was a single, young paediatrician, an immigrant from France; her biological father was a Canadian firefighter. Her biological mother named her 'Shelagh'. Like many therapies, this one is long and complex. I am addressing only small parts of it, not always chronologically, to illustrate and enhance the topic of this paper.

A few years into our work, Shelagh decided to open the adoption file and eventually met her biological mother. It turned out that her biological mother had named her by her own name, 'Shelagh'. She took care of her for the first weeks after birth, and then gave her to the children services for adoption. Afterwards, Shelagh moved among various foster homes until she was adopted by her current family at the age of six months. They immediately left her with a caretaker and went on a preplanned vacation for a few weeks.

During the first period of therapy, an obvious dramatic split in Shelagh's behaviour puzzled me: a good doctor during the day, binging and purging at night. One day, Shelagh decided to apply for a promotion in her hospital and shared that decision with her father. He responded with, 'But don't get disappointed if you don't get that job!' I thought, 'What's wrong with feeling disappointment if you don't get what you wish to get?' I realized that there was no option for Shelagh to own, let alone express, any negative emotion in the context of her adoptive parents. Shelagh had to be perfectly functional and perfectly happy, so her parents would be thankful for having adopted her, 'or else ...'

The mere thought of something negative brewing in her was accompanied by a deep threat of rejection. During this long period of therapy, Shelagh had become more and more able to own and express negative emotions. My role was to *not* abandon her and to convince her that she was indeed wanted, while slowly different layers in her emotional world unfolded. Containment occurred in the real relationship (Greenson, 1968) when appropriate and through mirroring and interpretation. Basic devotion was the issue here. It was not too difficult, partly because I liked her.

In the first few years of therapy, many of Shelagh's negative emotions were aimed at me. In my experience with borderline patients, they tend to create difficult-to-contain devaluations and attacks: 'You will abandon me once you know me. I will be unbearable to keep.' But what I experienced with Shelagh was different; as I described earlier, there was an underlying, clearly felt message: 'I know that I am difficult; please keep me.' I recall one of the strongest bonding moments in our therapy: Shelagh buried her face in her hands like a five-year-old girl and shamefully whispered in a scared five-year-old voice, 'I feel so *unlovable*.' Shelagh had recruited me to show her that she was, indeed, wanted. The understanding of the adoptee's archaic emotional experiences increased my capacity to contain much of the turbulence.

There were many real-life tests of my devotion: Shelagh went to France for a time-out of four months in order to check the option of moving there, to contemplate becoming a single mother, and to reach a decision about opening her adoption file. I promised her that when she returned to Toronto, her convenient time slot would be kept secure for her. During that time of contemplation, Shelagh decided to return to Canada, to open her adoption file, and to try to get pregnant. When going through expensive fertility treatments, she said that she could not pay for therapy. I was willing to be paid at a discounted rate when possible.

Once, however, I almost reached the point of re-enactment of abandonment by suggesting Shelagh terminate therapy. That occurred when Shelagh blamed me for trapping her in a long, intensive period of therapy in order to embezzle her. Coming to my assistance were Winnicott (1949) and Kernberg (1984), who liberated me to respond swiftly and definitively to this destructive attack on our working alliance. Once offered the option to end therapy, Shelagh used her control and chose to stay. Our working alliance has been restored.

Currently, Shelagh continues to thrive at her job; she has accumulated many professional and academic achievements. She has made new friends and maintains her friendships with old ones. She is raising her child to become what seems to be a healthy youngster. She continues to have a close relationship with her ageing parents and a somewhat remote relationship with her biological mother. Through the years, Shelagh's bulimia has shifted into what seems to be a lifelong struggle with excess weight.

Although not entirely a story with a happy ending, this therapy has some significant achievements, among them the development of solid trust that was built with much blood, sweat, and tears. Recently I gave Shelagh an objective reason to feel rejected by me by forgetting an appointment. I asked how she felt about that. She laughed.

> I know that you suck with calendars … When I compare my attitude to you now and in the past, it is totally different. I re-read some of the emails we exchanged through the years … I was so mistrusting, so angry. You said back then that the change would happen through our relationship, and I didn't understand it then. I do now.

Shelagh lives a full life. I found myself delighted to hear about the following encounter: Shelagh conveyed to a neighbour, with whom she had become friends, that she had a difficult personal history, including adoption and an eating disorder. The neighbour reacted with: 'I could not have guessed ... you always seem to be so perfect!' to which Shelagh responded, 'I know ... this is my *thing*.' When she told me about that encounter, her eyes shone, and she had a mischievous smile. I felt as if she was implying, 'I can be myself now; I dare to tell people about the *real me*.'

Discussion

In a famous social psychology experiment on conformism, Solomon Asch (1951) found that an individual subject within a group of confederates conformed to an obvious 'fake' opinion of others while performing a simple judgement about the length of a line. More often than not, the subjects distorted their own original assessment to accord with the invalid group assessment.

I would like to suggest that the individual's need to belong contributes to the tendency to conform to a group. For most subjects, the conformity is superficial: they know what the line's length is, but they may alter their judgement for the sake of keeping unanimity and avoiding disharmony with the group. For a few, the distortion is on a deeper level: the subject may be so influenced by the need to belong to the group that they lose the certainty of their own perception. Here, due to the threat of standing out, there is fragmentation: a part of one's true perceptual experience becomes split off, away from awareness.

Inspired by Winnicott's conceptualization of the 'False Self' (1965), I would like to suggest that people react to the internal pull, or the need to belong, in three different ways of conformity, which I call the *Roman way*, the *Chameleon way*, and the *Tattoo way*. The first type is characterized by a conscious adaptation: 'I want to belong, and I will do what is necessary for it.' 'When in Rome, do as the Romans do,' says the famous idiom. This is a simple tactic to manipulate the environment and increase harmony with others by taking a conventional pathway of behaviour. This tactic does not involve any fragmentation of the self or any 'ego distortion'. Sometimes, this is the tactful and polite way of being in a social environment, to behave in a way that is acceptable and harmonious with it. A subject in Asch's experiment may say to themselves something like, 'I know what I see, but I don't want to be different from other group members, therefore I am going to say what the other do and get this experiment over with.'

The second type, the Chameleon way, involves some confusion: I assume that the chameleon doesn't know that it changes its colours to fit the environment's colour. This physiological change happens spontaneously, without any consciousness or control. The result of this feature of the chameleon is that it is impossible to identify its 'true' colour. By suggesting this metaphor, I point to the idea that the Chameleon way offers a gradual increase in self-fragmentation, which creates a confusion about the self. In Asch's experiment, the conforming chameleon-like subjects doubt the length of the lines under assessment and start perceiving the lines in a way that fits the confederates' explicit judgement. When the self is not cohesive, one may think, feel, and behave like a chameleon that temporarily changes its colours to fit the colours of the environment. My metaphorical chameleon has a glimpse of self-awareness – 'I know who I am, but occasionally I am carried away by social or familial pressures.'

I would like to describe my own immigration experiences, as they relate mostly to the first type, the Roman way, sometimes sliding into the Chameleon way (when, for a little while, I convinced myself that I loved hockey).

Shelagh's all-good girl can be seen as the third type, the Tattoo way. This third type involves a deep fragmentation of the self: in order to belong, the person splits off essential parts of themselves. Here, the camouflage that aims to help the person belong to a social environment becomes metaphorically tattooed onto the skin of the individual. In contrast to the Chameleon way, the Tattoo way does not allow flexibility in changing colours once they have been tattooed onto the skin. Original, authentic, true parts of the self are split off and hidden, while the tattooed colours are showing to the outside world and are the only colours that are known to the person themselves.

Because there is no self-awareness of the split-off parts, this clinical situation resembles the *False Self*, as described by Winnicott. Here I concur with Winnicott's emphasis on the defensive dynamic behind the False Self. My patient, Shelagh, was indeed a perfect child to her adoptive parents. The split-off parts came to the surface in adulthood in bulimia. This was the problem that summoned her to psychotherapy and started the journey toward a slow recovery.

In the following section, I would like to address the aetiology of this, connect it to Winnicott's understanding of the False Self, and apply it to the specific situation of adoption.

In his description of the aetiology of the False Self, Winnicott (1965) attributes it to inadequate mothering. He writes:

> The mother who is not good enough is not able to implement the infant's omnipotence, and so she repeatedly fails to meet the infant gesture; instead she substitutes her own gesture which is to be given sense by the compliance of the infant. This compliance on the part of the infant is the earliest stage of the False Self and belongs to the mother's inability to sense her infant's needs.
>
> (p. 145)

As clinicians, we understand the myriad and complexity of reasons that lead parents to give up their children for adoption, and we acknowledge that they should not be judged for doing so. Nevertheless, providing psychotherapy to adoptees, we firstly have to hold on to their point of view. In this context, we focus on the newborn's need to adhere to their mother, to hear her pulse and her voice, feel her skin, smell her, and experience her touch. The newborn's needs are aimed at enabling them to develop a sense of security and safety in the world. Therefore, the act of giving up a newborn would be considered an extreme failure 'to meet the infant gesture'.

Often, in adopted children, this founding failure is only the *beginning* of an ordeal of repeated experiences of failure to meet their needs by moving them across a series of foster homes, agencies, etc. In Shelagh's case, she was cared for six weeks by her biological mother and was given to an adoption agency and moved to a few different foster homes until at six months she was brought to her adoptive parents, who immediately left her for a few weeks while they went on a preplanned vacation.

Depending on the child's predispositions (e.g., sensitivity and reactivity) and level of attunement, sensitivity, and wisdom on the part of the adoptive parents, sometimes a reversal of this process can occur, but adoptive parents often continue the pattern of failure to meet the child's spontaneous gestures and needs. Instead, they 'substitute' their own gestures, 'which is to be given sense by compliance' and which leads the way to the development of a False Self as described by Winnicott. I would like to suggest that the compliant adopted child splits off the undesired, unwelcome parts of themselves and becomes a 'perfect child'. A sense of belonging to the adoptive family is achieved at a great price: tattooing this perfection deep into the self while splitting off essential parts of the True Self. To paraphrase Miller's (1997) description of the *drama of the gifted child*, this would be an *extreme* drama of the gifted *adopted* child.

In therapy, through the meeting of minds (Aron, 1996), Shelagh slowly moved away from the Tattoo way and learned about and accepted dissociated parts of herself. She became able to increase her capacity to know and accept herself and became more trusting that she was, indeed, *wanted* and *lovable*. Perfectly functional in the outside world, Shelagh is now more able to embrace her own imperfections; she can smile and say, with a hint of self-irony, '*Seeming* so perfect is just *my thing*.'

References

Aron, L. (1996). *A meeting of minds: mutuality in psychoanalysis*. Hillsdale: Analytic Press.

Asch, S. E. (1951). Effects of group pressure upon the modification and distortion of judgments. In H. Guetzkow (Ed.), *Groups, leadership and men*, pp. 177–190. Pittsburg: Carnegie Press.

Brinich, P. M. (1990). Adoption from the inside out: a psychoanalytic perspective. In D. M. Brodzinsky & M. D. Schechter (Eds.), *The psychology of adoption* (pp. 42–61). New York: Oxford University Press.

Brodzinsky, D. M., & M. D. Schechter (Eds.). (1990). *The psychology of adoption*. New York: Oxford University Press.

Freud, S. (1961). The ego and the id. In J. Strachey (Ed. & Trans.), *The standard edition of the complete psychological works of Sigmund Freud* (Vol. 19, pp. 3–66). London: Hogarth Press. Originally published 1923.

Greenson, R. R. (1968). *The technique and practice of psychoanalysis*. New York: International Universities Press.

Kernberg, O. (1984). *Severe personality disorders: psychotherapeutic strategies*. New Haven: Yale University Press.

Kirschner, P. (2007). Sometimes a fatal quest: losses in adoption. In B. Willock, L. C. Bohm, & R. Curtis (Eds.), *On deaths and endings* (pp. 161–168). New York: Routledge.

Miller, A. (1997). *The drama of the gifted child: the search for the True Self.* New York: Basic Books.

Stern, D. B. (2003). *Unformulated experience.* Hillsdale: Analytic Press.

Weider, H. (1977). The family romance fantasies of adoptees. *Psychoanalytic Quarterly, 46,* 2–22.

Winnicott, D. (1949). Hate in the countertransference. *International Journal of Psychoanalysis, 30,* 52–69.

Winnicott, D. W. (1965). Ego distortion in terms of true and false self. In D. W. Winnicott, *The maturational processes and the facilitating environment: studies in the theory of emotional development.* New York: International Universities Press. Originally published 1960.

4   Identity struggles of a psychotherapist working on an international visa

Dayi Lian

How long does it take a person to feel they belong to a place? The answer varies. For some, it might only take months, more probably years, but for others, it may never happen. Such people may live out their entire lives feeling like outsiders.

Before moving to New York City in my mid-thirties, I was confident that with my life experience, fluency in the language, and understanding of the culture, I would not have a problem adapting to the new environment. No matter how much I had prepared for the change, however, there were additional challenges that I, a temporary immigrant, faced professionally and personally. These challenges put pressure on me and caused identity struggles on multiple levels and in multiple aspects.

Various articles have described the massive losses and profound disruptions of one's identity that one might experience in the process of immigration (Akhtar, 2006; Barreto, 2013; Kissil, Niño, & Davey, 2013). What I would like to address here is how moving to a foreign country affected my ethnic, professional, and cultural identity and how these influences in turn influenced my work with patients in psychotherapy, especially in psychodynamic psychotherapy.

Since the literature on the experience of foreign therapists is pretty limited (Barreto, 2013), this paper is a sharing of theories and personal experience that I hope might be useful for immigrant psychotherapists or therapists who are working with non-native or immigrant patients.

Ethnic identity: identity as a Chinese person

Immigrants and international students leave their countries for two reasons, either to survive or to strive, but before being accepted by the natives of their host country, all newcomers face the challenge of introducing themselves and explaining who they are.

Kirk and Okazawa-Rey (2006) mention that physical appearance is usually the most visible signifier of one's identity, and it affects others' perceptions, judgments, and treatment of us. Tatum (2000) mentions a similar concept: That which makes us "other" in people's eyes is always the aspect of identity that is the target of attention.

Take my own experience as an example: In a unique place like New York City that is very diverse and extremely fragmented by race and ethnic background, I realized that my skin color and ethnicity had become the first layer of my identity by which the new environment defined and positioned me. This experience was very different from my experiences in my original country, where, as a member of the majority, having the skin color and ethnic background of a Chinese person never stood out in my consciousness in any interpersonal situations.

Moreover, in this new environment, since in many situations there was no chance of or interest in a deeper introduction, skin color, to some extent, became the only obvious marker of identity. To be honest, I had never felt so identical to the other fourteen billion people who also identify themselves as Chinese. All the other things that were important in the past, such as class, education, profession, and personality, became invisible in the new environment.

Coming with this skin color identity, there are certain expectations and stereo-types. For example, like other Asians, Chinese people are supposed to be the "model minority"—hardworking, yet moderate and quiet—therefore when I was active and outspoken, it became very hard for the environment to position me, and an identity confusion arose on my side around how to position myself.

Even in the therapy room, the first thing my patients notice is my Asian name and non-white appearance. There is already fierce transference happening even before the therapy work starts. Particularly for some immigrant patients, there is already a strong idealization that with my skin color, I will have a better understanding and acceptance of their experiences and frustrations.

This accords with what Akhtar (2006) mentions—in the therapy room, skin color causes various projections and stereotypes, yet the therapist's "not from here" sometimes help them to win the trust of patients from minority cultures (Barreto, 2013) and provides a unique and enriching experience in therapy (Kissil, Niño, & Davey, 2013).

For example, an Asian immigrant patient had been bullied in her teenage years by her white peers. She mentioned that my skin color made her feel safe and trusting, which relieved her anxiety and made the work possible in the first place. In therapy, it took a while for us to work through this idealization and to help her realize her fear and anger towards the host environment, which had directly led to her ongoing isolation from her surroundings.

In contrast to the idealization, I also encountered devaluation and concern due to my race and ethnicity. A Chinese-American patient, holding onto a large amount of anger toward her Chinese immigrant parents, mentioned that she had noticed my Chinese name when I had contacted her and had considered changing therapists. This devaluation comes from the projection that, as a Chinese person, I will treat her similarly to how her parents do and will not be able to understand her. I am glad that she chose to stay with me, because she then had the chance to experience working with a Chinese person who was different from her parents; this, to some extent, also helped her to accept her own ethnic identity.

A different ethnicity is not only a different skin color or accent; it also affects how a person experiences and values themselves in a new environment.

Lobban (2013) describes a double consciousness in immigrants and believes that immigrants always view themselves via the eyes of others who belong to the dominant group in the environment. This view coincides with Sullivan's theory that a human being's sense of self is constructed in the constant exchange with the surrounding environment (Mitchell, 1988). According to Barreto (2013), the foreign therapist's living-in-between experience helps them to be more understanding and containing of others' similar experiences, which can lead to a new integration in the patients.

Both patients I have just described have internalized how the environment views them, particularly their racial and ethnic backgrounds. The first patient is obedient, as an Asian girl is supposed to be, yet feels angry and trapped all the time; the second patient attributes the conflicts with her parents mostly to their Chinese background rather than to her parents' interpersonal difficulties or family traumas. Such a negative view of her ethnicity also influences her self-esteem.

As for me, with the growing integration of my own ethnic identity in this new environment, I started to comprehend my patients' projections toward my skin color and to help patients realize that I am neither an enemy nor a magical savior. Their acceptance of my ethnicity also impacted on their acceptance of their own identity; even improved their experiences of their new environment.

For instance, a non-Chinese international student I worked with reported that everything she had learned about China from her own country was very negative. After working with me and experiencing encounters with other Chinese people in the city, however, she had a different, more accepting reaction to Chinese women. This new tolerance, in her description, also increased her acceptance of New York City, because coming here had opened her world and provided her with the opportunity to interact with people from many different backgrounds.

Professional identity: identity as a therapist

Moving to a new country is a ground-shaking experience in that it challenges one's experience of being in the world (Barreto, 2013). Since psychotherapy work relies heavily on shared cultural meanings (Akhtar, 2006), immigrant therapists face a double challenge, losing the cultural reference that grounds one's professional identity as well, which could lead to a feeling of uncertainty and doubt of one's ability to be effective therapeutically (Barreto, 2013).

On the other hand, coming from a different background provides the therapist with a unique chance to challenge a patient's social assumptions (Kissil, Niño, & Davey, 2013), and the therapist's curious attitude in therapy, as well as their own success in the acculturation process in the new environment, could also help to cultivate positive changes in their patients (Barreto, 2013).

While I was gradually settling down in the new environment and in the professional community in New York City, a second layer of my identity started to emerge. In a closer community, I was not viewed only as a Chinese person but as a psychotherapist and psychoanalytic candidate who is from China. There were lots of struggles around this professional identity as well.

As a newcomer, it took time for me to get familiar with the new system, and since most of the social norms are unspoken, there were moments when I felt very powerless and lost. For example, in my first year in New York, I experienced a medical scam towards which my initial reaction was shock and then powerlessness. Since I had no idea what kind of trouble it would cause me, especially to my legal stay in the United States, my first impulse when receiving the huge medical bill was just to pay the bill and save myself from any trouble.

My therapist back then told me that "Dayi, there is a reason why there are so many lawyers in this country." This opened a brand-new world in my mind, because, coming from a totally different social system, I not only had no experience but also had a spontaneous fear of dealing with lawyers and legal organizations. At that moment, my therapist's comment gave me the confidence and courage to start to navigate this system, trying to locate legal resources, such as the 311 hotline and low-fee legal advice. Looking back, I think what I internalized from my therapist was not only the assertiveness but also the confidence based on the understanding of social norms and a sense of having some control over this environment.

My lack of knowledge of the culture also made me doubt my own capacity to be a good therapist in this environment. With my limited understanding of social norms, it is sometimes a challenge for me to differentiate whether certain behaviors or situations are normal or problematic. For example, coming from a country where there are still many lifelong and guaranteed jobs, it can be challenging for me to differentiate whether the insecure feeling a patient has towards their job is a neurotic concern or whether it is true that in a competitive city like New York, people can be laid off at any minute. Usually in those moments, I think patients become my best teachers.

Aside from that, as a foreigner with a temporary working visa, there is also a strong insecure feeling within me. Particularly in the current political environment, there could be sudden changes to my working visa at any moment. Due to the unpredictable restrictions on foreigners' re-entry into this country, for a foreigner like me, some small things like taking a vacation abroad and coming back to work on time cannot be taken for granted. So as a therapist, each time I leave the country for a vacation or family visit, I worry that if I can't come back or I fail to come back on time, I will have to explain the situation to my patients. Will it be a trauma for them, especially for those patients who are already struggling in an underprivileged situation? Intellectually I am totally aware that one does not need to have a perfect life to become a psychotherapist, and accidents can happen at any time, but emotionally this is the first time I have doubted my capacity to be a psychotherapist, especially a psychodynamic therapist working in an interpersonal orientation.

It took me an entire year to fight the medical scam, and after that, coincidently, I had a new patient who was a first-generation immigrant from a Caribbean country. She came for therapy after the sudden death of her husband, but there was also a dispute with her late husband's company and the workers' union. Aside from the work on bereavement, I felt that the legal knowledge and the assertiveness I had just acquired from my own experience became super useful in my work with her. This made me feel a little thankful for the medical scam.

Cultural identity: identity diffusion of different cultures

When I no longer felt the pressure to adapt to or justify myself in my new environment, I felt that I belonged more to New York City. Yet with the help of therapy and psychoanalysis, I also became more aware that, even though I live an American lifestyle, deep down I strongly identify with my home culture, particularly in terms of spiritual belief, interpersonal relationships, and the understanding of life.

My generation in China grew up with the idealization that everything western is better, including the environment, social systems, and values about independence. I have such an idealization as well, and with my roots in Asian culture but my education and lifestyle in western culture, both of these two cultures are already part of me. It is hard for me to turn away from one and follow the other. I am stuck in between.

For instance, western philosophy emphasizes individualism (Soares, 2018), which values independence and assertiveness as well as freedom on the basis of a strong self-agency. Eastern philosophy believes in surrender, harmony with the surroundings, and that freedom is based on inner peace. This duality sometimes makes me confused about which direction in therapy my patients and I are going.

Moreover, since psychotherapy comes originally from western philosophy, there are also assumptions underlying therapy work. The values we promote and the behaviors we encourage in therapy may be different from those in another social context. For example, the concept of enmeshment is widely used to describe a dysfunctional family with diffuse boundaries, yet in some collectivistic cultures such as Hindu culture, it could indicate the family's lifelong intimacy (Akyil, 2011).

Such a difference sometimes causes confusion, even a shameful feeling in patients from a different cultural background. For instance, once my supervisor mentioned that a Chinese female patient had said that she felt confused when he complimented her on being ambitious, because ambition is perceived as negative when describing women in Chinese culture. Such a difference also made this patient feel ashamed of her native culture.

This sense of shame is not uncommon in immigrants and international students when they encounter differences from the dominant culture (Sue, Capodilupo, Torino, et al., 2007). Some may have an inclination to cut the connection with their culture of origin or with their parents, who might never have heard of a concept like "personal space," so as to belong to the host environment. This denial of part of their identity can sometimes lead to depression.

In therapy, therefore, I find that the challenge is not only to help patients adapt to the new environment but also to help them maintain a connection with the land that they have left behind, so that they can integrate what they are learning with what they have internalized from their culture of origin. The resolution comes when the different layers of self-representation find peace with each other.

Personally, I believe that pros and cons exist in every culture and social system. Like yin and yang, there is always black in white and white in black. Different characteristics are required when living in different social contexts, and there might be different costs and gains.

For example, in American culture, individualism is valued (Soares, 2018). In Chinese culture, family is considered to be an entirety, and family members are defined by each other in that they share the responsibility for the family's glory and suffer the same punishment in any humiliation. In such a collective culture, where personal space is not respected, a person needs a high level of flexibility and good interpersonal skills to balance all their relationships without being suffocated.

When working with patients from such a culture, the therapist might encounter resistance or doubts if they advise their patients to turn away from or directly confront their parents; instead, an exploration of the struggles relating to cultural identity could be very helpful. Moreover, patients might find it beneficial if the therapy or analysis could help them to achieve a mutual respect with their family and an acceptance of their original culture while, meanwhile, they learn how to establish proper personal boundaries and become more assertive yet flexible when encountering intrusion from their original culture.

Conclusion: integration

I am still integrating all my struggles regarding belonging and multiple identities, and there are many moments when I feel like I am going on an unknown adventure with my patients, trying to find the way in a dark cave, and the torch I hold tightly in my hand is not only technique or knowledge but also my own curiosity and courage to face the darkness and uncertainties. I also realize that the more assertive and entitled I feel in the new environment, the more empowered my patients can also feel.

References

Akhtar, S. (2006). Technical challenges faced by the immigrant psychoanalyst. *Psychoanalytic Quarterly*, *75*(1), 21–43.

Akyil, Y. (2011). Being a family therapist in the United States: multicultural competency through the lenses of an immigrant therapist. *Journal of Family Psychotherapy*, *22*(2), 157–171.

Barreto, Y. K. (2013). The experience of becoming a therapist in a foreign culture. *Journal of Humanistic Psychology*, *53*(3), 336–361.

Kirk, G., & Okazawa-Rey, M. (2006). Identities and social locations: who am I? Who are my people? In L. P. Rudnick, J. E. Smith, & R. L. Rubin (Eds.), *American identities: an introductory textbook* (pp. 9–15). Hoboken: John Wiley.

Kissil, K., Niño, A., & Davey, M. (2013). Doing therapy in a foreign land: when the therapist is "not from here". *American Journal of Family Therapy*, *41*(2), 134–147.

Lobban, G. (2013). The immigrant analyst: a journey from double consciousness toward hybridity. *Psychoanalytic Dialogues*, *23*(5), 554–567.

Mitchell, S. A. (1988). The intrapsychic and the interpersonal: different theories, different domains, or historical artifacts? *Psychoanalytic Inquiry*, *8*(4), 472–496.

Soares, C. (2018). The philosophy of individualism: a critical perspective. *International Journal of Philosophy & Social Values*, *1*(1), 11–34.

Sue, D. W., Capodilupo, C. M., Torino, G. C., Bucceri, J. M., Holder, A., Nadal, K. L., & Esquilin, M. (2007). Racial microaggressions in everyday life: implications for clinical practice. *American Psychologist*, *62*(4), 271.

Tatum, B. D. (2000). The complexity of identity: who am I? *Readings for Diversity and Social Justice*, 2, 5–8.

Part 2
Belonging and loneliness

5 Loneliness and belonging

The contradictory typologies of Islamist terrorism

Emad El-Din Aysha

Why has the Islamic State in Iraq and Syria (ISIS) been so successful at recruiting en masse, not only in the bordering nations of Iraq and Syria but across the world, from sub-Saharan Africa to Europe to the Philippines? The quick answer is the failure of the nation-state as a political reality in the Arab world and the failure of Arab nationalism as an ideology. A former member of the Qadafi regime, the moderate Ahmed Qadaf Al-Dam, explained that Iraqi and Syrian youths flocking to ISIS was tragic but understandable because of the repeated failure of regimes in those two countries to unite. (The Baath party as originally conceived, in Syria and Iraq, was meant to unify the two countries as a stepping stone towards Arab unity.) More generally, the disaffected, disillusioned Arab youth had no choice but to look to this nefarious organisation to fulfil their ambitions as Arabs and Muslims, for unity and prosperity and security, and to be taken seriously in the world and not targeted by foreign powers (Hassani, 2016).

The crisis posed by ISIS on its home ground in the Middle East, then, is explicitly a crisis of belonging. This is even more evident in the counter-narratives being deployed in Arab countries. Since losing the Tunisian general election in 2014, the moderate Islamists, led by the Ennahda party, have engaged in soul-searching and latched onto national belonging and the nation-state as common property, regardless of ideological allegiance. Prioritising local problems as the stuff of politics over high-sounding ideals is key to their reforms and self-criticisms (Mansour, 2014). Speaking from direct experience, residing in Egypt, there are official Friday prayer sermons broadcast on television arguing against the idea that the homeland is nothing more than a 'handful of dirt', as the Islamists say. Muslim clerics go to great lengths to try to instil a sense of national pride and belonging in people, all in the face of the pan-Islamist credentials of ISIS propaganda. Potential recruits are being called on by ISIS to *betray* their countries, something that may seem inconceivable to a Western audience, steeped in their brand of ethnic nationalism for so long. Belonging, moreover, is related to the sheer brutality of the organisation, its penchant for beheadings and suicide operations. The rational machinations of the leadership of ISIS can explain why these methods are used, but not why the young eagerly volunteer to be cannon-fodder for the organisation. Targeting civilians, whether by blowing yourself up in a crowd or by beheading them, is evidence of just how *angry* young recruits are towards the *whole* of society, and not just supposed collaborators or corrupt political elites.

Explaining ISIS, then, is a challenge to social science to explain how religious identity can outweigh national identity and how people can engage in acts of self-destruction at variance with rational self-interest and self-preservation. Insights from psychology and anthropology are called for. I have argued elsewhere for this approach when tackling the topic of Islamist suicide terrorism (Aysha, 2017) – suffice it to say that rationalist assumptions in social science are always fraught with difficulty. In the real world, notions of rationality are intimately tied up with *normalcy* (Isin, 2004; Dein, 1997; Fromm, 1944). Practices that seem irrational to us with a modern frame of mind, such as initiation scars, foot-binding and female genital mutilation, seem perfectly rational and reasonable to people in a community where this is the common practice (Goldenberg, Pyszczynski, Greenberg, et al., 2001, p. 428).

As to my previous work on Islamist suicide terrorism, the phenomenon was explained with reference to bodies of research in psychoanalysis pioneered by Erich Fromm (1900–1980), community and education psychologist Seymour B. Sarason (1919–2010) and psychologist and cultural anthropologist Ernest Becker (1924–1974), whose book *The Denial of Death* (1975) spawned terror management theory or TMT (Greenberg, Pyszczynski, & Solomon, 1986; Harmon-Jones, Simon, Greenberg, et al., 1997). Fromm explored the social psychology of modernity and the defence mechanisms employed by people in the face of the challenges posed by individualism. These mechanisms and worries in turn interact with mortality fears and other defence mechanisms people devise, both as individuals (covered by TMT) and members of religious communities (Sarason, 1993), to surmount these anxieties. The details will be recounted in this chapter, in addition to new material and research from psychologists, anthropologists and media propaganda analysts.

It is imperative this early on in the analysis to move out of the cultural frame of what is predominantly *Western* social science. One of the aforementioned psychologists, Sarason (1993), himself insisted on this, almost anticipating the situation today in the Middle East in his seminal work 'American Psychology, and the Needs for Transcendence and Community'. He cautioned social scientists and policymakers not to ignore culture and history as variables and not to ignore how Arabs-Muslims understand religion, stating the following:

> It is impossible for me in this paper to state and examine the implications of my argument for our foreign policy. It is obvious that the United States now has to deal with countries in the Mideast in many of which there is not only no separation between the need for transcendence with a divinity and the sense of a community, but in which there is little or no distinction between state and religion. We in our country simply cannot comprehend that way of seeing and living in the world, and psychology has been of no help at all. That inability to comprehend – indeed, our inability even to recognise what the problem is and will be for us – has had and will have enormous consequences for which

neither we or our national policy makers are prepared. A colleague of mine, Michael Klaber of the University of Hartford, put it to me this way: 'As long as Americans see our problems in the Mideast as centering around oil, they are missing the point: The problems are and have been in the most fundamental way religious and in ways utterly foreign to what we in this country ordinarily mean by religious.'

(Klaber, personal communication with Sarason, 1993, p. 200)

Cross-cultural comparative analysis taken from anthropology and psychology, then, is a must, supplemented by some first-hand knowledge of the region's culture and history. Given the complexity of the subject matter and the bodies of research consulted, the next section will be divided into three subsections. The closing section of this chapter will look into possible policy options and recommendations on dealing with the root causes of ISIS's popularity, political and psychological, especially in light of the experience of the war on terror and the second Arab Spring.

ISIS in comparative context: time, space, insecurity and agency

Religion and ideological violence

The first thing to realise about ISIS, despite the sensationalism of the headlines, is that there is nothing strictly speaking *unprecedented* about the organisation. There isn't that much of a difference in principle between the war-torn worlds of Iraq and Syria and southeast Asia during the Vietnam conflict. As brutal as ISIS is, it still has not reached the sheer genocidal proportions of the Khmer Rouge, for instance. What tore Cambodia apart and gave birth to the Khmer Rouge specifically was the foreign meddling of great powers in the destiny of an otherwise neutral country, and a pacifist Buddhist country at that. Moreover, acts of wholesale cruelty were not limited to the communist guerrillas. With the removal of Prince Sihanouk at the hands of the pro-American regime of General Lon Nol, popular violence broke out as peasants called for his return. In one famous incident a raging mob attacked two parliamentarians and sliced out their livers, later skewering the livers and selling them in the open marketplace (Palling, 1983). Even in Vietnam proper, young peasants recruited into the Viet Cong often engaged in acts reminiscent of today's ISIS, such as beheading local landlords and officials (Smith, 1983). This was meant to scare the locals into submission and convince villagers that the Southern Vietnamese regime could not protect them and that a communist victory was inevitable. Not to mention tapping into local socio-economic grievances against the rich and powerful. (See extended commentary on beheadings later in this chapter.)

Communism, moreover, is a universalist ideology and, much like Islamism, transcends borders and languages and calls on its adherents to place ideology over parochial nationalisms. Before the communists there were the anarchists, Europe's first designated cosmopolitan terrorists. Many were bombers who specifically targeted innocent civilians as a necessary means to an end, their motives documented and dissected in Joseph Conrad's *The Secret Agent* (1907).

Secondly, a clarification is called for here for the benefit of the Western reader. Islam is not only a supremely political religion, as Sarason points out, but it is also a supremely *footloose* religion. It is pan-regional in its very nature and its historical genesis. The *umma* (nation or community of believers) in Islam is an explicitly stated precept of the religion, with no ready equivalent in Christian discourse. We are taught as Muslims that what makes you better than other people – members of other religions – is piety, not the colour of your skin or your ancestry, however noble. Likewise, what makes you better as an individual Muslim compared with other Muslims is also piety, once again regardless of the colour of your skin or your ethnic or racial background. Arabic culture was the dominant culture of Islam from its earliest days, that is true, but the vast majority of Muslims, in fact, are not Arabs, but they have equal status to the original Arab founders of the Islamic *umma* provided they play by the rules of the religion. They can even outdo Arabs at their own game and rule the extended Islamic family, Arabs included, based again on piety and serving the cause – hence Saladin (1137–1193), who was a Kurd; the Mamluks (1250–1382, 1382–1517), a group of slave soldiers of diverse origins; and, of course, the Ottoman Turks, who took up the mantle of the Caliphate from the Arab Abbasids, the supposed descendants of the Prophet Muhammad (PBUH).

There were attempts in Christian history to politicise and universalise Christendom as a community, at the time of Emperor Constantine and the time of Charlemagne, but they came to nothing in the end. The power of the divide between Western and Eastern Churches continued, and the theological power of the Church itself over temporal political authorities prevailed for the longest time. Secularism and nationalism were then enshrined in European history with the termination of the Thirty Years War (1618–1648) by the Treaty of Westphalia (1648). Again, no ready equivalents of this experience exist in Arab and Muslim history. Pan-Arabism tried to play the role of pan-Islamism in the twentieth century, but it came to nothing again, which is in part why pan-Islamism has regained its lease of life.

Thirdly, it must be understood that ISIS is not only a pan-Islamist terrorist organisation but also that it is a *millenarian*, end-of-the-world movement. As I have documented previously, the movement relies on apocryphal sayings of the Prophet Muhammad (PBUH) about black banners held high by a movement at the end of time, during the cataclysmic confrontation with the Anti-Christ. That is why the banners and outfits of ISIS are black, just as the Abbasids also dressed in black when they exploited these apocryphal sayings in their day and age (Aysha, 2017, p. 96). This is pure propaganda on the part of ISIS, but it helps explain the movement's sheer ferocity when looked at from a psychoanalytic perspective and when bearing in mind the cultural-political context in which these more universal psychological problems play themselves out. Again, the key variable is belonging, with a crisis in belonging leading to social alienation and loneliness, and all characterised by a profound sense of *insecurity*.

Modernity and the apocalypse

A common sentiment you hear in Arabic countries is that 'this is not our land'; 'we're strangers in our own land', as if we're 'just passing through' a foreign land. Another common sentiment heard in Arabic countries is the identification of a country, a homeland, as a place where you feel safe – *amaan* in Arabic – in contrast to when you travel abroad.

The first sentiment is more strictly political, the second more social-psychological. If you live in a country where the government does not represent you, where it is impossible to get a job and make a living without connections, where's it's impossible to get anything done without bribes, where you live in an environment of urban sprawl and decaying utilities and public services, you will not have an automatic sense of belonging to that country. Political disenfranchisement by necessity leads to social alienation. It doesn't necessarily lead to violence or fighting back, but it does lead to a breakdown in national identity and people, especially the young, disassociating themselves from dominant norms and looking for their own brand of identity, caving in on themselves or searching for like-minded peer groups. This takes on an added urgency, however, when combined with the second sentiment, the kind of cultural and historical context in which the youth operate in the Arab world.

Former UN Secretary-General Boutrous Boutrous-Ghali, commenting once on sub-Saharan Africa, explained that citizenship is a modern notion and not necessarily attested to elsewhere in the world. In Africa, tribes are paramount and people don't think in universalistic terms, as individuals in a larger community with preordained rights to personal liberty and physical security. Consequently, members of a tribe or ethnic group do not feel safe outside their domain – when they are in someone else's domain, stepping into another tribe's or ethnic group's territory. This is actually a perfectly reasonable sentiment, since the state – the modern state that enjoys a legitimate *monopoly* on violence – is a recent invention in human history. In the past, people, whether individually or as communities, had to provide for their *own* security on a daily basis, especially when travelling.

The same holds true in the Arab world. You only feel safe in your tribe or your hometown or neighbourhood or amongst your extended family. The nation is a very modern construction. Having an automatic sense of belonging to society at large is *not* a given. The sense of belonging in Arab and Muslim countries, then, is often of the more microscopic variety (sects, clans, provinces) or macroscopic, the *umma* (Muslim world) or Arab world (pan-Arabism), with the nation-state sandwiched in the middle and trying to take root and predominate. The sense of insecurity this engenders, the sense that the nation-state can't or won't protect you, makes the young highly susceptible to Islamist movements and extremist ideologies.

In my previous research on suicide terrorism, I made the argument that modernity, not archaic religious beliefs, was the chief culprit behind Islamist terrorism. Islam is a religion that clearly forbids the targeting of civilians just as it clearly condemns (to hell fire) those who take their own lives. This is why researchers working on the Durkheimian thesis on the relationship between religion and suicide have found repeatedly that Islam has the lowest suicide rates globally (Shah & Chandia, 2010). Even within non-Muslim countries, like India, Muslims enjoy the lowest suicide rates of all, and across socio-economic classes (Simpson & Conklin, 1989, pp. 948–949, 962).

Modernity, however, is eating away at the social bonds that prop up Islamic values, a variable used by researchers to explain the still low but increasing number of suicides in Arabic and Muslim countries. Modernisation means urbanisation and secularisation, individualism and the breakdown of the extended family unit (Aysha, 2017, pp. 94–95). I have relied on Erich Fromm's classic *Escape from Freedom* (1941) to explain the psycho-dynamics of modernity as it presupposes the I/Other distinction. This pits the self-conscious individual against the entire outside world after doing away with the original groupings that people identified themselves with, such as caste, class, sect, trade, denomination, ethnic group, etc. (Fromm, 1955, p. 8). Psychological defence mechanisms ensue, and one key stratagem is the 'inflation of oneself psychologically to such an extent that the world outside becomes small in comparison' (Fromm, 1941, pp. 208–209). Hitler is the traditional example, of course – a common problem afflicting dictators in their formative years. But, interestingly enough, Fromm ties this psychological dynamic to 'apocalyptic traditions' as well. One reason why people flock to millenarian movements is that they make them feel special and unique and therefore capable of facing up to a world they find to be hostile. It is a self-styled form of belonging that combats the insecurity of modernity.

More specifically, millenarianism attracts certain people because they enjoy the

> images of the horrendous death and destruction rei[g]ned on the earth during the so-called last days, vivid and graphic accounts of the *unbearable pain and suffering* of nonbelievers, the burning and melting of the flesh [of] sinners, and the destruction of billions of lives of those who are not members of the *right religion.*
>
> (Wilson, 2009, p. 7; italics are mine.)

Such tell-tale psychological traits emerge repeatedly in other documented cases of millenarian violence. Terror expert Bruce Hoffman cites multiple examples from across the globe, from the white supremacist–survivalist movement in the US (2006a, pp. 82, 101–102) to the Aum Shinrikyo cult in Japan (2006a, pp. 82, 119) to Baruch Goldstein, who massacred Muslim worshippers in 1994 at the Ibrahimi Mosque mass shooting in Hebron. Hoffman explains that a potent mixture of 'messianic visions of redemption, legitimated by clerical dispensation and achieved through direct action entailing indiscriminate mass murder' was responsible because the act was perpetrated on the occasion of Purim, commemorating the historical figure of Mordecai from the fifth century BC. Goldstein stylised himself, and saw himself, as a 'modern-day savior' who would usher in the 'coming of the Messiah as foretold by Kahane' and, with that, a cataclysmic end-of-world confrontation with the forces of evil (Hoffman, 2006a, p. 100).

To return to the example of Vietnam, there is nothing specifically religious about any of this. As one US civilian adviser explained, Viet Cong recruits were often mild-mannered peasant boys who were transformed into brave and ruthless warriors who could engage in beheadings specifically because they were promised a way out of the feudal economy that consigned them and their forebears and their future offspring to servitude. In the process, the young Viet Cong is quite deliberately developed into a 'saviour' of his village and a *super*-nationalist, in direct defiance of Buddhist teachings on the sanctity of life (US Information Agency employee Everett Bumgardner, cited in Pearson, 1983). The interface of psychology and ideology is one and the same.

Bodily sacrifice and terror tactics

In the case of ISIS, insecurity is suffused with millenarianism. There is another apocryphal saying attributed to the Prophet Muhammad (PBUH) that the Muslim *umma* will divide into numerous factions at the end of time, and only *one* of these schisms will enter paradise because it is still adhering to the right path. Therefore the young feel they are joining the *only* group that will survive the end of the world and be guaranteed paradise, and since everyone else is to blame for the coming of the apocalypse due to their blasphemies, then that is all the more reason to punish them and so feed your ego in the process.

Next to the societal problems listed above brought on by modernity, there is also a more subtle political-religious factor involved in heightened rates of social alienation and suicide, reveals medical expert Mohsen Rezaeian. There is a sense of *disgust* with society among the young because 'some Islamic countries *only adopt Islamic law as a shell* and they do not apply the core of Islamic values', as evidenced by the toleration of 'poverty', a social ill Islam condemns as much as it does alcoholism or gambling. In the idealistic eyes of the young Islam advocates a 'fair distribution of wealth within the community' through such practices as charitable enterprises and taxes on the rich. When this doesn't happen, in spite of all the religious paraphernalia employed by the state and society at large, 'youngsters *especially males*' carry out the suicidal act 'using fatal methods such as hanging and self-immolation to *show their protest against* the unfair economic situations in their societies' (Rezaeian, 2014, p. 46; italics are mine). Family breakdown and urban dislocation contribute to this because they make it harder for people and institutions in Muslim countries to pass down 'Islamic values and principles to their new generation' (Rezaeian, 2014, p. 46; see also Rezaeian, 2008–2009).

In passive situations the young take out their anger on themselves, the most famous example to date being the Tunisian boy Bouazizi who burnt himself in public, protesting against social injustice and igniting the Arab Spring in the process. Many other copycat suicides have followed since, political and apolitical and among Muslims and non-Muslims. (The most famous non-Muslim to set himself on fire was an Israeli, Moshe Silman; Greenberg & Strous, 2012.) In the proactive frame, the young often take out that anger on society itself, run as it is by their elders. That's where the process of recruitment and indoctrination starts. As I have argued elsewhere, Islamist organisations are essentially peer groups that the dis-affected youth join in part because of their dissatisfaction with their families. The Islamist group becomes their *kin* that they are willing to sacrifice for, just like a son sacrificing for his family (Aysha, 2017, p. 93).

It is no coincidence that, to better indoctrinate young recruits, Islamist organisations – just like religious cults – *isolate* recruits by placing them in small, tightly knit squads, making the individual recruit completely emotionally dependent on the organisation (Aysha, 2017, p. 93). The very ideology of Islamist groups drives a wedge between recruits and society, portraying the outside world as antithetical to Islam, exaggerating out of all proportion the pre-existing social alienation that those who volunteer already feel (Al Raffie, 2012, pp. 19, 26; Al Raffie, 2013, p. 74). The twist in the tale is that just as you are willing to sacrifice for your brethren of choice, *they* in turn will stand up for you and sacrifice them-selves in kind, giving you a false sense of security in an uncertain world.

Jürgen Todenhöfer, a German journalist and politician who was one of the first to talk to ISIS members, found that the young recruits who were doing the beheading were ecstatic (Mansour, 2015). They said they were having the time of their lives because they were making history – doing something that mattered for the first time. The issue here is *agency* – feeling that you are taking your fate into your own hands. The exhilaration comes from an extreme sense of dis-empowerment and loneliness. The same paradoxical sense of empowerment can be found in suicide operations. Medical anthropologist Nancy Scheper-Hughes, researching the illegal organ trade coming out of Brazil's slums, found that the so-called donors all insisted that they were completely autonomous in their deci-sion and not coerced or tricked. They all insisted on their and only their *agency* (Scheper-Hughes, 2008; 1996). Note that the donors were invariably men, heads of households, and for them, cutting into their flesh was a form of sacrifice for their families. Even if you shorten your own life in the process, this does not ultimately matter because you are living through your children, a sentiment Arabs understand all too readily. In Arabic family life, children are referred to as *athar* (relics or remains after death) and your *imtidad* (extension, over time). Having children and sacrificing for them guarantees your immortality, just like sacrificing for your kin or extended family in an Islamist group.

That helps to overcome any emotional or moral reservations about suicide among otherwise pious Muslims. This was Sarason's key contribution to my original research on Islamist suicide terrorism. Just as he understood that Islam melded politics and religion, he understood more generally that religion was not a purely individual affair. By breaking out of the individualistic focus of religious studies, he came to see how religious persons need to feel they are not alone in the world through membership of a religious community and how this helps them attain a form of symbolic *immortality* through this membership (Aysha, 2017, p. 87). Even if they as individuals die, the community perseveres. The classic example he cited was Socrates, who sacrificed his life, his individual bodily integrity, in order for Athens to endure (Sarason, 1993, p. 195). TMT expands on this realisation significantly, since it is specifically through such symbolic substitutes – religious membership is only one such example – that people face down their mortality fears.

We could add that the slum-dwellers studied by Nancy Scheper-Hughes lived in a world very similar to that of war-torn Cambodia or Iraq. Death is around every corner, whether from police death squads or armed gangs or from typhus (Scheper-Hughes, 2010a; 2010b; 2010c). People coped with these grim realities through dark humour and religious rationalisations. (In the minds of slum dwellers, organ donation was probably the only thing that they hadn't been forced into in their lives.)

The same goes, essentially, for beheading. The logic behind it is a potent mixture of politics, culture and psychology. This is a modern example of the medieval tactic of 'atrocity propaganda' used by the Crusaders, where 'enemies were beheaded and their heads thrown into besieged cities or impaled on their lances to frighten the enemy. Sheer cruelty or an acute awareness of the role of psychological warfare? Perhaps a combination of both' (Taylor, 2003, p. 74). Propaganda and communications expert Nancy Snow (2014) has described ISIS beheading videos online as a very effective 'recruitment tool', if only because they 'wake up the senses', spreading across the Internet 'so quickly as to assume a form of violent hardcore porn'. Echoing Jürgen Todenhöfer and Nancy Scheper-Hughes's comments about agency, Snow explains that:

> All of us seek meaning in our fleeting lives. We want to be somebody, whether we're a fictional Cherry Darling with her machine-gun prosthetic leg in Quentin Tarantino's Grindhouse, or we are the very real Chechclear, a Dutch fighter for Isis proclaiming on a Tumblr post that 'Jihad is the best tourism.'
>
> (Chechclear, quoted in Snow, 2014)

Snow's analysis is also in line with Erich Fromm's insights: 'The blood it takes from so many of its innocent victims becomes transfused by a feeling of omnipotence. How many of us can say we are so dedicated and relentless in our non-violent pursuits?' (Snow, 2014).

We can add that many of these acts are couched political messages, both to the Muslim and the non-Muslim viewer. Sacrificing rams is a religious practice in Islam, and so these barbaric acts are meant to be Islamic-style sacrifices to the cause. (Again, this is not unprecedented. The 'flagellants' in the Middle Ages brutalised their own bodies in gruesome public displays during the Black Death, both to absolve Christians of their sins and to challenge the Catholic Church, which had failed to shield Christians from this divinely ordained pestilence; Cartwright, 1991, p. 42). As for the non-Muslim international audience, if you watch the summary executions conducted by ISIS in Libya, for instance, you will notice that the victims are dressed in prison fatigues. More specifically, the orange-red prison outfits that the detainees in Guantanamo Bay are forced to wear. ISIS is saying to the world, 'How are we any different from the Americans? And if we are savages, it is the overwhelming force that America is that has made us this way, forcing us resort to these methods.'

In conclusion

This is political chicanery, but it is also indicative of the nature of the beast and the psychological appeal it has. Combating such movements demands more than police tactics and military action by going to the very root of the problem – the crisis of belonging and why people feel lonely and disempowered in the modern Arab-Islamic world.

Bruce Hoffman once complained that the war on terror was not enough, since eliminating extremist figures and groups could just postpone the inevitable, with more movements and even more extreme tactics being adopted later by the next generation of fanatics (2006b) – prophetic words because he was talking about Al-Qaeda, which prefaced the far more violent and effective organisation that is ISIS. Now that ISIS is breathing its last, we hope, there is no telling what lies next. A soft power approach directed at the young, meant to win them over, is a better strategy in the long run, argues Hoffman (2008). The same goes for Arab regimes in their own smaller wars with extremist movements, but deeper-seated political and economic changes have to take place, too. The so-called second Arab Spring, in Algeria, Lebanon, Sudan and Iraq, may hold out some hope in this regard. In Lebanon and Iraq, in particular, two countries known for sectarian divisions in society and politics, the young have flocked to the streets to protest against corruption, regardless of the usual sectarian, tribal and provincial distinctions. Shiites and Sunnis alike are protesting against the ubiquity of corruption in the Iraqi state, just as Sunnis, Shiites and Christians are protesting side by side in Lebanon against the entire political class and all its key figureheads – President Michel Auon (Christian), the then Prime Minister Rafik Al-Hariri (Sunni) and parliamentary speaker Nabih Berri (Shiite). The slogans of the protest movements in both countries, moreover, come from Egypt at the time of the January revolution in 2011.

People have concluded, the young especially, that the older religious and tribal designations are no guarantor of security – social justice and legal equality – and that true citizenship and grassroots democracy is the only way out. The young also seem to have concluded that artificial religious and social designations, through joining the extended family of radical Islamist organisations, likewise will not put bread on the table and guarantee physical security and equality in front of the law. If these protest movements succeed, they could give birth to a new political order dedicated to representative democracy and economic prosperity and so resurrect more traditional models of belonging directed at the nation-state or more cosmopolitan forms of citizenship – the kind of civic nationalism characteristic of migrant states like Canada, the United States and Australia.

Only time will tell, but if the international 'audience' – academics, pundits, security experts and journalists as well as policymakers – can lend a helping hand, all the better. The hope is that this chapter will do just that – gain international attention for a domestic psychological problem that has international ramifications. Not to forget the home-grown problems of belonging and loneliness that modern countries themselves suffer from, which would explain why the most virulent members of ISIS are European converts to Islam!

References

Al Raffie, D. (2012, Autumn). Whose hearts and minds? Narratives and counter-narratives of Salafi Jihadism. *Journal of Terrorism Research, 3*(2), 13–31.

Al Raffie, D. (2013, Winter). Social identity theory for investigating Islamic extremism in the diaspora. *Journal of Strategic Security, 6*(4), 67–91.

Aysha, E. (2017). Islamist suicide terrorism and Erich Fromm's social psychology of modern times. *Journal of Social and Political Psychology, 5*(1), 82–106.

Becker, E. (1975). *The denial of death.* New York: Free Press.

Cartwright, F. F. (1991). *Disease and history* (8th ed.). New York: Dorset Press.

Conrad, J. (1907). *The secret agent: a simple tale.* London: Methuen.

Dein, S. (1997, August 23). ABC of mental health: mental health in a multiethnic society. *British Medical Journal, 315*(710), 473–476.

Fromm, E. (1941). *Escape from freedom.* New York: Farrar & Rinehart.

Fromm, E. (1944). Individual and social origins of neurosis. *American Sociological Review, 9*(4), 380–384.

Fromm, E. (1955). *The sane society.* New York: Owl Books.

Goldenberg, J. L., Pyszczynski, T., Greenberg, J., Solomon, S., Kluck, B., & Cornwell, R. (2001). I am not an animal: mortality salience, disgust, and the denial of human creatureliness. *Journal of Experimental Psychology: General, 130*(3), 427–435.

Greenberg, B., & Strous, R. D. (2012, August). Werther's syndrome: copycat self-immolation in Israel with a call for responsible media response. *Israel Medical Association Journal: IMAJ, 14*(8), 467–469.

Greenberg, J., Pyszczynski, T., & Solomon, S. (1986). The causes and consequences of the need for self-esteem. In R. F. Baumeister (Ed.), *Public self and private self* (pp. 189–212). New York: Springer.

Harmon-Jones, E., Simon, L., Greenberg, J., Pyszczynski, T., Solomon, S., & McGregor, H. (1997). Terror management theory and self-esteem: evidence that increased self-esteem reduces mortality salience effects. *Journal of Personality and Social Psychology, 72*(1), 24–36. doi:10.1037/0022-3514.72.1.24

Hassani, M. (2016, March 13). Qadaf Al-Dam warns of plans to divide the region via 'ISIS' and its sisters. *Arabs Today.* Retrieved from https://bit.ly/33FvkMF [Arabic]

Hoffman, B. (2006a). *Inside terrorism* (revised and extended ed.). New York: Columbia University Press.

Hoffman, B. (2006b, December 22). World: analyst assesses the global war on terror. *Radio Free Europe/Radio Liberty.* Retrieved from www.rferl.org/a/1073632.html

Hoffman, B. (2008). Unrestricted Warfare Symposium: 1.2 Al Qaeda on the run or on the march? In *Proceedings on Combating the Unrestricted Warfare Threat: Integrating Strategy, Analysis, and Technology, 10–11 March 2008* (pp. 27–43). Baltimore: Johns Hopkins University Press.

Isin, E. F. (2004, September). The neurotic citizen. *Citizenship Studies, 8*(3), 217–235.

Mansour, A. (2014, March 19). Abdelfattah Mourou … the experience of the Islamists in authority [Television series episode]. Bila Hudoud [Without Bounds], Al-Jazeera Satellite Channel.

Mansour, A. (2015, February 18). Jürgen Todenhöfer, a German who was guaranteed safe passage by Al-Baghdadi [Television series episode]. In Bila Hudoud [Without Bounds], Al-Jazeera Satellite Channel.

Palling, B. (Director). (1983, November 22). Vietnam: a television history (Episode 9) [Television series episode]. In Cambodia and Laos, PBS.

Pearson, A. (Director). (1983, October 25). Vietnam: a television history (Episode 5) [Television series episode]. In America takes charge (1965–1967), PBS.

Rezaeian, M. (2008–2009). Islam and suicide: a short personal communication. *OMEGA – Journal of Death and Dying*, *58*(1), 77–85.

Rezaeian, M. (2014). Suicide in the Middle-Eastern countries: introducing the new emerging pattern and a framework for prevention. *Middle East Journal of Business*, *9*(3), 45–46.

Sarason, S. B. (1993). American psychology, and the needs for transcendence and community. *American Journal of Community Psychology*, *21*(2), 185–202.

Scheper-Hughes, N. (2008). A talent for life: reflections on human vulnerability and resilience. *Ethnos*, *73*(1), 25–56.

Scheper-Hughes, N. (2010a, March 16). *A talent for life: on human vulnerability and resilience*. Talk delivered at the American University in Cairo, Downtown Campus.

Scheper-Hughes, N. (2010b, March 17). *Trafficking with the traffickers: undercover research on the organs trafficking underworld*. Talk delivered at the American University in Cairo, New Campus.

Scheper-Hughes, N. (2010c, March 22). *The terror and the tyranny of the gift: sacrificial violence and the gift of life*. Talk delivered at the American University in Cairo, New Campus.

Shah, A., & Chandia, M. (2010). The relationship between suicide and Islam: a cross-national study. *Journal of Injury & Violence Research*, *2*(2), 93–97. doi:10.5249/jivr.v2i2.60

Simpson, M. E., & Conklin, G. F. (1989). Socioeconomic development, suicide and religion: a test of Durkheim's theory of religion and suicide. *Social Forces*, *67*(4), 945–964.

Smith, M. (Director). (1983, November 1). Vietnam: A television history (Episode 6) [Television series episode]. In America's enemy (1954–1967), PBS.

Snow, N. (2014, September 3). ISIL beheading videos: the scariest part is how well their propaganda is working. *Alternet.org*. Retrieved from www.alternet.org/2014/09/isil-beheading-videos-scariest-part-how-well-their-propaganda-working/

Taylor, P. M. (2003). *Munitions of the mind: a history of propaganda from the ancient world to the present era* (3rd ed.). Manchester: Manchester University Press.

Wilson, C. A. (2009, February). *Erich Fromm revisited: the tension between religious humanism and religious pathology*. Paper presented at the annual meeting of the Midwest Political Science Association 67th Annual National Conference, The Palmer House Hilton (pp. 1–21). Chicago. Retrieved from http://citation.allacademic.com/meta/p_mla_apa_research_citation/3/6/0/7/7/p360776_index.html

6 The origins of terrorism

The obliteration of a sense of belonging

Nina E. Cerfolio

Introduction

This chapter serves as a psychoanalytic call to acquire a deeper understanding of the human aggressive and destructive instincts of terrorism. Another intent is to address the forgotten collective humiliation of the marginalized, which in turn often breeds terrorism. Terrorism is an act of pseudo–self-organization resulting from annihilation anxiety; the terrorist's push is to reconstitute a (distorted) sense of belonging. Sadly, hate is the glue that stabilizes the terrorist's tattered psyche with a (malignant) sense of object constancy.

"Why terrorism?" has become the modern-day version of the question "Why war?" that Einstein presented to Freud in 1932 (Einstein & Freud, 1981). Freud was absorbed in observing the impact of the collective violence of World War I on the human psyche. The psychoanalytic community, however, later became silent on the impact of the war, perhaps because of its own close encounter with the violence and loss experienced during World War II. As in World War II, victimized groups today, like the Chechens, suffer from dignity violations and a resulting sense of a loss of belonging, which contributes to the present-day trends of terrorism.

When we lose sight of the fact that we are all inherently valuable and matter as human beings, we allow our true dignity to slip out of our hands. Inequality, discrimination, and injustice are all violent acts in themselves that have been perpetrated by Russia's oppressive policy in Chechnya. Although the Chechens' basic human dignity can never be abrogated, Russia's oppressive political regime in Chechnya has violated the Chechens' self-worth while subverting Russia's own dignity. When those of us in the rest of the world turn our backs on the suffering of the Chechens, we deny the respect of the Chechens, and we also lose our own humanity in the process.

The Boston Marathon bombers, the Tsarnaev brothers, are an illustrative case of the societal consequences when the rest of the world turns a blind eye to the dignity violations endured by the Chechens and their resulting feeling of injustice. The risk of turning our backs on a population's suffering is that the next generation of Chechens will feel a deepening sense of disenfranchisement as their Chechen parents and grandparents struggle alone with the emotional and physical toll left by the war. It is this sense of unrecognized indignity that can breed the form of terrorism rooted in the mentality that becomes an honor code of "what is done to me, I will do to you."

How do we as psychoanalysts take the courageous first step to reach out to marginalized groups like the Chechens in an effort to witness their trauma and begin to lessen their sense of hopelessness and restore their dignity? Our efforts to start a dialogue of understanding by reaching out to the most isolated communities, where the people are being marginalized, is vital to begin to restore their sense of belonging to the world.

Susan Levine's (2016) *Dignity Matters* maintains that dignity is a basic human right, a vital need that is the birthright of every human being. Many of us have lost touch with our inherent worth because we were not treated with dignity as children. Our caretakers did not know the importance of honoring dignity or the lasting toxic effects of not honoring it. Levine examines the role of dignity violations in both therapeutic communities and nations in the understanding and treatment of trauma. Acknowledging the loss and violation of a population's dignity and working to restore it can be a powerful force in conflict resolution. She refers to Pumla Gobodo-Madikizela's (2015) interview with Eugene de Kock, the infamous white torturer of black South Africans during apartheid, and to Jessica Stern's interview with a terrorist imprisoned for life in Sweden (2014). Helping perpetrators acknowledge the harm they have done to others, as well as to their own selves, seeks to restore dignity (Coen, 2018; Hicks, 2011; Gobodo-Madikizela, 2015; Stern, 2014).

Working in the field of international conflict resolution, Donna Hicks (2011) has facilitated dialogue between communities in conflict. She describes an encounter with a member of a guerilla organization representing an ethnic minority that was fighting for independence from the majority government. The guerillas were able to stay in control of their territory even when they were significantly outnumbered by government forces because the guerillas were fighting to protect the dignity of their people. This pattern of unrelenting empowerment to restore the worth of its people despite being significantly outnumbered by the Russian army, which is equipped with superior military armament, is reverberated in the Chechens' struggle for independence from Russia.

Hannah Arendt, in *The Origins of Totalitarianism*, described loneliness as the common ground for terror and explored its function as the chief weapon of oppressive political regimes. Arendt maintained that when people lose contact with their fellow humans, as well as with the reality around them, they lose the capacity of both experience and thought. Terror can rule absolutely only over people who are isolated against each other (Arendt, 1968).

This isolation from the rest of the world is exemplified by the tyrannical Russian government's war in Chechnya. Starting in 1994, secret Russian black operations in Chechnya were attempting to keep the Soviet Union a single state (Dunlop, 1998), and as a result, the international community knew little about what was happening in Chechnya (Lenkvist, 2010). The powerful Russian military waged decades of wars and destroyed the private lives of Chechens through endemic torture, poisonings, and murders. As a result of this isolation, a collective desperate Chechen sense of not belonging to humanity developed. I first became knowledgeable about Chechen history when I was part of a team that went to Grozny during the Second Chechen War.

To understand the situation of the Chechens, it is essential to be familiar with the Chechen milieu and history. A 6,000-square-mile corner of the northern Caucasus, Chechnya is one of seven republics within the Russian Federation. Chechnya has struggled for centuries under Russian domination, and its most recent declaration of independence in 1991 led to the First Chechen War, which ended in 1996. One of the main cultural differences responsible for the ongoing conflict is religion. Instead of the Russian Orthodox religion practiced in much of Russia, the majority of Chechens are Sunni Muslims. Another factor one can speculate about, though it is rarely spoken of, is the oil- and mineral-rich Caucasus mountain range, which Russia exploits and will never relinquish. In contrast to Moscow's modernization, most of the Chechens are farmers, who live a rural life without evidence of industrial prosperity, making the Russian suppression of the Chechens easier. The history of hostility between Russia and Chechnya dates back to 1785 and Empress Catherine the Great, and it continued during the twentieth century, when Stalin deported half a million Chechens using freight trains and a quarter to a third of them did not survive (Dunlop, 1998; Flemming, 1998; Fredholm, 2000). This experience created the special emotional bond known to people subjected to genocide, that "never again" sentiment that reduces the whole world to the struggle of survival, and has served to unify the Chechens over many generations (Politkovskaya, 2003).

In August 2005, our group visited Chechnya because we wanted to better understand the negative psychological impact of war on children, including their loss of a sense of belonging. Our team consisted of the founder of the International Track Club, a running club for disabled athletes, and myself, a psychiatrist now in private practice. Previously, I was the medical director of a high-traffic psychiatric emergency room and walk-in clinic at St Vincent's Hospital in New York City. We focused on Chechnya, since the Chechen War has been one of the most dangerous, misunderstood, and underreported in the world today. Our team visited the wartorn republic, which was surrounded and controlled by the Russian military, for ten days to start a running chapter for disabled children in Grozny, the capital of Chechnya. During our stay, we also provided medical care to many of the refugee Chechens in the Caucasus. Upon our return, despite numerous refusals of their exit visas, I fought for three years by cajoling bureaucrats to bring three disabled Chechen children, whom we had met during our visit, to New York in 2009 for further medical treatment.

Even though there was a far greater need for intervention than we could provide, I believe that by reaching out to even one child and attending to his or her needs, we slowly began to contribute a sense of connection. There is a tremendous need for medically and psychodynamically trained aid workers in Chechnya. The risk of non-intervention is that the next generation of Chechens will feel a deepening isolation—the obliteration of a sense of belonging and connection to humanity—as they struggle alone with the emotional and physical toll the war has taken.

Similar to the Chechen children who were victims of a Russian authoritarian regime, aid workers, who were seen as challenging their Chechen policy, also became collateral damage. As a result of my role in Chechnya as an aid worker, I was poisoned with what I suspect was anthrax by an FSB (formerly KGB) agent (Cerfolio, 2016). For seven years after becoming ill, I lived in a liminal space between life and death. I no longer enjoyed a sense of belonging to the living, as my foothold in this world had become tenuous. As opposed to Middle Eastern physicians, most American physicians have limited knowledge of and experience with anthrax, which made it more difficult to receive medical help and to recover. Both the lack of available medical knowledge and the lack of validation by significant people in my life of my poisoning and illness expanded my sense of marginalization and identification with the Chechen sense of not belonging. As an example of what happens when targeted, I hope in writing this chapter to provide an adaptive response of containing trauma without resorting to retaliation. For me, that response came in the form of a spiritual awakening (Cerfolio, 2017). My response consisted of a glimpse of an active awareness of transcendent aspects within myself that created a profound interconnectedness with the numinous, something much larger than myself, which was essential to my recovery.

Another wish is to bring a deeper awareness of the underpinnings of terrorism, which is a desperate, maladaptive attempt of last resort; as a result, one can simultaneously develop a distorted sense of belonging by raising public awareness of the struggle of the victimized. In an attempt to witness their suffering and begin to foster a sense of belonging, the third purpose is to report on our mission in the Caucasus to provide aid to the abandoned Chechens.

True belonging is fostered by good-enough mothering to create a sense of justice, beauty, and love. This sense of belonging is needed whether we are in dire circumstances or just leading peaceful lives. Everything I write about in this chapter is applicable both to the biographies of our home-grown shooters and to our own personal stories of garden-variety and persistent disregard of others. Our team taking time to care for the Chechens, who have been ostracized and marginalized, may be helping to plant a seed to diminish the Chechens' feeling of isolation and begin to stop the cycle of retribution. By the United States and the international community becoming more aware of and involved in providing stability in Chechnya, a sense of Chechen belonging—the greatest bulwark against the lure of terrorism—will begin to develop. Our work as psychoanalysts is cut out for us.

The Chechen conflict and its influence

The First and Second Chechen Wars with the Russian military have fostered a deepening sense of Chechen degradation and alienation from the freedoms of the world. This growing sense of not belonging to humanity is compounded by several factors, including the Russian government's lack of acknowledgment of the whereabouts of Chechens who were kidnapped and disappeared. Many of the Chechen children we met recounted traumatic memories of when their fathers were kidnapped and never heard from again and their mothers raped. Because of the lack of knowledge of the location of the victim's body, it is more psychologically difficult for the survivor to validate the death, relinquish their hope of survival, and mourn the loss of a loved one. This phenomenon of delayed mourning also occurred with 9/11 family members, who continued to desperately hope that their family members survived the World Trade Center disaster, in part because they were unable to locate their loved ones' bodies.

One key moment that obliterated the already tattered Chechen sense of belonging occurred in 1999—a phenomenon called the Russian Apartment Bombings,[1] which killed hundreds and injured thousands of Russian civilians. The Chechens' sense of hopelessness in response to being framed by Russia for the 1999 Apartment Bombings and then invaded by the Russian military has deepened their embedded depiction as terrorists and redoubled their sense of not belonging to humanity.

From this point in their history up to the present day, the Chechen sense of isolation has increased, as their struggle has been largely ignored internationally; much of the violence that occurred in the Second Chechen War was not reported by the world press due in part to the political agenda of Russia and the United States. Both Russia and the United States were willing to erroneously depict the Chechens' fight against the Russian army in the north Caucasus as "terrorism" with no acknowledgment of Russian provocation (Goldfarb & Litvinenko, 2007; Dunlop, 2014; Satter, 2016; Anderson 2017).

Our team found that by understanding the Chechen history and culture by engaging with individuals—listening and paying attention to their experiences—we could begin to grasp the Chechen sense of hopelessness that can breed terrorism.

At the time of our visit in 2005, the Consolidated Appeals Process[2] estimated that 90 percent of the people living in Chechnya could not leave due to Russian military occupation, and more than 2,000 children under the age of three would die each year as a result of inadequate medical care, which has created a Chechen sense of annihilation anxiety and not belonging. More than 30,000 children had already been injured or killed because of the war or land mines spread throughout the Republic. As a result of the actions of the Russian military, the Chechens experienced acts of murder, kidnappings, and violence on a daily basis, which increased their sense of loneliness and isolation. To highlight how horrific have been the effects of the wars, UNICEF reported that from 1994 to 2008, 25,000 Chechen children lost one or both parents (Seierstad, 2008), expanding the Chechen sense of not belonging and hopelessness.

Our Chechen mission

Once we arrived in the north Caucasus, our American group expanded to include a Chechen who was deputy minister of Chechnya for "Unusual Circumstances," a

Czech interpreter, and a Russian "journalist," whom I came to realize was an FSB agent. Because we were in a war-torn area where Russian approval was required, we were constantly "escorted" by this Russian FSB agent. We all stayed in a general's home in Ingushetia, which was protected by twenty-foot brick walls that separated us from the surrounding bucolic farmland. Prior to our arrival, unbeknownst to me at the time, Doctors Without Borders had abandoned the area after one of their female doctors was kidnapped and killed.

As the only physician on our team and in the area, I provided medical care to the Chechen refugees we visited, who were displaced throughout Ingushetia and lived in old, abandoned Soviet train cars and tents that were home to thousands of Chechens. During our stay, I voiced my desire not only to write about the Chechens' plight but to ensure that our aim of bringing home three Chechen children whom we had met in Grozny so that they could receive more extensive medical aid in the United States would be successful, as this care was sorely lacking in Chechnya.

Around the middle of our trip, I developed flu-like symptoms—fever and muscle soreness. Days later, my symptoms included nausea, vomiting, lethargy, dizziness, diarrhea, and extreme weakness; I was delirious and unable to move out of bed for three days. Immediately after becoming sick, diagnosing myself based on the severity of my symptoms as if I were my own emergency patient, I knew that I had been poisoned (Cerfolio, 2016). The poison had probably been in my food, but at the time I did not know the specific poison. I later learned that many of my symptoms were consistent with acute gastrointestinal anthrax exposure; at the time, I realized it was not just food poisoning, as out of our group of seven adults and three children—all of whom were eating the same food—I was the only person to fall ill. After my initial symptoms, I subsequently developed chronic inflammation, recurrent pneumonia and gastrointestinal parasitic infections, arthralgia, an autoimmune disorder, and twenty food allergies.

Despite my becoming ill and there being no medical resources available in the area, I was resolute in continuing our Chechen mission. I could not bear to abandon these children. In addition to surviving starvation and oppression as a result of living in a war zone, the Chechen children I had met in 2005 in Grozny had suffered medical injuries including the loss of limbs by land mines and artillery fire. Ruslan, for example, was scrawny, walked with a limp, and had the wide-eyed stare of a small hunted animal who expected nothing but trouble. Ruslan had a left above-the-knee amputation, a right arm above-the-elbow amputation, and part of his penis blown off when he was ten years old by stray artillery fire that struck him in his backyard play area. Four years old when the war first started, he was five when he saw his village destroyed and his father kidnapped, never to be heard from again. In 2009, after bringing him and two other Chechen children to New York, we were able to provide Ruslan with prosthetics that were suction-based and decreased his edematous stumps, as well as other medical care (Cerfolio, 2009). Ruslan's childhood trauma was typical of many of the Chechen children we met, who suffered from unattended debilitating medical problems and had at least one parent who was abducted, never to be heard from again, or tortured by the Russian military. The Chechens' sense of humiliation was not unique to other people subjected to genocide, where the aggression is driven to destroy their personhood (Cerfolio, 2009). Nor could the Chechen sense of shame in their survivor's psyche be wished away by our team's respectful ideas and medical aid. The violence and persecution perpetrated in the war produced a collective sense of Chechen trauma in those who had been denied any agency. The violent suppression by the more powerful Russian army led to a deeper penetration and fragmentation of the Chechen survivor psyche and tattered soul (Hoffman, 2004).

By recognizing the indignities perpetrated on others and their lack of opportunity, I believe it is possible to begin to slowly chip away at the present trends of terrorism. We took one small step towards this goal. We organized a five-kilometer Hope and Possibility race from Nazran to Magas, Ingushetia, a neighboring republic to Chechnya. It took place two weeks after we left the north Caucasus. More than 200 Chechens, including invalid children and refugees, ran for Hope and Possibility on September 11, 2005. This race marked the first time a Muslim republic had banded together to run in defiance of terrorism.

Despite our efforts and hope of breaking the cycle of violent retribution, one of the race participants was murdered. A deaf Chechen woman, a teacher and founder of a deaf school for refugee Chechen children in Ingushetia, was run over by a speeding government car that left the scene of the crime. While we were in the north Caucasus, we had visited her in her one-room school while she proudly served tea. She had told us about her deaf daughter, who was a student at the school. Taking this hit-and-run murder as a warning from the Russian government, the Chechens did not hold this race against terrorism in the north Caucasus again. This situation mirrored the more famous tragic stories of truth tellers who tried to reveal the horrors of routine life in Chechnya.[3]

The murders of Alexander Litvinenko and Anna Politkovskaya, who both reported on the framing and torture of Chechens, served to deepen the Chechen sense of alienation, injustice, and loneliness. The biographies of Litvinenko and Politkovskaya serve as the most well-known examples of how state-sponsored terrorism tries to strip people of their personhood and dignity. Russian oppression in Chechnya has created a republic under immense stress about to explode. When there is no justice for the loss of basic human rights, how does this affect the young Chechens growing up? The destruction of war and the consequent reaction of rage, with the burning desire for vengeance for the purpose of righting a wrong and to seek justice, is the most important cause of terrorism.

Nation-states have caused far more harm and suffering than non-state terrorists. Since 1999, in Chechnya alone, it was estimated that up to 200,000 Chechen civilians have been killed, while another 5,000 Chechen civilians are missing and 40,000 members of the Russian military have been killed.

There are societal consequences when a population like the Chechens develops a sense of not belonging, marginalization, and misunderstanding. As a result of civilians being bombed—with no way of making it stop—exploited, killed, and defeated in war by a more powerful Russian army, a collective sense of Chechen shame was created. The scapegoating and framing of the Chechens for the Russian

Apartment Bombings in order to justify waging war in Chechnya is yet another example of this vicious oppression. Most American lawmakers turned a blind eye and showed no interest in these bombings, with the exception of Senator John McCain (Anderson, 2017).

Putin declared solidarity with the United States by subsuming war in Chechnya with the fight against terrorism (Trenin, 2003). The West, by misunderstanding the war in Chechnya as part of a global fight against terrorism, is in effect condoning the loss of dignity and basic human rights by the destruction and oppression of a republic (Trenin, 2003; Shafee, 2015). This global indifference sends a message to the young Chechens that there is no way to act moderately: If you care about your country, you must become a terrorist.

The Chechen sense of not belonging, including a sense of not sharing in the freedom to experience the inherent rights of humanity, a history of betrayals, and an eye-for-an-eye mentality, are exemplified by the April 2013 Boston Marathon bombings. The Tsarnaevs' background was one of dislocation. The father was Chechen; the mother was Avar, another Muslim ethnic group, indistinguishable from the Chechens in the eyes of their Russian rulers but a different population nevertheless. The mother was never fully accepted into the Tsarnaev family because of those Muslim ethnic differences (Murphy 2015). Her ostracism was part of the reason the family continuously moved around in a desperate zigzag to find security, from Siberia to Kyrgyzstan, from Kyrgyzstan to Kalmykia, back to Kyrgyzstan, then to Chechnya, back to Kyrgyzstan to flee the war, then to Dagestan, then to the US. The parents emigrated in 2002 via refugee status to the United States and settled in Cambridge, Massachusetts.

During one of the Chechen wars in the 1990s, their father was tortured in Chechnya in one of the many Russian camps and as a result often hallucinated that KGB agents were following him. He and his family were granted asylum to the United States (Sacchetti, 2013; CBS, 2015; Martinez, 2015; McPhee, 2017). The Tsarnaev father was later diagnosed with Post-Traumatic Stress Disorder by an American psychiatrist, who testified to the father's torture in a useless effort to change Dzhokhar Tsarnaev's death sentence to life in prison (CBS, 2015). By refusing to spare Dzhokhar the death penalty, we continue to foster the bitterness we have sown only to reverberate it in unforgiving messages.

My goal is not to condone the Tsarnaev brothers' horrible act of human destruction but to provide a background of the Chechen psychological, historical, and political milieu that obliterates a Chechen sense of belonging and in turn can breed terrorism. The killing of innocents did nothing to further the brothers' cause. The act was despicable, no doubt. The brothers not only demeaned their victims in order to carry out the killings but dehumanized themselves in the process. They disconnected from the part of themselves that felt the horror of taking someone's life.

James Jones (2008) points out that to the extent that one is identified with those who are victims of violence, the humiliation that results from a sense of not belonging can be experienced vicariously. An example of this vicarious identification, the Tsarnaev brothers were descendants of ethnic Chechens deported to

Central Asia in the Stalin era (Gessen, 2015). The brothers struggled to assimilate in the US. Dzhokhar, the younger brother, was charming but was a master of mirroring everyone's expectations of him, and he struggled to develop a substantial connection to himself and others. Few people noticed his slow deterioration into a stoner who was failing at a mediocre college. Perhaps in an attempt to create a sense of belonging and connection, he began to forge a Russian-speaking Chechen-centric identity. Living marginalized immigrant existences and feeling like outsiders (Murphy 2015), the brothers grew to hate the United States, which led to their growing rage and radicalization.

Tamerlan, the older brother, was the perfect candidate for recruitment by the US government with a promise in regard to his citizenship. Broke, desperate, and with a new American wife and baby girl to take care of, he spoke fluent English, Russian, and a dialect of Chechen. Despite being on several terrorist watchlists, the FBI recruited Tamerlan as a "mosque crawler" to inform on radical separatists here and in Chechnya during six months that he spent in Russia. But upon his return to the US, the FBI broke their promise of Tamerlan's citizenship (McPhee 2017).

The US's betrayal of its promise of Tamerlan's citizenship may have destroyed his final hope of belonging and thrown him into annihilation anxiety. A basic human reflex when humiliated is to humiliate the perpetrator. Tamerlan's severe panic may have been experienced as an unmanageable affect, difficult to contain. His desperate attempt to deal with his chaotic feeling of the abyss of annihilation anxiety was to expel his terror on the perpetrators, the US. The sense that the Tsarnaevs might have felt that they did not belong is evident in the younger brother writing a note, scrawled on the interior of the boat where he was hiding from the FBI, that stated that the Boston Marathon bombings were "retribution for the US military action in Afghanistan and Iraq." He called the Boston Marathon victims "collateral damage," alluding to the innocent citizens who have been casualties in US-led wars around the world.

Tamerlan's inability to integrate into American society created a deepening sense of his impotence and alienation. His sense of not belonging, combined with his sympathy for the rebellion in the Caucasus region, contributed to his motivation for retaliation in the Boston bombing. Through the bombings, the brothers saw a chance to not only to have a sense of belonging to something greater than themselves and become significant but also to declare war on a great power (Murphy, 2015). This need for revenge is not unrelated to the behavior of our own homegrown shooters, who feel alone and lonely. The brothers may have felt a collective sense of shame as a result of the United States' wars waged against Muslims that was compounded by the international community largely ignoring the Chechen War. The Tsarnaev brothers' sense of despair may have left them more vulnerable to the lure of terrorism as not only a means to raise awareness of the Chechens' struggle for survival against a much more powerful Russian adversary but also as retribution for all the civilians who were killed or injured during the Chechen, Afghanistan, and Iraq wars.

The collateral damage that grows and festers from a sense of not belonging goes well beyond the people killed and injured, spreading through time and space via those left behind to deal with loss, outrage, and grief. The Tsarnaev brothers serve as an illustrative case of the additional collateral damage that nation states have created, as they felt the only way that they could find meaning in their suffering and shame was to act it out on others whom they identified as members of the "guilty" state.

In order to assuage the feeling of absolute loneliness that often breeds terrorism, we need to find, individually and in groups, the courage and passion to demonstrate that they are not alone and that others care. Reaching out to the Chechens, the medical team aspired to slowly chip away at the chronic hopelessness and despair that often breeds desperate acts of violence. We hoped that this important therapeutic intervention would present a different paradigm that would take root in even one Chechen's life and encourage them to envision a more hopeful future. I believe that even one person's effort to reach another who is marginalized and suffering reverberates to assist all.

Implications for therapeutic interventions

Richard Galdston (1987), in "The Longest Pleasure: A Psychoanalytic Study of Hatred," maintains that hatred affords a homeostatic adaptation of the impulsive reaction of retaliation.

Hatred enables the ego to retrieve aggression through a process comparable to mourning libido lost with a disappointing object. Hatred can be distinguished from anger, which is a time-limited response to a proximal irritation that passes. The ability to hate is a skill indicative of ego development to the level of object constancy.

Through their hatred, the brothers were able to hold on to a disappointing object, the US, which they felt had betrayed them and take revenge. The brothers' hatred served as a prosthetic device to maintain a steady relationship with an object (the US) that they could hold on to. This holding on to an object provides a distorted sense of belonging to something greater and security in being united against a common enemy. Hate was a glue that stabilized the brothers' tattered psyches with a malignant sense of object constancy because the hated object, the US, was a constant target. The brothers' hatred created a false sense of self-organization, providing a sense of equilibrium for their ephemeral, unsettled life.

The sequence of humiliation leading to revenge is helpful in understanding the United States' response to the events of September 11. For many people in this country, the events of September 11 were experienced as a major humiliation. Our customary sense of invulnerability was shattered. We were attacked by our own planes on our homeland and suffered a major defeat. Robert Lifton (2005), in "Americans as Survivors," describes our first response to September 11 as involving a sense of individual and collective fear and vulnerability and feelings of injured national pride and humiliation.

Lifton describes the process of mutual narcissistic injury and humiliation followed by retaliatory violence as a primary way that Americans have responded to the trauma of September 11. This national response for revenge was expressed by President Bush on September 14, 2001 when he visited the World Trade Center site and said, "The people who knocked these buildings down will hear from all of us soon" (Carroll, 2004). Lifton (2003) also points out that Osama bin Laden, Al Qaeda, and the Islamist fundamentalists have engaged in a parallel process and cycle of revenge.

The downward cycle of violence and retaliation needs to be disrupted by the United States taking the first step in acknowledging our violent acts perpetrated after 9/11 in Iraq and Afghanistan. Without taking responsibility for our government's acts, the feeling that we are innocent victims of unprovoked acts of terrorism and justified in taking our revenge will only spur the endless spiral of violence and retribution. In addition, the West should encourage the Russian leaders to negotiate with the Chechens instead of fighting them (Fredholm, 2000).

While the political solutions to the Chechen crisis are worth addressing, the need for psychoanalytic understanding is paramount to help build bridges between groups and move beyond generalizations to view one another as human beings from varying cultures who have experienced different realities. There is a great need to work with groups and to restore the emotional meaning of the traumatic events that was ruptured by the traumatization.

Whether for the victims or groups within society, the need for greater reflection about terrorism and the feelings engendered by it in order to encourage psycho-political dialogue is paramount. It is unprocessed losses and psychological trauma that maintain the divide between warring communities. To begin to restore dignity by honoring suffering and to encourage a sense of belonging, the need to create space to recognize, reflect on, and witness the impact of terrorism is paramount.

Notes

1 The defected Russian KGB agent, Alexander Litvinenko, revealed that the 1999 Apartment Bombings were manufactured acts of terrorism and were actually planted and staged by FSB (former KGB) agents and not Chechen terrorists, so that Russia could wage war on "terrorism" in Chechnya to bring Putin into presidency (Litvinenko & Felshtinsky, 2007; Dunlop, 2014; Satter, 2016; Anderson, 2017).
2 The Consolidated Appeals Process includes numerous United Nations organizations, including the International Organization for Migration, the Red Cross, and the United Nations International Children Fund (UNICEF).
3 Alexander Litvinenko divulged Russian horrors such as the support of terrorism in Chechnya and worldwide by the KGB and FSB and their routine use of deadly poisons to kill dissidents (Litvinenko & Felshtinsky, 2007; Politkovskaya, 2006). Litvinenko accused Putin of ordering the murder of Anna Politkovskaya, who resolutely reported on the torture of Chechens and political events in the Second Chechen War (Politkovskaya, 2004).

References

Anderson, S. (2017, March 30). None dare call it a conspiracy. *GQ*. Retrieved from www.gq.com/story/moscow-bombings-mikhail-trepashkin-and-putin

Arendt, H. (1968). *The origins of totalitarianism*. New York: Harcourt.

Carroll, J. (2004). *Crusade: chronicles of an unjust war*. New York: Metropolitan Books.

CBS News. (2015). Doctor: Boston bomber's dad claimed he was tortured, had PTSD. *CBS News*. Retrieved from www.cbsnews.com/news/boston-marathon-bomber-dzhokhar-tsarnaevs-father-had-ptsd-doctor-testifies/

Cerfolio, N. (2009). Multimodal psychoanalytically informed aid work with children traumatized by the Chechen War. *Journal of The American Academy of Psychoanalysis and Dynamic Psychiatry*, *37*(4), 587–603.

Cerfolio, N. (2016, December). Loss, surrender and spiritual awakening. *Palliative and Supportive Care*, *14*(6), 725–726.

Cerfolio, N. (2017). My mystical encounter with a wild gray whale. *Psychoanalytic Perspectives*, *14*(2), 265–269.

Cerfolio, N. (2019). Spiritual knowing, not knowing, and being known. In B. Willock, I. Sapountzis, & R. Coleman Curtis (Eds.), *Psychoanalytic perspectives on knowing and being known in theory and clinical practice* (pp. 117–127). New York: Routledge.

Coen, S. (2018). Between action and inaction: the space for analytic intimacy. *Journal of the American Psychoanalytic Association*, *66*(2), 312–336.

Dunlop, J. (1998). *Russia confronts Chechnya: roots of a separatist conflict*. Cambridge: Cambridge University Press.

Dunlop, J. (2014). *The Moscow bombings of September 1999: examination of Russian terrorist attacks at the onset of Vladimir Putin's rule (Soviet and post Soviet politics and society)*. Stuttgart: Ibidem Press.

Einstein, A., & Freud, S. (1981). *Why war 1932? An exchange between Albert Einstein and Sigmund Freud* (6th ed.) American Psychological Association. Ottawa: Shalom Press.

Flemming, W. (1998). The deportation of the Chechen and Ingush peoples: a critical examination. In B. Fowkes (Ed.), *Russia and Chechnia: the permanent crisis* (pp. 65–86). New York: Palgrave Macmillan.

Florin, D. (2010). Book review of A. Babchenko, *The Colour of War. Caucasian Knot*.

Fredholm, M. (2000). The prospects for genocide in Chechnya and extremist retaliation against the West. *Central Asia Survey*, *19*(3–4), 315–327.

Galdston, R. (1987). The longest pleasure: a psychoanalytic study of hatred. *International Journal of Psycho-Analysis*, *68*(3), 371–378.

Gessen, M. (2015). *The brothers: the road to an American tragedy*. New York: Riverhead Books.

Gobodo-Madikizela, P. (2015). Psychological repair: the intersubjectivity dialogue of remorse and forgiveness in the aftermath of gross human rights violations. *Journal of the American Psychoanalytic Association*, 63, 1085–1123.

Goldfarb, A., & Litvinenko, M. (2007). *Death of a dissident: the poisoning of Alexander Litvinenko and the return of the KGB*. New York: Free Press.

Hicks, D. (2011). *Dignity: its essential role in resolving conflict*. New Haven: Yale University Press.

Hoffman, B. (2004). *After such knowledge: memory, history, and the legacy of the Holocaust*. New York: PublicAffairs.

Jones, J. (2008). *Blood that cries out from the earth*. New York: Oxford University Press.

Levine, S. (2016). *Dignity matters: psychoanalytic and psychosocial perspectives*. London: Karnac Books.

Lifton, R. J. (2003). *Superpower syndrome: America's apocalyptic confrontation with the world*. New York: Thunder's Mouth Press.

Lifton, R. J. (2005). Americans as survivors. *New England Journal of Medicine*, 354, 2263–2265.

Litvinenko, A., & Felshtinsky, Y. (2007). *Blowing up Russia: terror from within*. New York: Encounter Books.

Martinez, M. (2015). A tale of two Tsarnaevs on eve of trial in Boston Marathon Bombing. *CNN*. Retrieved from www.cnn.com/2015/01/02/us/boston-marathon-bombing-dzhokhar-tsarnaev-trial/index.html

McPhee M. (2017). *Maximum harm: the Tsarnaev brothers, the FBI and the road to the Marathon bombings*. Lebanon, NH: University Press of New England/Fore Edge.

Murphy, C. (2015, April 7). From Chechnya to Boston: tracing the Tsarnaev brothers' motivation. Vanity Fair. Retrieved from www.vanityfair.com/news/2015/04/the-brothers- masha-gessen-tsarnaev-brothers-book

Politkovskaya, A. (2003). *A small corner of hell: dispatches from Chechnya* (A. Burry & T. Tulchinsky, Trans.). Chicago: University of Chicago Press.

Politkovskaya, A. (2004). *Putin's Russia: life in a failing democracy*. London: Harvill Press.

Politkovskaya, A. (2006, March 1). Poison in the air. *The Guardian*. Retrieved from www.theguardian.com/world/2006/mar/01/russia.chechnya

Sacchetti, M. (2013). After FBI probes, questions on granting of asylum. *Boston Globe*. Retrieved from www.bostonglobe.com/metro/2013/07/04/wake-marathon-attack-questions-about-safe-harbor-for-ibragim-todashev/iTe3zMwBZxh46u9l5N2SWL/story.html

Satter, D. (2016). *The less you know, the better you sleep: Russia's road to terror and dictatorship under Yeltsin and Putin*. New Haven: Yale University Press.

Seierstad, A. (2008). *The angel of Grozny: orphans of a forgotten war*. New York: Basic Books.

Shafee, F. (2015). Misperceptions about the conflict in Chechnya: the influence of Orientalism. *Securutologia*, *2*, 27–42.

Stern, J. E. (2014). A case study of a Swedish neo-Nazi and his reintegration into Swedish society. *Behavioral Science & the Law*, *32*, 440–453.

Trenin, D. (2003, November 19). The forgotten war: Chechnya and Russia's future. *Moscow: Carnegie Endowment for International Peace*. Retrieved from https://carnegie.ru/2003/11/19/forgotten-war-chechnya-and-russia-s-future-pub-1402

7 The unbearable transience of belonging

An essay on Coppola's *Lost in Translation*

Arthur Caspary

Sofia Coppola's film *Lost in Translation* (2003) is about the struggle to feel alive in a world that both existentially and culturally all too often promotes estrangement from others and ourselves. Coppola has said:

> It's about misunderstandings between people and places … It's about things being disconnected and looking for moments of connection. There are so many moments in life when people don't say what they mean, when they are just missing each other, waiting to run into each other in a hallway.
>
> (Thompson, 2003, para. 4)

This is a funny film about two desperately alienated people who, in what might be seen as a remembered interlude, briefly find each other. Although Coppola deservedly won an Academy Award for her screenplay, her most articulate and poetic voice is that of the camera. She shows us her characters' subjectivity: their loneliness, their longing, and their hidden despair. The sometimes-languid action, the minimalist dialog, and the emphasis on the visual suggest that which is implied rather than explicit, that which is interior rather than manifest. Coppola invites us to use our eyes to find interiority.

The first part of the film establishes Charlotte and Bob's dilemma. They lack passion and direction, and neither feels that they can be authentic with others. Bob is an aging, fading man who seems bewildered and lost. He is distant from his wife, sliding in his acting career, and seems to career from situation to situation. Charlotte is a young woman who is ignored by her husband, but she is also discovering that she is only beginning to truly see him and that she doesn't like what she sees. She feels aimless and formless. She spends her days wandering through a foreign city that she is not a part of or silently looking out through her hotel window, separated from what she sees. Charlotte and Bob belong nowhere and to no one.

The famous opening shot of Scarlett Johansson is a visual essay on the alienation of objectification. Her torso and legs are cut off and all we can see are her buttocks through transparent pink underwear. There is a pull to become a voyeur; desire becomes safe because its object is nothing more than just that: captured, a non-subject.

Coppola develops Charlotte and Bob's state of alienation in a number of ways. At times Tokyo is pictured as shallow, jarringly garish, and bizarre. In order to accentuate the city as emblematic of alienation, she initially populates it with characters like the garrulous director of a commercial that Bob is acting in who goes on a long, angry diatribe in Japanese. But the interpreter softly tells the shocked and intimidated Bob that what the director really said was simply for Bob to move his hand. Bob's reaction conveys comic bewilderment barely concealing mute terror. He knows there's more, but it's lost in translation. He's left, estranged, to wonder.

Another device that Coppola uses is the juxtaposition of the silent insularity of empty, bland hotel interiors with the busy intensity of the outside landscapes. The still eloquence of Charlotte's solitude is captured by an image of her silhouetted in front of the window as the glass mutes the city. She is like Salinger's Franny: a lost girl. She can only wander the vivid streets of Tokyo. She is always a tourist, an outsider. As she seeks fulfillment, she visits shrines but doesn't feel anything. Her ennui is related in part to her increasing emotional estrangement from her husband. But the cause of her disaffection is not simply that she feels ignored by a man with whom she is disillusioned. The marriage is only a facet, and perhaps an expression, of her greater dilemma. She cannot find anything she can or wants to do. She is adrift.

Mirroring the image of Charlotte mutely silhouetted in front of the hotel window is another scene in which Bob silently peers through a rain-spotted taxi window, insulated from the neon colors of the night. There is no discourse, no other, no aliveness. In both scenes the reflections are impersonal; there is no one to know them, to translate their experiences so that they are known as subjects and thus to affirm their identities. Unfound, they fall into a state of anomie. Bob and Charlotte are feeling out of place because their identities are out of place. There is no translation for this. They, in other words, need each other and each other's gaze. The initial gaze serves more as a diversion, but it evolves into an experience—that of feeling because of what one brings and not because of fame or looks.

Charlotte's and Bob's sense of disaffection is not just with their careers and families. They cannot connect with a sense of vitality within themselves, nor can they feel engaged with the people around them or the society that they live in. Neither feels that there is anyone who sees and is interested in them. Charlotte's husband's preoccupation with his career and Bob's acting in commercials to sell whiskey both evoke the emptiness of consumerism. Coppola introduces the characters of a blond pop star and a frenetic TV host who serve as icons for the silliness and shallowness of pop culture. In a very real sense, Charlotte and Bob have nowhere to turn.

That the film tells its story by showing as well as telling seems appropriate, as we all first meet the world not through words but rather through the maternal body, face, smell, and song. While it doubtless makes Ayn Rand roll over in her grave, evolution has genetically designed us to seek belonging with others. Winnicott (1974) finds that we are experientially intertwined with our mothers, provided that they are good enough to be safely taken for granted and thus not thought about. Kohut (1984) emphasizes how essential caregiver empathy is for the development of a cohesive self. Kohut also reminds us that throughout our lives we never cease to need to be known and responded to by other people. Stern (1985) provides us with empirical evidence that we are pre-adapted from birth to engage with a human environment. And Beebe and Lachmann (2002) use persuasive experiments to demonstrate the ways that the self arises from the internalization of caregiver–infant relational patterns. While psychoanalysis lives in a theoretically pluralistic time with multiple competing voices in animated, sometimes Manichaean, discourse, nearly all schools of thought recognize that to be human is to be interdependent and that our reality, whether in the analytic hour or everyday life, is mutually created. We also recognize that the experience of vitality is contingent upon a meeting of minds (Aron, 1996) in transitional space (Winnicott, 1974), whether it occurs face to face, body to body, or in the experience of being swept up by music, art, or film. We are built to belong.

Despite our canon of famous relationships via correspondence, our most satisfying relationships are deeply embedded in the visual. Perhaps this is more so in Western societies. There is no privileging the sighted over the non-sighted, and I suspect that touch can serve the same functions as sight. Words function as easily as walls as they do as bridges, and I believe that Coppola builds much of the film on this premise.

A Japanese acquaintance once told me that her culture's "inscrutability" is an adaptation to the overcrowding that occurred due to rapid population growth in a small island nation. She suggested that to be "unread" both provides emotional privacy and masks society-threatening aggression. This aspect of Japan allows Coppola to use the culture as a backdrop to magnify her characters' isolation. However, in many cultures, facial expressions are essential for conveying affective states, and it has been argued from a Darwinian perspective that this was an adaptive factor, as knowing the state of mind of others allowed us to live in groups and thus survive as a species.

In general, psychoanalysis has privileged the verbal when considering the enhancement of the self in treatment and privileged the somatic when considering the development of the self in infancy. However, Winnicott (1974) made an important point when he commented that babies sometimes live in their bodies and sometimes live in their mothers' faces. He argues that it is the mother's capacity to recognize the subjective state of the baby and to reflect that understanding to the baby through gaze, rhythm, and tone of voice that allows the baby to gradually gather together the bits and pieces of his or her experience into a cohesive self. Thus, from almost our very beginnings, the gaze is essential to the development of our sense of belonging. And belonging is essential to being.

In the film, the first contact between the protagonists takes place in the elevator. Bob is acutely aware of his otherness as he awkwardly looms over the surrounding people and, in what seems to be a moment of respite, looks over at Charlotte. Later, in the bar, she rather desperately looks away from the painful banality of the people at her table and sees Bob. Here, too, her gaze brings relief.

The deadness that Bob and Charlotte feel would be seen through the lens of psychoanalysis as a malaise associated with, among other things, the inability to know and be known by others. We use words like "inter-subjectivity" and what Martin Buber (1923/1996) described as "I–thou" to describe the experience of mutual recognition of one another as subjects rather than as the objects of our preconceptions. If we are able to mutually recognize and accept that, despite our obvious similarities, our perspectives, motives, and intentions are different, we can populate the space between us with a kind of creative play that is the very definition of a feeling of vitality. For this to happen, there must be mutual recognition.

Charlotte and Bob have a tentative conversation in the New York Bar, where, using humor to smooth the rough edges, they hesitantly try to find out what aspects of their selves can safely be revealed. In one sense, this is quite ordinary. It happens any time we meet someone new, be it someone at a party, a neighbor, a potential lover, or a shrink. If we dare to go beyond the necessary but deadening constraints of social ritual where we are mostly certain of the outcome, we tend to experience the fear and excitement of hope. By translating the language of the other, we allow ourselves, little by little, to know and be known.

As I wrote this, my wife commented on how differently Coppola's father visually expressed the effects of alienation, and I was reminded of his use of violent imagery in *Apocalypse Now* (F. F. Coppola, 1979). Perhaps when facing emptiness, men tend to move toward action, toward aggression, while women, when faced with emptiness, move to stillness and yearning. To the extent that this generalization is true, I think that women are the stronger, the more courageous in the face of alienation. The narrative of the characters' respective alienation is developed by Coppola as she shows Bob awkwardly encountering a histrionic prostitute and later shows a photo shoot wherein the director screams in staccato fashion at Bob while his assistant softly translates that he simply wants Bob to move slightly. She shows Charlotte wandering alone through the city.

This begins to shift as Charlotte and Bob find each other in the ersatz oasis of familiarity represented by the bar and begin to tell each other their stories. Coppola neatly avoids miring the film in the treacle of sentimentality by using the tartness of irony. But their stories do get told, and Charlotte and Bob begin to be heard. Gradually they get to know each other and, as they connect, something quite ordinary and yet quite extraordinary happens: They become subjects to one another.

Up to this point of the connection between Charlotte and Bob, the visual action in the film tends to convey disjunction, misunderstanding, and a jangled sense of being in the world. The relationships between the various characters are filmed as physically out of sync, awkward, and unfulfilling. After Charlotte and Bob meet, there is a visual sense of growing synchrony. The gestural dance becomes increasingly more reciprocal; gaze and facial expression convey empathy and warmth without sentimentality. The screen more frequently shows two or more figures. Exciting sights and sounds are shared and created mutually. I also think that the space between the audience and the screen becomes more available to be mutually populated with shared meanings. One expression of this is when Charlotte and

Bob become accomplices in organizing an escape from the people and forces that emotionally empty them out. The metaphor for their internal escapes from alienation is to leave the hotel literally and to get involved with people who are actually engaged with one another.

Now, the camera is closer, there is movement, and the visual representations of characters are not so rigidly differentiated from each other. There is more fluidity and synchrony in the characters' interactions. Their movements are more relaxed and less contrived and reflect the ongoing nature of their involvement. This is a reciprocal dance, not a stage full of solo performers. They do not seem to view each other through lenses of preconception but rather are able to be interested in finding out about one another, not just as someone older or someone one-dimensionally sexual. The implicit eroticism is comfortably taken for granted because it is not based on objectification. There is the unstated assumption of choice. The group scene shot in front of windows no longer suggests estrangement but rather functions as a container for life.

When Bob sings "(What's So Funny 'Bout) Peace, Love, and Understanding?" by Elvis Costello and the Attractions (1978) at a karaoke bar, we see it concurrently through a funny, ironic lens and as a deeply felt lament and affirmation. This is what play looks like; it feels good, it's spontaneous, it doesn't take itself too seriously, and it is often about the only really important things. We can only play together when we recognize each other as subjects, and when we do, we feel alive.

In the scene when Bob carries a drunken Charlotte to bed, both eroticism and trust are suggested. There is an implicit acceptance that the external realities of their differences impose a barrier that, if transgressed, would result in something being lost. This is the reality principle. There is nothing precious or idealized about their relationship. They engage in the mundane realities of sore toes and achy bodies, but now they become lively and warm because they matter to each other. Whereas before, the alienation of language evoked frustration, anxiety, and sometimes meanness, now we see Bob react to the same frustrations in quite different ways: In the scene with a lady in the hospital waiting room, the frustrations of that which is lost in translation now evoke shared humor and mutuality. In a small, funny moment of shared humanity, Bob thanks a stripper and, in doing so, changes her from an object to a subject.

Bob and Charlotte watch *La Dolce Vita* (Fellini, 1960), another film about alienation. The Italian soundtrack is dubbed in Japanese. But now, rather than identifying with the film, they recall their own moments of meeting. As they lie in bed, Bob offers her the vantage point of experience. While not dismissing the reality of her lostness or flinching from the necessary compromises of life, he tells her that he's not afraid for her. The fragility and bravery of the moment are captured when he tentatively touches her foot. She doesn't flinch and neither do we, the audience.

In Kyoto, Charlotte watches a very formal wedding and sees a highly stylized kind of touch continued from antiquity. But now I imagine that she is able to sense something human. She joins the community of those who hope as she ties a fortune to the tree. Throughout this visit, she is filmed as alone, but I don't experience her as alone because I know that she knows that she lives in the thoughts of someone else. This knowledge is a big part of what gets us through our days.

We see the resuscitation of hope as Bob, talking on the phone with his wife, attempts to tell her that he yearns for something more. But this is not a fairy tale. She sharply rebuffs him, reminding him that this is the life that he has built and the life he will return to. As therapists, we know we have a tendency to weave ourselves into problematic relational configurations that express unconsciously remembered attempts to cope with times when things went very wrong back when we were developing our own selves. We had to go into hiding.

Sometimes we can rewrite the theater of our relationships, often to the great benefit of those we love. Sometimes we also come to realizations that allow us to find moments when we can partially, perhaps briefly, come out of hiding from behind the curtain of defensive strategies. But when we are momentarily able to hope that we can be found and then discover that no one wants, or is able, to see us, we scurry back to the safety—to paraphrase T. S. Eliot (1915)—in which we prepare a face to meet the faces that we meet.

After the failed attempt to connect with his wife, we see Bob's return to a sense of alienation. He seems to have lost the resilience that was hinted at after his connection with Charlotte. Attachment theory addresses the issue of how essential it is that we internalize a sense of relatedness characterized by what Erikson (1950) has called basic trust. With this achievement, we tacitly experience ourselves as worthy of being treated well and have the capacity not only to develop relationships that confirm this belief but also to possess an internal resilience that allows us to maintain an experience of ourselves as cohesive and worthy even in the face of the inevitable injuries that life inexorably inflicts.

The metaphor for this in *Lost in Translation* is Charlotte's injury that Bob cares for. Mothers heal skinned knees and bruised self-esteem with warmth and empathy as well as antibiotic cream. But wounds also heal by not losing sight of the movement of time. Trauma, especially relational trauma, freezes the moment of fragmentation in the unconscious, and we then live our lives as if the terror is still present and always will be. If we have internalized the expectation that turning to others in hopes of being found and healed will inevitably lead to retraumatization, we protect ourselves from trust. We imagine others as threats to be manipulated or avoided and/or as audiences to applaud our preferred versions of ourselves. While some measure of this is inevitable, when this fear-induced non-relatedness predominates, we are trapped alone in a house of mirrors that gives us nothing new, nothing nourishing, and we are left, like Bob in the cab, hidden, depleted, and listless.

When I use words like "being found," I'm trying to get at that singularly important and most frightening of experiences: to know and be known by another person as a subject with different perspectives and feelings. Their image of you can be quite different from your preconceptions. Hegel once said that what we desire most yet fear the most is to be known. Mitchell (1993) wrote of hope and dread in psychoanalysis and in life. When things have gone badly, we are too frightened to be found. Instead, we have to settle for stimulations that ward off terror at the cost of always being just one step ahead of despair. These necessary compromises leave us running in place, always yearning and rarely knowing it.

Bob, shaken by the failure of his hope with his wife, retreats into the illusory solution of a one-night stand with a stranger. As is so often the case with our abortive attempts to dodge the abyss, he wakes alone in bed, both literally and existentially. Charlotte takes the one-night stand as a betrayal. She thought she was important to him. Then she was dropped. But what counts here is that they survive the necessary retaliatory cruelty, aided and abetted by the forced proximity of a convenient fire alarm. While they wait, they hate each other, they talk, and they forgive. There was damage; there was reparation.

But there is also the existential fact of loss. And, of course, this is not simply an artifact of the forced transience of Charlotte and Bob's moment of belonging. Loss is always there—in change, in betrayals (both enduring and ephemeral), in necessary leavings, and ultimately in death. It is a small consolation to know that without the binaries of life and death, of having and losing, neither would have meaning. Up would have no meaning without down. The hall scene, in which Charlotte and Bob stand together in a moment full of pauses and off-center kisses, becomes a visual poem about just how impossible it is to negotiate that metaphorical tearing of human tissue, that is, the experience of real loss. So very much is at stake.

Toward the end of the film, in the lobby, when Bob, deadpan, accuses Charlotte of stealing his jacket, none of us wonder what loss he's really talking about. And it is not gratuitous that he literally turns away from his visual reflection in the admiring eyes of an attractive woman to symbolically find someone who has found him as a full other. Their awkward conversation in the lobby reiterates the theme of just how much is inevitably lost in translation.

But here's the thing. Coppola won't settle for the tidy closure of simple tragedy. With the whispered message that Bob leaves with Charlotte, we are left unresolved. In doing so, Coppola hints at the ephemeral uncertainty of hope. She won't let us rest.

References

Aron, L. (1996). *A meeting of minds*. Hillsdale: Analytic Press.

Beebe, B., & Lachmann, F. (2002). *Infant research and adult treatment: co-construction interaction*. Hillsdale: Analytic Press.

Buber, M. (1996). *I and thou* (W. Kaufmann, Trans.). New York: Touchstone/Simon & Schuster. Originally published 1923.

Coppola, F. F. (Director). (1979). Apocalypse now [Motion picture]. United States: Omni Zoetrope.

Coppola, S. (Director). (2003). Lost in translation [Motion picture]. United States: American Zoetrope.

Costello, E. (1978). (What's so funny 'bout) peace, love, and understanding? On Armed forces [LP]. Columbia Records, New York, New York.

Eliot, T. S. (1915). The love song of J. Alfred Prufrock. *Poetry Foundation*. Retrieved from www.poetryfoundation.org/poetrymagazine/poems/44212/the-love-song-of-j-alfred-prufrock

Erikson, E. (1950). *Childhood and society*. New York: Norton.

Fellini, F. (Director). (1960). La dolce vita [Motion picture]. Italy: Astor Pictures.

Kohut, H. (1984). *How does analysis cure?* Chicago: University of Chicago Press.

Mitchell, S. (1993). *Hope and dread in psychoanalysis*. New York: Basic Books.

Stern, D. (1985). *The interpersonal world of the infant*. New York: Basic Books.

Thompson, A. (2003, Fall). Tokyo story. *Filmmaker Magazine*. Retrieved from www.filmmakermagazine.com/archives/issues/fall2003/features/tokyo_story.php

Winnicott, D. W. (1974). *Mirror-role of mother and family in child development in playing and reality*. New York: Penguin.

Part 3

Groups, culture, and the environment

8   Birnam Wood

Robert Langan

Prologue

To approach the topic of "belonging," I first thought about Freud's (1919/1959) experiential distinction between the heimlich and the unheimlich, the comfortably homey and the disconcertingly uncanny. The psychoanalytic catch is that the comforts of home can themselves become strange if secrets are discovered, lies and omissions revealed. To "share" a secret can mean paradoxically to join in keeping it from others or to reveal it to others. Psychoanalysis addresses secrets we keep from ourselves. There is a way that even our most intimate selves are stories, based on the make-believe knowing of what's what. We are, after all, cast into a world not of our own making with parents we did not choose telling us who we are. Yet we are born from nowhere, there to return. Outside knowing, the unconscious looms. The belonging safety of the heimlich can seed demonization of the unheimlich, and so provoke dualistic me/not-me confrontation evermore. That is, unless we dare to recognize ourselves all as strangers in a strange land (Exodus 2:22), alike in our being different, and so dare to extend to each other a hand.

I thought I might explicate these ideas with reference, say, to the Buddhist equivalence of self and no-self, form fundamentally being emptiness; or with reference to Wittgenstein's notion of family resemblance; or with reference to examples of losing oneself to find oneself in varieties of religious experience. But instead I began to feel that rather than write about belonging, I should much rather describe an identificatory experience of coming to belong, to show how the redemption of separateness lies in our bonding with others. So I chose to write a story. Here it is. You can decide whether it belongs.

A Story

"Birnam Wood"

The boys were all Boy Scouts. The boys were at their summer getaway, Boy Scout Camp Birnam Wood, high on the national forest Angeles Crest for two weeks away from home and Mom and the family usuals, testing independence, with three-blade pocket knives in their pockets, thirteen and older, with Bowie knives in a sheath on their khaki canvas brass-clasp-buckled officially issued membership-identification-required-for-purchase belts. Carry your Scout card. Identify other Scouts by shaking hands with the middle three fingers extended in the secret handshake. Bowies could with practice be flung from the tip, flipping through the air until chunk stabbing deep into the bark of a tree. The tree suffers silently. We can protect ourselves if attacked by a bear in the woods. They learned in camp gathering wood and building fires and how to cook, how not to burn the forest down around them, how to catch a fish from the stream and gut and eat it, how to lash a stick-and-leaf shelter together, how to tie knots in a rope to rescue a friend who had fallen over a cliff and needed rescuing, not forgetting that the fallen friend could be yourself.

The boys knew one another from all going to the same school, but better from their tighter association in Troop 361, the school-sponsored affiliate of the national Boy Scouts of America, with its weekly Friday night troop meetings of seven patrols of five to eight boys each with a patrol father for guidance, and troop weekend games and field trips and the summer getaway, and weekly patrol meetings as well, focused on each Scout earning merit badges (swimming, canoeing, compass orienteering, first aid, and more and more) to advance through the ranks from just-joined Tenderfoot to exalted Eagle Scout, exemplar of achievement, merit badge sash festooned with embroidered circlets depicting swimmer in the waves, paddler J-stroking in canoe, compass honed true north, bandages Red Crossed, and more and more and more until the Eagle flies. Aspiration enticed, path outlined, belongingness secretly assured. Just stick with the program. (Let Mother hope the boy not grow out of the uniform and all the insignia have to be resewn.)

Walter and Roger (both aged thirteen) were senior in the ranks, both having risen to Star Scout and thereby ascended to the Officer Patrol, Walter the Drill Leader, Roger the Scribe, responsible for dues-keeping and recording of deployments in the Troop Log. Only the rest of Walter's and Roger's patrol had not come to the camp-out. Some had conflicting family vacations. One guiltily acknowledged an invitation to a girl's birthday party. Walter's father was the Assistant Scoutmaster, in charge of the deployment of Troop 361 to Birnam Wood. Like many of the other fathers, he had been a soldier in World War II and wanted to impart soldierly values to his son. Roger, when asked, had no father, readying the assumption that his father was dead, denying the fact that his parents had divorced before he could remember and that his father, though living, was dead to him, unmet and unseen. It was Roger whose young uncle would substitute for a father at father-son Scout banquets. It was Roger who felt himself on the periphery. He had told only Walter about his father. Walter kept the secret.

Walter and Roger had been given the serious responsibility of supervising the other boys whose rag-tag patrols had not shown up in force for the camp-out. The older boys got, the more likely they were to shirk Scouting. So when a full patrol did not muster, the rag-tags were gathered together to form a patrol of the occasion, a grab-bag of leftovers. On arrival, cabins were assigned. Walter's father took him and Roger aside to explain that they would be in charge of the boys assigned to Woodpecker Cabin, with no adult available to spend the night with them. As ranking Scoutmaster, he was obliged to sleep in the main lodge in earshot of the sole telephone. In case of emergency at Woodpecker, they were to report to a father in a nearby cabin. He knew he could trust them with this responsibility.

So camp routine began, with reveille and the raising of the flag, breakfast in the mess hall, the obligatory morning swim, merit badge activities and hikes and crafts and games, the evening meal, the lowering of the flag, and the nightrise campfire with songs and skits and stories, then to bed.

Below the dark starry sky above the treetops brushing chill in the air, central campfire tumbling to embers, last notes of "Taps" fading from the bugle, the cries of patrol leaders summoned their members. Walter repeatedly called out "Woodpecker," Roger at his side, privately amused at the seeming birdcall. In answer, there came Tony, just thirteen, a chubby fellow with a ready grin; Brad, small for his age of twelve, but able to do a forward mid-air somersault from a standing position; Charlie, eleven, shy so that no one seemed to know him very well; Simon, also eleven, a quiet one as well, but all ears and eyes, taking everything in; and ten-and-three-quarters-year-old Peter. Boys were supposed to be eleven to be admitted into the Scouts, but an exception was made for Peter because his older brother was already in the troop. He joined, and his brother promptly quit for newfound interests in high school.

Walter called out a formal roll call, while Roger checked off the names in his patrol log. No one said "President" instead of "Present." Walter called for presentation of flashlights. Everyone's worked. Walter leading, Roger bringing up the end of the file, their beams of light flashing this way and that, they set off through the trees on the narrow path past other cabins into the darker woods at the periphery of the camp, where the Woodpecker Cabin stood visually isolated, ringed in its own grove of Douglas Firs.

It was a log cabin, with an entry door in the middle of one face, a small paned window at the back, four double bunk beds, and a single bed for the counselor. A woodburning stove stood before the window, firewood available but unused in the summer. There was no electricity.

Roger had selected the counselor's single bed by the door, Walter a top bunk near the back window, the other boys lower and upper bunks, leaving two free. Everyone had a clear sightline to everyone else, but the only lights were their flashlights. It was cold.

Walter remembered, "I forgot to have us stop at the outhouse. Does anyone need to pee?"

Brad responded, "Who needs the outhouse? We can just pee in the bushes."

"We're not supposed to do that. Besides, there aren't any bushes here. It's just trees and pine needles all over the ground."

Tony volunteered, "Trees were made to pee on. Doesn't everyone know that?"

Brad added, "My dog knows that. Trees and fire hydrants."

Everyone laughed, including Walter. Only Roger knew Walter's secret, confided when they first shared a pup tent at age eleven: Walter had just managed to stop peeing in bed. But if he did that night in his sleeping bag, he wanted

Roger's promise not to tell. Roger promised. In the morning, no pee to tell about. But Roger never told.

Walter continued, "No one needs to pee, then?" Heads shook no. "Well, I'll step out to pee on a tree." He did. When he approached the chosen tree, he pocketed his flashlight and felt the dark and the cold clasp him. As his eyes adjusted, he sensed his surround of tree after tree fading to unseeable sentinels of the night, the forest miles deep, branches swaying, and the sound, over his trickle of urine, of the quiet swish of the wind against countless upheld needles. Finished, with a shiver down his spine, he hurried back inside, carefully latching the cabin door.

Hanging their clothes on pegs pounded into the log walls, the boys stripped down to their underwear and zipped themselves into their sleeping bags—except for Charlie, who risked goosebumps to pull on the pyjamas his mother insisted he bring. He was glad they weren't ones with the feet sewn into them. He was glad no one teased him for being different.

Keeping an arm outside their sleeping bags, they played at chasing each other's flashlight beams across the timbered ceiling. Brad wanted to change it into a game with rules and winners and losers, but the others lost interest.

Tony asked, "Did you see that recruiting flyer with the photo of me getting my First Class promotion?"

"That came in the mail?" Murmured assents.

Charlie asked, "Wasn't that embarrassing? You had sweat stains under your armpits the size of saucers!"

"Who cares? What I was really worried about was that my grandma visiting from Italy was there, and I thought in front of everybody she was going to hug and kiss me and pinch my cheeks. Now that's embarrassing."

"Why didn't she?"

"My parents must've held her back. I like her, but she hardly speaks English, so it's all kissy goo-goo." The boys joined in noises of retching.

Brad asked, "Did you start to use deodorant? I have. It helps keep the sweat down."

"I haven't noticed it smells much, but maybe I should give it a try. Could I use yours?"

"Sure, but I didn't bring it to camp." Roger and Walter volunteered that they used it on school days but hadn't brought it to camp either.

Peter, the youngest, said, "My brother uses it all the time, but he's shaving now, too. Dad gave him a razor and shaving cream and the whole family went into the bathroom for pictures of his first shave. He was pretty embarrassed, I tell you."

Simon spoke up from his quiet reserve of attention, asking generally, "Does anyone get embarrassed when they make us go naked for morning swim?"

"I do!" declared Charlie. The routine was for the three troops currently at the camp to take turns, going troop by troop to leave their clothes in the changing area, rinse off with soap in the showers, wade through the disinfectant foot bath, and frolic in the heated outdoor pool, where there would be too many of them really to swim.

Walter vouched, "I think it's to make sure that we all bathe with soap, so that we don't go home after two weeks and freak out our mothers." More laughter.

Roger observed, "Also you get a chance to have a good look at what your body changes look like down there, going from no hair to lots. I mean, we're all going through the same thing sooner or later."

"I kind of like being naked, especially outdoors," offered Brad, "because you're just you, like a deer in the woods. And besides, everybody's naked and we're all boys, so there's no need to cover up."

"But you know what doesn't happen?" asked Peter. "No one ever gets a boner!"

Amidst a general groan of protest, Charlie exclaimed, "Oh no," and Simon and Peter agreed. "Now that's really embarrassing. I'd die!"

Roger recounted, "You know once at school Miss Sigurdson called on Andy Gibbs to come up to the blackboard for an arithmetic problem, and he did this Groucho Marx walk all the way with a big grin. Everybody thought it was funny but kind of stupid and he told me later he did it to hide his hard-on."

"That's true," said Tony. "You never know when the little friend might pop up to say hello. I remember the first time in fifth grade assembly standing for salute to the flag. I happened to lean forward against the chair in front of me and boing!"

"I usually wake up with one."

"Me, too."

"Me, too."

"I sort of discovered it," confided Brad, "in the shower—I mean the shower at home, with the soap and all. Did you know you can hang a washcloth on it?"

"I've done that," confessed Walter. "And one time when my father was in the bathroom shaving, I stepped out of the shower kind of to show him."

"What'd he say?" chimed several.

"He said, 'My, you're getting to be a man, aren't you?' and went on shaving."

"That's all he said?"

"That's all."

"Maybe he was embarrassed?" wondered Peter.

Walter mused, "Maybe. You know, we've never had the birds-and-the-bees talk. Has anybody with their dad?" No one had. "I remember once asking him where babies come from and he said, 'From love between a man and a woman. You'll find out more as you grow up.' And that was that."

Simon hesitantly asked, "Well … where do babies come from?"

"You don't know?"

"Sort of, but not really …"

Charlie intervened. "I don't want to hear this!"

To which Walter replied, "Then plug your ears. And Roger, this is a job for you." Charlie did not plug his ears.

Roger cleared his throat. "A while back, I was in a used bookstore and came across this book, *Ideal Marriage*. It was written by a doctor for newlyweds and it's all about sex! I mixed it in with another couple books so the clerk didn't really notice and let me buy it."

Tony protested. "So you make babies with a cookbook? Come on, Roger, out with it!"

"So your wife lies down and spreads her legs, and you get on top of her with a hard-on and slide it inside her. And you push it in and out and it feels really good."

Brad mused, "It must be like doing push-ups on top of her. Maybe that's why they make such a big deal about push-ups in gym class." Laughter.

Roger continued. "And then it feels really really good, and this stuff called sperm comes out of your dick, and then you're done. Though the doctor says something about maybe taking a shower for personal hygiene."

Simon, abashed, wondered, "My mother would do something like that?"

Charlie concurred reluctantly. "Must be only a few times in her life to make a baby." He paused, puzzled, then asked, "But how does doing that make a baby?"

"Oh, yeah, that," Roger responded. "The sperm actually has like a zillion teeny tadpoles in it—I mean really teeny, like you need a microscope to see them. And they swim around until one of them finds the mother's teeny egg and joins up with it, and that grows and grows inside her belly for nine months until out comes baby!"

"And so here we are," concluded Walter. "Each one of us started out as a little squirt." This time, no one laughed. They shared a bafflement at the mystery of creation.

Peter was worried. Hesitantly, he began, "You know, my brother told me about getting a boner and how to make it feel good going up and down, how to beat off, but when I do it … I mean at the end, nothing comes out, no sperm. Am I all right?"

Roger reassured him. "Yes, you are perfectly okay. It's because you're still too young to come. When you start getting some hair, then it'll start to happen."

"What does it look like, the sperm?" asked Peter.

Tony intervened. "Wait a sec. I'll show you." He thwacked vigorously against the inside of his sleeping bag half a dozen times, then extended his arm in the air, fingertips touching, for all to see. "Have a look."

Flashlights convened on the hand, something shiny and sticky wet on the fingers.

"I don't believe it! You can't come just like that."

"Gross!"

"You're kidding us, aren't you?"

"I can't believe you'd show everyone!"

And Charlie declared, "You are not supposed to play with yourself."

"Well," responded Tony with mock frostiness, retracting his arm, "I'll just take my toys and go home."

Brad quipped, "Don't you mean 'Go home to your toy'?" There was uneasy laughter.

Roger resumed. "It says in the Boy Scout Handbook …"

"Holy moly, you've actually read that, too?"

"Well, parts. If you hunt up 'sex' in the index—and it's there; it wasn't in the old edition—there's a short paragraph saying it's best not to think about it because it can become a 'bad habit.' I think they mean beating off—or masturbation, it's called. And instead you should do some other project, like putting together a model airplane."

Peter protested, "But my brother said it was okay to do, just something private, and he was almost an Eagle Scout before he quit."

Tony proposed the dilemma, "So you're sitting there in your room and you think, 'Let's see. What do I want to do? Make another model airplane or do something that feels really good? Hmm.' "

Brad added, "Maybe the project should be masturbation. You could get a merit badge in it!" Laughter broke out.

"The patch on your sash could be a penis standing at attention," says one.

Said another, "But you'd have to explain when it wasn't there on your sash for Inspection, 'I'm sorry, Sir. I earned it but it keeps coming off.' " Hoots rose among them.

They calmed down.

Tony, once again extending his arm, quietly announced, "Okay, the first time it was just spit, but this time it's the real thing." The flashlights homed in on his hand, and the whitish, thick fluid clung between them as he moved his fingers.

Roger acknowledged, "That's what it looks like."

Walter confirmed, "Yes, that's the real thing."

Tony retracted his arm. No one said anything. The spots of light meandered around the ceiling. They had become secret sharers, bonded in silence.

Simon, who half knew from his own body but half didn't, having avoided the confusing feelings, dared to ask, "What does a hard-on look like?" The latent question was whether you can show yourself to, or be yourself with, others.

Tony protested, "No way! I am not going there! That's private!"

Walter wondered, "But why is that private and showing a glob of sperm isn't private? I don't get it. We're all boys, aren't we? What's the big deal?" The others suddenly knew what was about to happen even before Walter did.

Walter unzipped his sleeping bag and uplifted his erection skyward. The flashlights homed in on center stage. Walter sang a fanfare, "Dut di-di-dah di-di-dah."

Brad gleefully exclaimed, "It's just like mine."

"Same as me."

"Me, too."

"Me, too."

"Me, too," agreed the others.

They felt a common belonging. And an initiation of sorts, a shared secret.

Walter concluded, "So we're all pretty much alike, aren't we?" Yet he began to feel only half-proud, now half-embarrassed. "Okay, show's over." He zipped up.

Walter reverted to his more comfortable role as patrol leader, even the tone of his voice changing: "Okay, it's time for lights out. Shall we have a story from Roger?"

Murmurs of assent. This had become a routine after Roger had volunteered a story their first night together in the cabin.

"All right," Roger said. "Give me a minute to think." They lay in the dark in their beds, the whispering of their surround of trees emerging from the background. They were glad to be together, not alone.

Roger began: "Once upon a time—this was when everyone was poor, in the Great Depression, before the War—there was a bunch of runaway boys who'd met in a freight car. They were wandering around the country, hopping on trains. So this one time they came to a hobo camp and were begging for food, but the …"

"What's a hobo?" asked Peter.

"Like a bum, a homeless man with no job. There were lots of them then … So the hoboes were all fighting and drinking and wouldn't share any food, and the boys decided to make their own camp in the woods. They set off, and in this deep grove of trees discovered an empty log cabin! They decided that's where they'd spend the night.

"But as they were falling asleep, they heard the trees creaking and whispering in the wind, then realized they could understand what the trees were saying. They were hissing, 'You boys have killed our brothers to make your log cabin. You are sleeping among their bones.' The boys cried out that they hadn't built the cabin, they'd just found it, but the trees answered, 'Then you shall pay the price for your fathers' crimes.'

"The boys wanted to run away, but the trees had moved! There was a big tree trunk blocking the only door and three tree trunks against the window. The trees said, 'You cannot escape. When you wake in the morning, each of you will have become a tree in our secret grove.' And that's just what happened. The end."

After a stunned silence, Walter said with irony, "Gee, Roger, thanks a lot. That makes it really easy to fall asleep."

But fall asleep they did, and in the morning no one awoke as a tree.

Nonetheless, after life's long shuffles of when and where, each would end up encased in the wooden crate of a coffin, probed for nourishment by the gentle roots of trees.

The End

Epilogue

Can I show myself to, or be myself with, others? Am I the same or other? Have I a refuge in sameness or exile in difference? Do I belong or not belong?

These are the latent questions with which the boys grapple. "Boy Scout" (do not fail to capitalize) is a shared identity, a belonging to the larger polity (like practice for Citizenship, a potential merit badge). It is a claim to recognition, promising some certainty as to who I am in others' eyes and who those others are who stake my claim. We wear the same uniform, know the secret handshake, share a code of conduct and an aspirational ranking. We pledge allegiance to the flag of the US of A. The path to the future is paved, belonging assured.

But (there is always a "but") when certainty overrides its tenuous grounds, the uniform can entrap the person. The sins of the fathers can curse the sons with a bygone soldierly prescription for living in a world of poverty and war, of haves and hobo have-nots, of loyal conformists versus unbridled renegades. The comforting certainty of "Just like mine!" and "Me, too!" obtrudes on the uncertainties of difference. The future is fundamentally unpredictable. Bodies change involuntarily. Accidents fall off cliffs. Bears sometimes attack. The only certainty, one way or another, is death. Born alone to die alone, we all belong to the grim reaper.

This existential perspective (Langan, 1995; May, Angel, & Ellenberger, 1958) distinguishes three simultaneous and interrelated worlds of being. First is umwelt, where one finds oneself embodied with physical reality all round, obligated to take it in as food, air, and water and to find in it safe space to live. The experience of being oneself in one's own world, a subjective and private consciousness within yet apart from that outer world, minds eigenwelt. As well, the separation of the solitary thinker occurs in the perpetual midst of all those other chattering people out there, present or not, with whom one finds oneself in the mitwelt, the cultural interchange of humanity.

How is it to be oneself with another? The question grows complicated: Which self with which other, and when and where and to what purpose? The other person can be one's smiling mother and her open arms, or a distant silhouette caught in the crosshairs of one's rifle scope, or a passing pedestrian, or an attentive waitress, or one's very best friend. The continuum of being-with runs from person as thing to person as self, from emotional distance to the closeness of intimate affiliation (Langan, 1999).

Winnicott (1971/1986) descries a developmental leap in the continuum. Early "object relating" treats the other person as a projective object, a thing to be manipulated. Tyrant baby rules from the high chair—or tries to, even if tantrums over frustrated gratifications have little effect. We can only hope baby grows up, achieving transition to the "object usage" that recognizes the other person as a subjective partner in a shared reality. The other person is not shackled to one's expectations but greeted openly person to person. The other is allowed to be, and valued for being, other.

Ghent (1990) maintains that many relationships under therapeutic purview exemplify a sadomasochistic retreat to "object relating." Sadist and masochist follow their scripts in monotonous repetition of their roles, thereby each substituting a false self for the deeper intimacy of "object usage." Nonetheless, "there is, however deeply buried or frozen, a longing for … surrender, in the sense of yielding, of false self" (p. 109). This surrender is not a defeat but an opening, a transcendence, a liberation. It is what the boys in Woodpecker Cabin dared to do.

Winnicott (1971/1986) generalizes:

> Of every individual who has reached to the stage of being a unit with a limiting membrane and an outside and an inside, it can be said there is an inner reality to that individual … if there is a need for this double statement, there is also need for a triple one: the third part of the life of a human being, a

part that we cannot ignore, is an intermediate area of experiencing, to which inner reality and external life both contribute. It is an area that ... shall exist as a resting-place for the individual engaged in the perpetual human task of keeping inner and outer reality separate yet interrelated.

(p. 2)

That resting-place is the playground of illusion, an "intermediate area between the subjective and that which is objectively perceived" (p. 3).

It is transitional space, that trap-door in the mitwelt that proffers a falling through, a letting go, a surrender of presumptions and certainties the better to allow unthought possibilities and undreamt vistas. In this space occur the deconstruction and reconstruction of realities, the molting of selves, the selective incorporation of others' thoughts and feelings, manners and styles, strengths and weaknesses. This space is the arena of interbeing. Perhaps it needs its own name, zwischenwelt, world of the between. (Or, via Tibetan Buddhism, the bardo.)

Whereas the worlds of outside, inside, and with stay locked in the grip of dia-chronic now-then time and dualistic here-there space, interbeing invites a suspension of usual time and space. The medieval Scholastics called it the nunc stans and hic stans of being, the ever-present moment of now and here that cups the flow of time and space.

Interbeing is "out of this world" and relates directly to the experience of truly loving relationship. It is a "falling in love." We belong to one another. Two sense themselves as one. There is a quality of naked meeting. Buber (1923/1970) described it as I and Thou, touching on its overriding immediacy, intimacy, and intimation of the sacred. The Buddha woke to it as enlightenment. (See Langan, 2006.)

Interbeing entails a capacity to rest intimately between knowing and not knowing both self and others. Too much knowing devolves into a closed-system world of checklist descriptors and infallible truths. Too much not knowing invites the chaotic limbo of psychosis. But a balanced receptivity to the flow of experi-ence, inner and outer, lends itself to a continuing maturational growth. Interbeing vitalizes engagement with life.

In this light, clinical diagnosis is less a matter of categorization than an assessment of how stuck or not are a patient's habits of mind. Psychotherapy becomes a disruptive interchange of ways of being. Maturational change con-tinues through life, but with markers and measures idiosyncratic for each of us.

What did the boys in Woodpecker Cabin dare to do? They dared to risk shame and embarrassment by surrendering protective reserve. They broke boundaries. They revealed secret fears and doubts and forbidden questions. They supported and informed one another. They showed as well as told, with a measure of trust between them. They felt all alike, glad to be together. They faced fate in the abrupt, inescapable grip of marching trees. And that evening, without knowing it, they determined truly to live their lives before they died.

Another end

References (explicit and implicit)

Bachelard, G. (1994). *The poetics of space.* Boston: Beacon Press. Originally published 1958.

Boy Scouts of America National Council. (1958). *Boy Scouts of America: handbook for boys 1958.* Irving: Boy Scouts of America.

Buber, M. (1970). *I and thou* (W. Kaufman, Trans.). New York: Charles Scribner. Originally published 1923.

Conrad, J. (2003). The secret sharer. In J. Conrad, *The secret sharer and other stories: 'twixt land and sea and tales of hearsay* (pp. 86–126). London: Folio Society. Originally published 1912.

Farber, L. H. (1966). *The ways of the will.* New York: Basic Books.

Freud, S. (1959). The uncanny. In J. Strachey (Ed.), *The standard edition of the complete psychological works of Sigmund Freud* (Vol. 17, pp. 253–264). London: Hogarth Press. Originally published 1919.

Frie, R. (2017). *Not in my family: German memory and responsibility after the Holocaust.* New York: Oxford University Press.

Ghent, E. (1990). Masochism, submission, surrender: masochism as a perversion of surrender. *Contemporary Psychoanalysis, 26*(1),108–136.

Golding, W. (1954). *Lord of the flies.* London: Faber and Faber.

Heinlein, R. (1961). *Stranger in a strange land.* New York: G. P. Putnam.

James, W. (1987). *The varieties of religious experience: a study in human nature, being the Gifford Lectures on natural religion delivered at Edinburgh in 1901–1902.* New York: Library of America. Originally published 1902.

Kanwal, G., & Akhtar, S., Eds. (2019). *Intimacy: clinical, cultural, digital and developmental perspectives.* London and New York: Routledge.

King James. (1865). *The Holy Bible containing the Old and New Testaments: translated out of the original tongues: and with the former translations diligently compared and revised, by His Majesty's Special Command.* Oxford: Oxford University Press. Originally published 1611.

Langan, R. P. (1995). I thou other: fluid being in triadic context. *Contemporary Psychoanalysis, 31*(2), 327–339.

Langan, R. P. (1999). Coming to be: change by affiliation. *Contemporary Psychoanalysis, 35*(1), 67–80.

Langan, R. P. (2006). *Minding what matters: psychotherapy and the Buddha within.* Boston: Wisdom.

May, R., Angel, E., & Ellenberger, H. F. (Eds.). (1958). *Existence: a new dimension in psychiatry and psychology.* New York: Basic Books.

Mendis, K. N. G. (1979). *On the no-self characteristic (anatta-lakkhana sutta).* Kandy: Buddhist Publication Society.

Shakespeare, W. (1956). *Macbeth.* Baltimore: Penguin Books. Originally published 1623.

Van de Velde, Th. H., MD. (1947). *Ideal marriage: its physiology and technique* (20th ed.). London: William Heinemann Medical Books. Originally published 1928.

White, E. B. (1997). Once more to the lake. In E. B. White, *One man's meat* (pp. 198–203). Gardiner: Tilbury House. Originally published 1941.

Winnicott, D. W. (1986). *Playing and reality.* London: Tavistock. Originally published 1971.

Wittgenstein, L. (1958). *Philosophical investigations* (2nd ed.). Oxford: Blackwell. Originally published 1953.

9 From attachment to detachment

The transformation of "belonging" in the kibbutz

Zvi Steve Yadin

> Before night falls—come, oh come all!
> A unified stubborn effort, awake
> with a thousand arms. Is it impossible to roll
> the stone from the mouth of the well?
>
> Rachel the Poetess (Rachel Bluwstein)

It is no wonder that the words "longing" and "belonging" have a similar sound. When people live alone, they naturally long for the company of others—for inter-personal relationships, for membership in a clan; in short, for belonging. A lone person is like a single thread; by gaining a sense of acceptance as a member of a group, this slim strand is interwoven with the others and the individual is granted the strength of a rope.

Belonging was a common experience for members of the kibbutz (the Hebrew word for "group"). The kibbutz was designed as a voluntary democratic commu-nity where individuals work on a noncompetitive basis; every member finishes working at the same time, and everyone is supposed to achieve the same results. As a result, no one suffers and all share in the output. After its inception, the movement spread its wings and these collective communities blossomed and took root throughout the country of Israel. This chapter analyzes vignettes of modern Hebrew literature related to the kibbutz as it follows the transformation from the members' sense of belonging to their own little communities with total commitment to the collective, to the privatization of their property and a radical shift in social and economic values. My research (Yadin, 1984) focuses on the psychological aspects of these changes as illustrated in the work of a group of young writers who were born in Israel in the 1920s, lived on kibbutz, and started publishing their stories around the time of the establishment of the State of Israel in 1948. They were the first generation of writers who were born into and grew up in a blossoming Jewish secular and national culture. Hebrew—which had just been revived as a modern spoken and literary language in the late nineteenth century—was their native tongue; they knew its roots and layers and brought new life and style to the biblical language.

The literature of this generation reflects the strong sense of attachment that was central to the early period of kibbutz life, followed by the slow erosion of the founders' values and the gradual detachment from traditional engagements within the kibbutz (as well as in the broader Israeli population). In their early works, the emphasis for these authors was on the "we": the attachment of the individual to the young Jewish community, intensified by the strong bond of belonging to the kibbutz as well as to the militia force that would soon become the Israeli Army. They started publishing stories about their battles against the neighboring Arabs who, after Israel's statehood was declared, attacked the young country from all sides. They also wrote about kibbutz life, searching their souls about their own place in the kibbutz, their struggles in relation to others who joined the kibbutz later, and their relationship to Israeli society as a whole. After the War of Independence—the protracted military conflict that began the day after the establishment of the state and ended in 1949—the values of the kibbutz began to change, and the authors slowly began to shift their focus from the "we" to the "I."

The literature of the kibbutz demonstrates the ongoing inner struggle for members between their personal wishes for self-actualization and the needs and the demands of the community. My analysis suggests that these major changes in group psychology may shed light on the inclination of individuals to strive for individuality and for the freedom to be whoever they want to be. Though group members often choose to make compromises during challenging times by giving up their liberty to better serve the community, this literature indicates that they revert to the desire for personal freedom when external pressures are relieved.

The kibbutz, the militia, and the community: the culture of "we"

The group of authors whose works I discuss is referred to as the "*Palmach* generation," since most served in the *Palmach* (Hebrew acronym for "strike forces"), the elite fighting unit of the Jewish underground army during the British Mandate in Palestine (formally in force between 1923 and 1948). As a result, they shared a strong sense of belonging both to the kibbutz and to the militia force. The theme of the collective runs loud and clear in the *Palmach* anthem: "**We** are ready when the command is given / Always **we**, **we** the *Palmach*." The emphasis was on "*we; always we.*"

The "we" as depicted by these authors was characterized by small groups of kibbutzniks (kibbutz members) who were the protagonists of their stories. Their early literature, which explicitly championed the values of belonging to the collective, was labeled as "mobilization" or "propaganda" literature. The literary critics of the *Palmach* generation judged them harshly, depicting them as members of a solipsistic tribe who believed that everything revolved around their actions and focused their writings on just a few subjects related to their narrow world. The critics proposed that this new trend in Hebrew literature resulted from the loss of Jewish cultural life in Europe and represented an attempt to replace it with the secular folklore of Israel. On the positive side, the critics noted that the *Palmach* writers brought fresh language and expression to Israeli literature, tapped into the new style of Jewish life, and depicted the rugged landscape of the country.

Still, the writers of the *Palmach* generation were blasted for alienating themselves from previous generations and especially for being influenced by the translated Russian literature of World War II. One book that had a marked impact was the novel *General Panfilov's Reserve*, based on the real-life character Ivan Panfilov, a Soviet general noted for his courage during the battle of Moscow who later became a posthumous hero in the Soviet Union. It became a major influence on the *Palmach* and later on the young Israeli army, where it was used as a standard tactical handbook for the Israeli Defense Forces (Shahal, 2007).

It should be emphasized that the "we" mindset predominated during a period of deep uncertainty for the young Jewish community prior to the establishment of the State. At that time the Arab communities in Palestine were feeling threatened by Jews who were settling and building across the land; they established their own militias and fought to deter the new settlers from establishing their homes. Fighting for survival, members of the *Palmach* had only one option: united *we* stand, divided *we* fall. Attachment to the collective was heightened by economic factors; the nascent Jewish community had scarce resources and people were drawn to the kibbutz as a source of vigor and security. The young pioneers were ready to sacrifice individualism in order to accept *equality of outcome*, where each person lives under the same economic conditions, to ensure an equal chance within a structured framework of rules.

In their early stories, the authors of the *Palmach* generation portrayed the hero as a man who contributes to society, bravely battles the nation's enemies, and struggles to break new ground under adverse life conditions; he immerses himself within the community and obliterates his own individuality. In later novels, however, the focus gradually shifts as the authors begin to tackle the struggle between the individual's needs and desire for self-expression vs. the demands of the kibbutz community and the Israeli collective as a whole. I addressed the "we"/ "I" dynamic with the *Palmach* authors in a series of private conversations (1982– 1984). Moshe Shamir, a prominent writer who later became a member of the Israeli Knesset, described it as follows: "There is a pendulum in all literature and in every artist that swings between the personal/intimate and the social/belonging sides of human nature. I too am tossed by this pendulum." When I questioned the others about their perspective on the collective culture of their time, I gained a more nuanced understanding of the reality of the "we." The writer Nathan Shaham, whose works are explored in this paper, explained that "the notion 'we' should not imply blind loyalty to a certain group. The need to question each other is part of your self's survival. But maintaining your 'self' does not mean obliterating it to the 'we.'" Izhar Smilanski, another prominent author and Knesset member, expressed his view that the "we" becomes second nature when a crisis arises. "But when the storm is over," he added, "the individual sheds the new habits, returns to his nature, and reverts to his original qualities," that is, the pendulum shifts back to the personal side of the spectrum. The author Yigal Mossinson described the spirit of the "we" as "a culture of small groups, sitting around the bonfire, discovering the new land, and walking in the steps of the Bible." He sees the "we" as a product of unity brought about by the battles his generation fought together, but he too reflected on its temporal nature: "When the War of Independence was over, the family feuds started."

Always we: the evolution of Nathan Shaham

The *Palmach* generation produced a vast body of literature; to narrow the scope, I focus on the works of Nathan Shaham, a prolific writer and the only one of his generation who remained on the kibbutz through the end of his life. Born in Tel Aviv in 1925, Shaham began living on Kibbutz Bet Alfa in northern Israel in 1945 and published for seventy years until his death in 2018. Like others of this group, he served in the *Palmach* during the 1947 War of Independence. In fact, the title of one of Shaham's (1952) early novels, *Always We*, echoes the words of the *Palmach* anthem. The novel's protagonist is a kibbutz member and a soldier who fights in the war. As one might predict, he freely surrenders his individuality to the norms and will of the collective, with an understanding that this identification is the right step to take in demanding times. Shaham's (1948) first book of short stories, *Grain and Lead*, epitomizes the genre of propaganda literature. The title itself fuses the two foundational pillars of the *Palmach* generation: grain, a reference to agriculture, and lead, a reference to bullets and the battlefield. At the time of the book's publication during the War of Independence, months of battles against the Arab forces surrounding the new state had claimed the lives of thousands of Israeli soldiers. During this extended period of bloodshed, it is no surprise that the values of courage and self-sacrifice prevailed in the literature. One striking passage in *Grain and Lead* exemplifies this theme. A young soldier returns home from the battlefield and pays his condolences to the father of his friend. He later reports on his visit:

> I told him how his son was killed in the battle ... I praised his courage ... I know that all of those who matured during the years of the *Palmach* ... they are people that can be trusted not to lose the essential moment of the battle ... They will be happy to run against the barrage of the bullets.
>
> (p. 7)

Here the author, the narrator, and the hero all speak with one voice. The message of the story served as oil to the wheels of the young state in the process of formation. The early literature of this generation put its full weight behind the ideology of belonging to the collective—the cognitive aspects of "belonging"—while ignoring the individual's emotional life. Accordingly, the protagonist of this novel (along with others of Shaham's early works) is not fully developed as a character; he is more of a symbolic figure who epitomizes the ideals so critical to the formation and defense of the State.

The very title of Shaham's *Grain and Lead* uses a metaphor that encapsulates the idea of the individual as a unit of the collective; as a single stem of wheat swaying in the breeze along with innumerable others, a stalk that is ultimately harvested, shelved, and stored together with the rest of the crop. In reality, however, an individual is not a sheaf of wheat; the human soul can be stifled but it cannot be suppressed forever. Submerged beneath one's duty to serve as a cog in the collective machine, it appears that the individual's desire to live freely prevails and will eventually emerge after dire times are over. After the war ended in 1949, the bonds of battle loosened and the pressures of self-defense lifted. Tens of thousands of new immigrants from diverse cultures—European Jews, Holocaust survivors, displaced refugees from Arab states—flooded the young country that was no longer under siege and sought to manage their lives in privacy. The *Palmach* literature, too, began to reflect the new trend from the "we" to the "I." Shaham, along with other writers, started to expose the first chinks in the armor of the idealized collective and to explore the inner lives of characters who struggle with their choices rather than conform and submit without question to the collective.

When the storm is over: from "we" to "I"

The first whisperings of these social changes unfolded in Shaham's (1956) novel, *A Stone on the Well's Mouth*. The title was inspired by the biblical story of Jacob, who, during his wanderings through the fields of Canaan, came upon a well protected by a stone (Genesis 29:1–3). In the ancient Middle East, where water was scarce, the wells were covered with heavy, rounded flat stones to prevent evaporation and contamination by shifting sands. They were not opened frequently; rather, it was customary to assemble all the flocks and roll the stone away from the mouth of the well to water all the sheep at one time. Shaham used the metaphor of the stone to convey that only when the "we" have been gathered can the burden can be lifted to sustain life. Here, Shaham refers to the far-left political groups of that time; in his view, they were the only movements upholding the basic kibbutz values that the right wing had largely abandoned by the mid-twentieth century. Interestingly, psychoanalysis was of great influence on that far-left movement called the "Young Guard" (*Hashomer Hatzair*), in part through the efforts of Siegfried Bernfeld and Otto Fenichel to integrate Marxism with psychoanalysis (both were important members of the Vienna Psychoanalytic group of Socialists and/or Marxists).

Despite this metaphorical reference to the collective, *The Stone Over the Well's Mouth* marks a true departure from the earlier "propaganda literature" of the *Palmach* generation. The novel describes the lives of the pioneers who immigrated to Israel at the beginning of the twentieth century and established the kibbutz movement. Shaham explained to me (personal communication, 1983) that, rather than portraying them as heroes, his goal was to demonstrate that the kibbutz founders were not the giants they depicted themselves as, nor were they a seamless community. In reality, they were fractured into separate groups with divergent political views that frequently engaged in internecine squabbles. In the novel, the commitment of the individual to the collective is portrayed as more ambivalent than in Shaham's earlier works. According to Shaham, the common goal of the kibbutzim was conquering the work of the land and maintaining the values of egalitarianism and reciprocal assistance. Agricultural labor was elevated to the status of religion, replacing the Jewish religion with a secular one. But, he explained, work in the fields was difficult; when European immigrants of the 1920s unaccustomed to manual labor realized that their volunteerism would become mandatory duty, some were overcome by despair and took their own lives. Many had been forced to stay in the kibbutzim and towns despite their personal dissatisfaction because they were no longer welcome in their countries of origin. If not for the outbreak of World War II, Shaham added, these "pioneers" might have deserted the Zionist utopia and returned to their parents' homes and more comfortable lives in Europe.

The "uprooted ones"

After 1949, a new type of character began to appear in the works of the *Palmach* authors: the "uprooted ones" (*telushim*). These fictional characters were based on the new, post-Holocaust immigrants; people who came to live on kibbutz and tried to connect and integrate with the "we" but nevertheless felt detached from the community; some left and tried their luck outside the kibbutz. Loneliness, the antithesis of collective togetherness, becomes an issue for some of these fictional kibbutz members. For the first time in the kibbutz literature, we encounter protagonists who choose to look inside themselves rather than to the community in search of their national and private identity. Correspondingly, these characters are far better developed than those in Shaham's early novels. In his story, *The Other Side of the Wall,* Shaham (1983b) describes the loneliness of a 24-year-old woman who joins the kibbutz. She is quiet, bookish, and goes unnoticed; she describes her isolation as "being smothered in a closed room." She does not fit in to the "we" norms of the kibbutz:

> Around here they don't like emotional, dreamy, hypersensitive girls who carry on dialogues with themselves in writing. Just the opposite. Admiration goes to those girls who can work on a tractor or in the machine shop, who can listen to a dirty joke and response with boisterous laughter.
>
> (p. 106)

The protagonist secretly becomes an erotic guardian over her married neighbor's clandestine extramarital affair that takes place on the other side of a thick bordering wall. The isolated young woman begins to live vicariously through the couple's trysts, documenting in her diary the visceral experiences she gathers by eavesdropping. The narrative shows the futile expectations of the lonely kibbutznik who has no real interpersonal contact and yearns to belong to a body bigger than herself.

Another "uprooted" character is a young man named Shai who can no longer find his place in the kibbutz after he returns home from the battlefield of the War of Independence (*Veterans' Housing*, 1958). He leaves the kibbutz for the town to forge a path as a civil servant, where he quickly learns that the old socialist values no longer hold; instead, his fellow workers turn their backs on other kibbutzniks. His manager confides in him that "the 'we' are not the 'we' anymore … friendship is not what it used to be." Shai competes for a promotion with a former high school classmate who avoided the army and spent his time studying in the United States after high school, while Shai contributed those years to his army service. This individualist classmate wins the coveted position, driving home the novel's message that dedication to the collective no longer carries weight in the new system; instead the new ethos is "each man for himself."

Shaham continued to raise questions regarding the place of the individual in the collective framework in many other novels and stories (*Veterans' Housing*, 1958; *Citrus Scent*, 1962; *Green Autumn*, 1979; *Bone to the Bone*, 1981; *Still Silent Voice*, 1983a). The tension between the "we" and the "I" is powerfully portrayed in his novel *First Person, Plural* (1968). Shaham interpreted the title to me as: "First-person, comma, plural. It means, everybody for himself and nevertheless plural." In fact, the transformation described in the novel was one of the first indications of a trend that would take place in the kibbutzim decades after the book's publication. Built on the pattern of the film *Rashomon*, the story uses a plot device involving three characters representing three generations: the kibbutz founders, the middle generation, and the *Palmach* (the author's) generation. Each protagonist provides alternative and contradictory versions of the same event. When Alfred, a kibbutz member and Holocaust survivor, is notified that he will receive financial reparations from Germany, the protagonists wrestle with the question: who is entitled to the money—the victim or his kibbutz? The author presents three different points of view ranging from the individualist to the collectivist. The conflict is ultimately resolved—not by the decision of Alfred, who wanted to send the expected reparations to his poor relatives in the city, but by an unexpected change in Germany's reparations policy that allowed the money to be given directly to the survivor's relatives. The resolution of the unfolding drama by forces external to the kibbutz makes the situation acceptable to all members.

Cutting the cord

Within the framework of the collective, the individuality of kibbutz members was expressed for many years in just one constricted section of their domain: the private gardens in front of their homes. All other institutions—even the children's dormitories—were communal; parents would spend only two hours in the afternoon with their children and were unequivocally banned from putting them to bed. As the children grew older, days could pass without an opportunity for parents to see them. In the movement's heyday, the most important and prominent building—the dining room—stood at the center of the kibbutz. Members had a strong sense of attachment to the collective dining room, the "big breast" that was always available for nurturing and support.

In 1985, seventy-five years after the first kibbutz was established, a sudden economic crisis in Israel sent shock waves across the kibbutz movement and forever changed its members' sense of belonging. Feelings of attachment were replaced by detachment from traditional engagements. Many kibbutzim started charging for meals in the collective dining room, while some shut it down completely, forcing members to start making their meals at home. People with financial means began to purchase their own new cars (originally, valuable items like cars were communally owned), among other luxuries. Instead of working together toward a common goal, members were encouraged to find employment outside the kibbutz, and disparity in living standards became the new norm. The traditional children's dorms were abolished, and families gained full responsibility for their children in their homes. People who were used to living in a sheltered environment found themselves scrambling to stay afloat; the umbilical cord had been severed by the capitalist surge that penetrated the socialistic camp. *Equality of outcome* was replaced by *equality of opportunity*, where there is no transfer of income from the wealthy to the needy and people live in a state of constant competition and discrimination.

Today, the majority of kibbutzim are converting to a model (the "renewed kibbutz") where members are paid differential wages and each kibbutz defines its own mission statement. The current notion of "we" is not fully based on the original values of the kibbutz; instead, much more weight is given to the particular needs of each individual. Only a small minority of kibbutzim continues to preserve the original values and abide by the "collaborative model" (Shapira, 2008). While the younger generation was quick to embrace the philosophy of privatization, it was traumatic for many older members who had spent most of their lives in the kibbutz; it shattered their illusions that relationships revolve around the "we." The fabric of the utopic socialistic society of the "we" was unraveled for the new "I."

Concluding remarks

What I take from this review of the *Palmach* generation's literary work, and from my conversations with many of its authors, is that the essence of kibbutz society was characterized by participation in daily physical labor that was instrumental in developing the collective's means of production and economy, coupled with the personal security acquired through membership. There was a famous fable in the kibbutz literature of that time called "the manure fable"; the message was that the first generations of the kibbutz were "manure for the fields of the land of Israel." They sacrificed their own personal level of comfort for a mission larger than themselves: establishing settlements, cultivating the land, and paving the way to harvesting its fruits. The emphasis was not on aspiring to develop many "I-Thou" relationships (as Buber would put it), but rather on creating the solidarity, the communion, the mental notion of "we." Even the interpersonal relationships on the kibbutz, as depicted in the literature, appear to be a byproduct of the effort for communal day-to-day comfort rather than ends in themselves (see Rifkin, 2010). Beyond the revolution of the kibbutz movement, Israeli society as a whole underwent a transformation in the latter half of the twentieth century: from its inception as a socialist country influenced by the USSR, where citizens revered the collective and had feverish faith in their society's moral superiority, to becoming a "little America"—a capitalist society that accentuates private property, capital accumulation, wage labor, and competitive markets. By the 1960s, a new "anti-hero" Israeli begins to appear in the works of Shaham and others—a radically different character from the mythological *sabra* (colloquial for a Jew born in Israel) that the *Palmach* generation depicted during the War of Independence. The Israelis' identification and sense of "belonging" became that of a culture far different from that of the tribal bonfires and group sing-alongs of the kibbutz.

On a personal note: though I did not grow up in a communal settlement, I lived in a semi-kibbutz environment as a teenager in an agricultural boarding school affiliated with the socialistic Labor movement. The school integrated half-day classroom studies with a half day of agricultural and livestock work. Students were given the power to manage different aspects of their own community life; for example, we elected our own committees, organized the general assembly of the community for discussing the social agenda, arranged our work schedules, and published a daily newspaper. I entered the school after my bar-mitzvah and experienced it as a 24/7 pressure cooker with its unending demands for conformity. At times I would push back against the unspoken but very real boundaries and express my own opinions. One day, for example, I voiced my frustration in the school paper that our daily work in the fields went uncompensated. My protest was unsuccessful, and the management ignored my grievance. On another occasion, I made it clear that I wanted to further my academic studies rather than help establish a new kibbutz in the Israeli desert (which was an expected goal of the school and its graduates). In fact, after completing my three years of the compulsory military service—after high school graduation—I pursued psychology studies at the university.

Still, despite my grievances about the pressure to conform in a communal society, I am aware that my generation has lived in Israel with a sense of existential self-confidence. This country is the origin of my identity, and I find that I miss some safeguards of the old socialistic Israel: a community that insured easy access to the health system; a country where the elderly could retire with dignity, even if they had just minimal resources; a place where people spent days on their porches—not behind shaded windows, walls, and gates—that invited ample opportunities for interpersonal engagements; a society where people lived simply and were satisfied with little. The bright side today is that the young generation of Israelis, many of them the children of my own generation (whose members were born with and immediately after the State of Israel was established), are an integral part of the young international Western community. They utilize social media to share feelings, coordinate their own gatherings and travels, and receive instant information about their individual needs. Overall, they appear to feel less obligated to the "we" than do members of my generation and my parents' generation.

References

Bluwstein, R. (n.d.). Here on earth. *Poemhunter*. Retrieved from www.poemhunter.com/poem/here-on-earth-2/. Originally published 1927.

Rifkin, L. (2010, June 5). Adult children of the dream. Jerusalem Post. Retrieved from www.jpost.com/Jerusalem-Report/Adult-Children-of-the-Dream

Shahal, Y. (2007). Isaac Babel – a war correspondent. Kesher, 35, 5e–7e. Retrieved from www.tau.ac.il/humanities/bronfman/files/kesher35/kesher35-english.pdf

Shaham, N. (1948). *Dagan ve-oferet* [Grain and lead]. Tel Aviv: Sifriat Poalim.

Shaham, N. (1952). *Tamid anahnu* [Always we]. Tel Aviv: Sifriat Poalim.

Shaham, N. (1956). *Even al pi ha-be'er* [A stone on the well's mouth]. Tel Aviv: Sifriat Poalim.

Shaham, N. (1958). *Shikun vatikim* [Veterans' housing]. Tel Aviv: Sifriat Poalim.

Shaham, N. (1962). *Reyah hadarim* [Citrus scent]. Tel Aviv: Sifriat Poalim.

Shaham, N. (1968). *Guf rishon rabim* [First person, plural]. Tel Aviv: Sifriat Poalim.

Shaham, N. (1979). *Stav yarok* [Green autumn]. Tel Aviv: Sifriat Poalim.

Shaham, N. (1981). *Etzem el atzmo* [Bone to the bone]. Tel Aviv: Am Oved.

Shaham, N. (1983a). *Demamah dakah* [Still silent voice]. Tel Aviv: Sifriat Poalim.

Shaham, N. (1983b). The other side of the wall. In *The other side of the wall: three novellas* (L. Gold, Trans.). Philadelphia: Jewish Publication Society of America. Originally published 1977.

Shapira, R. (2008). *Transforming kibbutz research*. Cleveland: New World.

Yadin. Z. (1984). Dor Ha-Palmach *during its development* (Doctoral dissertation, Bar Ilan University, Israel).

10 Belonging

The conundrums of interfaith marriage

Renée Cherow-O'Leary

During the siege of Jerusalem by the Romans in 66–68 CE/AD, Rabbi Yochanan ben Zakkai, a sage, witnessed the implosion of the Jewish people. In order to save Judaism, the Talmud recounts, ben Zakkai arranged a secret escape from the city hidden in a coffin so that he could negotiate with Vespasian, at the time a military commander who later became Emperor. He was able to get the commander to agree that the leaders of the Jewish faith could be moved to Yavneh, where they might re-create Judaism after the inevitable destruction of the temple that ben Zakkai foresaw. When that destruction came to pass, in the year 70 CE, true to the pact, the Jews moved to Yavneh, far from Jerusalem, to begin anew and determine how to live in a post-Temple world (The Talmud, n.d.).

Ben Zakkai organized a Jewish Council, a school, and the re-establishment of the Sanhedrin, the Jewish legal authority, so that they could decide how to adapt Judaism to a new situation where there was no central Temple in terms of laws, calendar, and liturgy. He helped persuade the Council to replace animal sacrifice with prayer, moving from a ritual full of sensory experience to one of symbolism. He also understood that roots must be developed. To him is attributed the quote, "If you are holding a sapling in your hand and someone tells you, 'Come quickly, the Messiah is here!', first finish planting the tree and then go to greet the Messiah."

Since the Messiah in Judaism has not yet come, Jewish religious authorities are now facing another upheaval—one of demographics—caused not by external hatred but by internal transformation of what was once an insular community. The denomination of Conservative Judaism, particularly (in the middle between Orthodox and Reform movements of the faith) is at the crossroads of deciding whether to plant trees or cut them down. This soul-searching is occurring because of interfaith marriage. I speak of this both personally and communally. I grew up in an Orthodox shul, had an early, unhappy marriage to an Orthodox man when I was twenty years old, and, after a "get," a Jewish divorce (and a civil one), graduate school, the feminist revolution, and life in an era of deep social change that all of this encompassed, met my Irish Catholic husband of forty years (a psychoanalyst, John O'Leary, whom some of you know) working on a political campaign. We married in the 1970s, a time when intermarriage was still quite rare. We could not find clergy who would officiate and so wrote our own vows in an Ethical Culture ceremony (Ethical Culture, n.d.). My husband did not convert, nor did I expect him to. We have raised two Jewish children who have an extended Catholic family in Ireland and in New York. The Irish family welcomed me and my family welcomed them. John entered joyfully, and with the warmth for which he is known, into the Jewish world of study and activism that is a significant part of my life.

We blended our lives and found other intermarried couples who became our friends. We now have three young grandchildren, coming out of a religious and cultural experience totally different from John's and mine—our immigrant parents and grandparents, our Hebrew School and Catholic school, the vividness of the Holocaust, the attention paid to ritual and to the Pope. These grandchildren raise the question that has in many ways always roiled the Jewish community—what does it mean to be a Jew now, and what might it mean forty years hence—in 2060? In effect, the question is: what does it mean to *belong* to a people, and perhaps a religion, today, in a world more diversified than ever, where the market-place of ideas is a click away? What type of education and activities encourage belonging to that group? And why, why should anyone belong to that group and not to another somewhere else?

These questions, always fraught, began to take on an insistent urgency in 2013, a fast-moving seven years ago, when the Pew Center on Religion & Public Life released "A Portrait of Jewish Americans," which shocked the dire demographers of Jewish life who deplored intermarriage ("marrying out") as destructive of Jewish continuity (2013). In this seminal study based on 3,475 phone calls with Jews across the country, 22 percent described themselves as atheist, agnostic, or having no particular religion. They identified as Jewish on the basis of ancestry, ethnicity, or culture. Intermarriage was a related phenomenon: 79 percent of married Jews "of no religion" had a spouse who was not Jewish, compared with 36 percent among Jews identified by religion. Moreover, among Jewish respondents who had gotten married since 2000, nearly six in ten had a non-Jewish spouse. One-third of intermarried Jews who were raising children said they were not raising those children Jewish at all.

When the Pew Report came out, it was a watershed moment for Jewish life in the twenty-first century. It confirmed what was sensed and known but not spoken. How should synagogues and religious institutions respond? Of course, these questions were moot for members of the most Orthodox factions of the community. And reform rabbis, though conflicted, were given the option to choose individually whether they would officiate at interfaith marriages, out of conscience, but their choice was without penalty. However, Conservative clergy had to *refuse* to perform intermarriages or risk being expelled by the Conservative Rabbinical Assembly and be isolated from the benefits of communal credentialing (Rabbinical Assembly, n.d.).

It was only in 1983 that the Conservative Jewish movement began to ordain women as rabbis and as recently as 2007 when they began to ordain gay rabbis, male and female. There still is no ordination for intermarried people who might want to become rabbis. And there is still only matrilineal descent accepted to answer the question of who is an authentic Jew. Even with Jewish patrilineal descent, a newborn child of a non-Jewish mother must be bathed in a mikveh, a ritual bath, and, in effect, be converted to Judaism, if the mother did not convert.

(Jewish Virtual Library, n.d.)

What to do? In these seven years, Judaic leaders have had to look long and hard in the mirror and, as never before, make choices about following the halacha (the letter of the law) or finding ways to recognize both pragmatically and spiritually that another way must be found to reach intermarried families. Like ben Zakkai at Yavneh, a creative reinterpretation of belief and practice was required that maintained the spirit and richness of Judaism and yet could still accommodate the present reality in a diverse and complex America. This is especially true in the big cities, where Jews reside, are educated, and are, by and large, widely accepted and have accrued great economic and social power. We are beginning to see a radical rethinking of intermarriage in the Conservative Jewish community. In the past year alone, two highly respected rabbis in New York City have left the Rabbinical Assembly over the issues of officiating at interfaith marriages. They have spent innumerable hours in conversations with their congregations, writing philosophical treatises about Jewish law and the relationship to the "stranger" (for you were strangers in Egypt), and currently some are devising new rituals and ceremonies of welcome and rites of passage not only for weddings but other moments of transition. (My husband and I are connected to both of these synagogues—B'nai Jeshurun, where we have been members for over twenty-five years, and Lab Shul, where I am on the board [Congregation B'nai Jeshurun and Lab Shul, both in New York City]).

There is also the growing complication in North American Jewry of relationship to Israel. Israeli policy has moved decidedly to the far political right, recently, for example, declaring Israel a primarily Jewish state and downgrading the status of its Arab citizens. Orthodox rabbis govern marital decisions there. Religious intermarriage is exceedingly rare among Jews in Israel and must be performed outside of the land of Israel. Marriages between members of different faiths conducted in other countries are recognized in Israel, but even Jews from different factions (i.e., ultra-Orthodox and secular) tend to be isolated from one another socially there. Most Jews, Muslims, Christians, and Druze in friendships and family relationships stay within their own religious communities.

Belonging used to mean to belong to the collective Jewish People. But now, belonging is a complex set of choices raising questions—what do I accept, what do I reject, where do I fit, what is the purpose of my impulse to belong? For the partner in a marriage who is not Jewish by birth, these questions have added resonance.

The Belonging Project in the Department of Psychiatry and Behavioral Sciences at Stanford University says in its literature:

the importance of the feeling of belonging has been demonstrated through empirical work on human resilience and identity formation and on factors that protect emotional health and personal wellbeing, even in the context of adversity and trauma ... Clear evidence has shown that individuals ... who feel they are disconnected and not part of the larger community—what the researchers call "thwarted belongingness" are vulnerable to alienation and disaffection ... People want to be a part of something greater than themselves and establish sustaining relationships.

(The Belonging Project)

The tension in interfaith marriages to choose how and where to belong is exacerbated—for both partners. A person who converts often feels the belonging more strongly than one born into a faith. The convert has worked hard to learn what classic belonging involves (through training and education and rules). However, two secular Jews may take their belonging, such as it is, for granted, and it may require little of them to call themselves Jews, perhaps even cultural rather than religious Jews, which is a growing trend.

Another book written in 2013 has a very different rationale explaining the changing nature of who is a Jew. The book, by distinguished Indiana University Jewish Studies professor Shaul Magid (now at Dartmouth), is called *American Post Judaism: Identity and Renewal in a Post-Ethnic Society*. He says:

While ethnicity remains a strong source of identity both in America and other countries around the globe ... this is changing, in large part the result of the *dissolution of historically culturally homogenous societies* ... America is steadily being transformed from a multicultural and ethnocentric society to a *postethnic* society. "Ethnicity," depending on how the term is defined, will survive but will become something other than purely a consequence of attribution of a particular trait or even biological descent. A multiethnic society will produce *new ethnicities* that are created by a combination of descent and consent, ascription and affiliation. Disassimilation will often occur before ethnicities are totally reconstituted, because disassimilation is not a return to a pre-assimilated ethnic mode as much as a revision, *taking into consideration the changes assimilation has invariably produced*. Disassimilation among ethnic groups that have already lost a sense of "pure" ethnicity due to intermarriage and assimilation will generate new ethnicities and not erase ethnicity as a category of social identification.

(Magid, 2013, pp. 17–18)

"The perennial tension between assimilation and distinctiveness has entered a new phase" (p. 29). Magid celebrates the openness of America's multicultural society, which has encouraged a mix of identities ... The cultural boundaries in America have become so porous that Jewishness, he says, may be seen as "free floating," open to be appropriated by anyone—including reappropriated by Jews! (p. 33).

In the classic Exodus story, when God took the Hebrew slaves out of Egypt, He did not immediately bring them to the promised land, although if you look at a map, physically it was not that far away. Instead, the slaves wandered in the desert for forty years until a new generation was born who could forget Egypt and anticipate a new way of life, who had the courage that it would require to start over and be able to implement a new beginning. The desert wanderers were in an in-between place, between what was and what will be.

When ben Zakkai took his fractured community to Yavneh after the destruction of the Temple, he worked to build institutions that could replace, even transform, what had gone before. He knew his generation of Jews was transitional but also foundational. They could remember the past but knew that their role was to invent the future.

Shaul Magid sees this generation of Jews in the same way. He unequivocally states that Zionism and the Holocaust, two seemingly immutable anchors of Jewish identity, will no longer be centers of identity formation for future generations of American Jews. "My claim," he states:

> is that we are living in the rupture that creates the "in-between" ... These in-between spaces provide the terrain for elaborating strategies of selfhood— singular and communal—that initiate new signs of identity and innovative sites of collaboration and contestation in the act of defining the ideas of a new society ... this is a Judaism in a world where identities are mixed, where allegiances are more voluntary than inherited, where our capacity to conceptualize will simultaneously embrace and engage—not resist or reject—the new ...
>
> (Magid, 2013, p. 5)

I would like to leave us with Magid's progressive, utopian vision, but since 2013, we have regressed, in my opinion. Many people think that the place where the huddled masses yearning to be free lift their lamp beside the golden door, as Emma Lazarus said in the nineteenth century poem about America on the Statue of Liberty, is in jeopardy (Lazarus, n.d.).

Instead, we might consider intermarriage as a harbinger of a solution for the separation that is being propagated among groups. Intermarriage is based on a voluntary coming together, rooted in love and the culmination of a process that is committed to knowing the other and loving that person as yourself. It offers an opportunity of transcendence beyond literal categories. According to a recent issue of *National Geographic* with the theme of race (2018), in the fifty years since the legal case of *Loving* v. *Virginia* struck down state laws banning inter-racial marriage, newlywed intermarried couples with partners from another racial, ethnic, or religious group went from 1 in 33 to 1 in 6! If our hearts can stay open during this in-between time, a new America may yet be born.

References

The Belonging Project, Department of Psychiatry and Behavioral Sciences at Stanford University, Palo Alto, CA. *Stanford University*. (n.d.). Retrieved from https://med.stanford.edu/psychiatry/special- initiatives/belonging.html

Congregation B'nai Jeshurun Jewish Home Project. (n.d.). *B'nai Jeshurun.* Retrieved from www.bj.org/community/the-jewish-home-project/

Ethical culture. (n.d.). *New York Society for Ethical Culture.* Retrieved from https://ethical. nyc./about/

Jewish Virtual Library. (n.d.). *Patrilineal Descent.* Retrieved from www.jewishvirtuallibrary. org/patrilineal-descent

Lab Shul proposal on interfaith marriage. (n.d.). *Lab/Shul.* Retrieved from https://labshul. org/portfolio/joy-a- proposal/

Lazarus, E. (n.d.). "The New Colossus" on the pedestal of the Statue of Liberty. *Wikipedia.* Retrieved from https://en.wikipedia.org/wiki/The-New-Colossus/

Magid, S. (2013). *American post-Judaism: identity and renewal in a post-ethnic society.* Bloomington & Indianapolis: Indiana University Press.

National Geographic. (2018). Issue on race: case on *Loving* v. *Virginia.* Retrieved from www.nationalgeographic.com/magazine/2018/04/interracial-marriage- race-ethnicity-newlywed

The Pew Center on Religion & Public Life. (2013). Retrieved from www.pewforum.org/ 2013/10/01/jewish-american-beliefs-attitudes-culture-survey/

The Rabbinical Assembly. (n.d.). Retrieved from www.rabbinicalassembly.org/about-us-0

The Talmud. (n.d.). Story of Rabbi Yochanan ben Zakkai. *My Jewish Learning.* Retrieved from www.myjewishlearning.com/article/johanan-ben-zakkai/

11 Secure uncoupling

A proposed theory of belonging after divorce

Joy A. Dryer

"Out beyond ideas of wrongdoing and rightdoing there is a field. I'll meet you there," Rumi (1207–1273) (2004, p. 38).

> For decades I have been working in therapy and in mediation with couples before and after they have divorced. Post-divorce, some couples hate each other's guts. Others figure out how to get along better post-divorce than before. I was perplexed by the difference. What can clinicians do to promote this better outcome?

The "belonging" theme of this book frames this contrast. Belonging can be a helpful lens through which to discuss how you can belong *in* love and in relationship *or* belong *out* of love but still in relationship, but one that is now *uncoupled*.

In this chapter, I propose a theory of secure uncoupling. While the couple may no longer belong to one another, as when married or in a long-term committed relationship, they can still belong to a joint effort by which they work together in an intersubjective space. It is a safe, and even creative, space. It is Rumi's field in the quote above. No rightdoing or wrongdoing, just an open field. The goal of secure uncoupling is to develop such a space between the partners that transcends the individuality of either person. Not yours or mine, but a shared play space.

Two couples highlight the difference: Brian and Betty developed a state of secure uncoupledness. Jack and Jill did not.

"Get outta my face. There you go exaggerating again. Blaming me! I did NOT say Johnny could NOT get the Fortnite video. I SAID I had to think about it. That you and I need to talk about it. Damn! You're always maligning me to the kids!" Jack's voice was low and gravely. His eyes squinted darts toward Jill.

Jill's pointy pupils glared back. "You lie. You don't try to talk to me. It takes days before you answer my texts. That's unacceptable! Every day Johnny nags me. And where are YOU? Traveling! Off to meetings in LA or Dallas."

I stop them: "What's happening now?" Back to defensive mode, fight or flight … Well, just fight. Actually, they're in kill or be killed mode. I refocus on the process. I remind them, "You're both in amygdala highjack. If every subject triggers weapons of mass destruction, then we'll never get to negotiate any agreement that's workable and meaningful to you both."

They stop to catch their breath. Well, I think, at least they can self-regulate, albeit minimally, even if they cannot mutually regulate. I consciously slow my own breathing. Two years divorced, and they still act like snipers in a South Asian jungle!

The line from Rumi floats in and out of my brain: "Out beyond ideas of wrong-doing and rightdoing, there is a field. I'll meet you there." How do I help them meet in that field? Aye ... even *know* that such a field exists? Where there's no judgment. No criticism. Mutuality ... even teamwork! Some Theory of Mind (Fonagy, Gergely, Jurist, et al., 2004) where they can see, even if not accept, the other person's perspective. Where they can belong to, and cooperate around, a shared set of values and beliefs (Gottman & Silver, 2015) in their children's best interests.

"How shall we plan the party after graduation?" Betty pulled out her spiral notebook and favorite multi-colored pen.

"Don't go getting all obsessive on me now." Brian offered a little wink at her.

Betty squirmed, laughed a little. "Okay. I just wanna get the details planned before I leave for my workshop."

"Oh. What's the date on that?" Brian pulled out his phone and added Betty's workshop dates. "We need to talk to Brenda first. What does she want? I mean, how many of her friends will be staying?" Brian asked. "I really want to keep the costs down," he added. "We're launching the new product line in three months and I'm worried ..."

"Yeah. I know," Betty interrupted. "You've always worried about having enough—enough money in particular. But just to remind you—and I'm one who knows"—she chuckled—"that you've always prioritized your finances, managed them well, and done what you wanted."

"Yes. I DO plan carefully. And watch the bottom line." Brian leaned toward Betty. "Okay. One step at a time. Let's talk to Brenda first."

Context: a post-divorce contrast

Like Jack and Jill, Brian and Betty had been divorced for almost two years. Each couple had returned to couples' mediation to work out some parenting issues around their kids. Jack and Jill can barely sit in the same room together. They trigger emotions in the other, dysregulating their ability to feel or to think clearly. In contrast, Brian and Betty gently tease one another (Betty's obsessive planning, Brian's constant worry about money in spite of his excellent business skills). They cooperate as a team toward a common goal (planning their daughter Brenda's graduation party).

During their marriage and now uncoupled, Jack and Jill remain like snipers in a forest. Slinking along, alert to danger, spotting the enemy, squatting, aiming, firing, you're dead. (Not unlike the dangerous situations depicted in the video game their son wanted for Christmas!) Again in contrast, Brian and Betty's marriage was like a meandering stream, whose tributaries wandered off into yonder cornfield and silently disappeared among the stalks. Little connection. Little pleasure. And yet, once divorced, Brian and Betty found a healthy way to fall *out* of love and to develop together a state of secure uncoupledness. Unlike Jack and Jill, Brian and Betty found Rumi's field.

How do we understand such a couple whose relationship is healthier post-divorce than it was while married? How does a divorced couple get to that shared space? This chapter asks how to take the next step. How do individuals earn security via attachment repair when they are no longer married? How do they develop trust and security with one another when they are now uncoupled?

Theory: roots of secure uncoupling

This theory of Belonging Uncoupled is rooted in four foundational modes of thinking that swerve around and tangle up with one another like bumper cars in a multidimensional playground. These are at the back of my mind both as separate theory threads and as intersecting and interrelated threads weaving implicitly and explicating in and out of the clinical material.

Attachment theory and psychoanalysis

Modern attachment theorists and contemporary psychoanalysts believe that intrapsychic, internal processes determine the discrepancies between actual and psychic reality. Our egos create defenses (A. Freud, 1936/1993) to protect us from distorted expectations, both conscious and unconscious, and perceived dangers, both internal and external. Sigmund Freud (1926/1959) taught us that our anxiety, a biologically determined epiphenomenal experience, sounded the alarm to such dangers like the canary in the mine. The fundamental danger of losing the object, real or perceived, theoretically connects attachment and psychoanalytic thinking. Thus the interpersonal aspects of both theories connect adults' caretaking misattunements and failures to the resulting range of characterological and relatedness problems in their children.

More specifically, current research takes a developmental view that how people respond in relationships in general is moderated by how they regulate their emotions as well as their attachment style (Main, Kaplan, & Cassidy, 1985). See how Bowlby's (1969/1982) internal working models describe the self-regulations of emotional variations responsible for attachment styles (Birnbaum, Orr, Mikulincer, et al., 1997).

Earned security

All four of the people I describe above grew up with caretakers whose attachment interactions with their children were varying degrees of dismissing or preoccupied. And yet, from research, we have learned that couples can earn security within a relationship, even though their individual attachment histories may indicate insecure attachment styles. Main and Goldwyn (1984–98) described a group of parents whose problematic and painful childhood histories would ordinarily have associated them with an "insecure" category rating on their AAI assessment. However, their stories and their ability to describe attachment-related experiences were coherent and collaborative. As researchers, they called this group of parents "earned secure." They demonstrated that *attachment repair* was possible. Siegel (1999) noted that such couples often benefited from emotionally significant relationships with close friends, romantic partners, and/or therapists. Levy, Meehan, Kelly, et al. (2006) demonstrated that attachment style is improved in psychotherapy.

Intersubjectivity

An intersubjective (Atwood & Stolorow, 1984/2014) post-modern approach emphasizes how psychic phenomena and interactions are contextual. It bridges the personal and the shared between self and others.

For example, sitting in a room with Jack and Jill, you can experience their intersubjective tug of war. Each of their individual forms of insecure attachment were triggered by the other into a black-and-white struggle between the *me* and the *you*: the *you* gets lost, and the attachment remains at a stalemate of insecurities. It may be a combination of projection and identification where Jack and Jill may see a self *in* the other, and *my* way is the right way. To preserve a sense of self, each retreats into *my* way as the right way. *My* way or the highway. This is a polarized opposition experienced as eat or be eaten, or kill or be killed (Benjamin, 2004). Right or wrong, they cannot *decenter* (Aron & Benjamin, 1999) from identifying with only one position: only I am right, *or* if you are right, I must be wrong. Theirs was an intersubjective stalemate fueled by insecure attachment styles with fight/flight defenses.

Social constructionism

Expanding the horizon of our mind's eye, social constructionists (Bretherton & Munholland, 1999) frame human perspective, knowledge, and meaning as more than existing in reality but additionally constructed by society.

Distinguishing between the attachment and intersubjective systems supports the *cultural intelligence* hypothesis (Boyd & Richerson, 2005; Tomasello, Carpenter, Call, et al., 2005). This explains how humans became a dominant species during the Pleistocene era through their ability to cooperate rather than compete. The attachment system kept individuals alive within the protective dyad. And this intersubjective system enhanced teamwork to keep the group alive.

Neuroscience

The neuroscience of how our brains are wired informs all these viewpoints. Such wiring has developed to reduce threat and to seek safety, as we have learned from Porges' research (2011). Evolutionary strategies selectively pressured mutations that increased social understanding and advanced intersubjective communication.

In this way, the neocortex and mindreading abilities expanded among our Great Ape relatives.

One study in particular integrates the above-mentioned viewpoints. The authors Cortina and Liotti (2010) propose a dialectical view of our human brain. The main function of attachment is to seek protection to facilitate survival of the individual. The main function of intersubjectivity is to communicate, at intuitive and automatic levels, with members of the same species and to facilitate team-work and group survival. Stern sums it up (2004, p. 105): "This intersubjective approach promotes group formation and coherence. It permits more efficient, rapid, flexible, and coordinated group functioning. And it provides the basis for morality to act in maintaining group cohesion, and language to act in group communication."

Fonagy and Target (2008) help us understand how this dichotomy between a dyadic attachment and a more complex intersubjectivity can work when they describe the neurobiology of how the brain reacts under the stress of trauma. When a baby is traumatized by an attachment figure(s), the attachment system and mentalizing abilities operate inversely. That is, the interpersonal trauma induces a hyperactivation of the attachment system closely associated with subcortical *right*-brain structures. At the same time, dramatically reduced are mentalizing activities, linked to the complex intersubjective prefrontal cortex and the *left* brain. They quote Arnsten (1998)'s article suggesting that learned helplessness induced by trauma, or other uncontrollable stress, triggers a bimodal reaction turning *on* or *off* parts of the brain and peripheral nervous system. Catecholamine neuromodulators (that is, dopamine, norepinephrine, and epinephrine) are released in the central and peripheral nervous system and *turn on* the amygdala, the emotion center, and *turn off* the mentalizing functions in the prefrontal cortex. In the peripheral nervous system, the heart and skeletal muscles are turned *on* and the stomach is turned *off* to prepare for fight or flight. Thus numerous researchers now support the view that the attachment and intersubjective mentalizing systems, while obviously interrelated, are functionally and developmentally distinct (Gergely & Unoka, 2008; Cortina & Liotti, 2010).

Application: creating a secure uncoupled state

How do these theories show up with legs and practical boots on the ground? How does a couple like Brian and Betty, defensively siloed inside their own head spaces when married, *earn security* and learn a collaborative dialogue between them once they uncouple? How do they then develop an intersubjective play space? They no longer belong to one another. Yet they learned to belong to a joint effort that found Rumi's field and cleared a workspace together. How does that happen?

Growing up, neither Brian nor Betty felt seen or known by their parents. This affective misattunement, this silence, repeated in their marriage. The pain of their divorce and their separate need to find out what went wrong propelled each of them to seek answers.

They were each separately, then together, very motivated to accept my guidance toward learning how a secure functioning relationship could be achieved and maintained.

Earning security

Over the course of a year, they became more accepting of how scary it was to know and be known by another mind. Affect attunement paves the road to feeling safe and intimate with another. You can learn if and how your feeling state is recognized, acknowledged, and shared by the other. You can learn which subjective states are shareable and which are not. Trevarthen (1998), for example, argues that humans have an innate ability for empathic contact by *matching* the timing, intensity, and micro-momentary shifts of behavior, that is, the dynamic patterns of rhythm, shape, and activities, across all sensory modalities. This foundation of intersubjective connection is preverbal and dialogic.

Step by step, I gradually taught them about secure functioning. First step: they learned to remain quiet yet attentive while the other talked. Each learned to make eye contact. They learned to recognize the other's bid for attention, to feel open to the other's feelings, positive or negative. They tried to understand the other's psychic and actual emotional state and respond to it by acknowledging or elaborating on it. They learned to recognize and acknowledge difference and conflict and to repair disruptions not just by acquiescing (Ghent, 1990), but by negotiating in a sincere attempt to find common ground. They found that this attunement-disruption-repair cycle (Tronick, 1989; Beebe & Lachmann 1994; Tavormina, 2017) is the foundation of knowing and being known by another's mind, and the source of intimacy and intersubjective connection.

The second step was to acknowledge that disruptions always happen, large and small. The repair is what is essential—how to bring their emotions back into their tolerable range, into their Window of Tolerance (Siegel, 2007). Once each learned to identify emotions, especially those that can contradict or sting, can shame or blame, they could practice stepping back from conflict.

All these basic intersubjective experiences were new to them as they struggled through their separation and divorce discussions. A year of hard work laid the foundation for their desire to collaborate and to cooperate in a new space where their newfound teamwork mattered, especially co-parenting their daughter, Brenda. It is not that they stumbled into Rumi's field. They worked hard clearing away unrealistic expectations and false assumptions, as if in a forest with thick underbrush. It was hard work, but they cleared a common open ground.

Brian and Betty's learning journey illustrates the fundamentals needed to belong to a secure functioning relationship, where teamwork reigns and individual needs breathe in the other's presence. What is "good for the goose" needs to be "good for the gander," as the saying goes. Negotiation, not combat, is the goal. So, to *belong*, you need to feel safe. You can experience a sense of belonging in a *secure functioning* relationship even when uncoupled, as Brian and Betty discovered. Here are the three principles of secure functioning that frame the process Brian and Betty worked through.

Emotion regulation

Regulating your emotions helps you tolerate ambiguity, unpredictability, difference. When you have the ability to regulate your own emotions or help the other to do so, this involves your ability to step back, count to ten, and return to some rational thinking where you can make better-informed choices. Self-regulation, and mutual regulation when possible, protects against a black or white difference becoming a disruption, then disjunction, even sliding recklessly into a kill or be killed mentality. Regulating your own emotions, while the other is doing so too, helps you feel safe and behave respectfully, consistently, and predictably.

You can see how defenses in this attachment system are triggered every time Jack and Jill interact. Even a minor lack of communication can trigger their limbic system to turn on, often escalating into full *amygdala highjack* mode where their mentalizing functions turn off!

"I ask you to tell me your travel schedule by the first of each month. But NO-o-o-o. Never happens." (Here comes Jill's transference projection.) "It's like a continuous 'fuck you' to me. You don't care how much you inconvenience me." (Then the full amygdala highjack.) "I'm thinking that you don't really wanna see your kids no matter how much you say you do."

(Jack cannot soothe or repair: he is in defensive fight mode.) "You never understand how my meetings get scheduled only a few days ahead. A week if I'm lucky." (Escalation happens quickly for him too.) "I compensated YOU for paying off my student loans. So I pay YOU eight grand a month. I need to go to the meetings to earn a living to pay YOU." (Here is Jack's full amygdala highjack hammering home his resentment and sense of betrayal.) "While I support this whole damn family, you pad around in your PJs all day!"

In contrast, Brian and Betty sound as if they have been understanding the other's perspective their whole lives. They both learned to save feelings, time, brain resources, and money by cooperating and appreciating each other's feelings. They can even be playful and tease each other about the other's neurotic needs, such as Betty's need to sequence well-controlled plans and Brian's ever-present worry about finances.

Differentiating boundaries: between self and other, between actual and perceived reality

Each person recognizes the other as a separate center with thoughts and feelings of his/her own. Having this *Theory of Mind* (Fonagy 2001) acknowledges various perspectives. With this ability, the other's viewpoint is recognized, acknowledged, and respected. That is, you need to surrender your own viewpoint in order to see from the other's viewpoint, whether or not you agree with that point of view. I call it "walking around to view from the other side of the mountain." This is not a *submission* to another's power but a choice to *surrender* (Ghent 1990) control, or viewpoint, in a positive sense.

Feelings aren't facts. Each of us is entitled to our feelings, but that does not make them real or true outside our head and *in* the world. In the above quoted interchange, Jill is sure that Jack wants to torture her by *not* communicating his schedule, when he'll pick up the kids, etc. They do not practice repair, empathically soothing the other, correcting misinformation, and thus differentiating between actual and perceived reality.

Safety

Thus differentiating and holding self-other boundaries and regulating emotions helps both people feel safe. Holding safety between you, as a transition play space, can contain both complexity and flexibility. These are the characteristics of collaboration and cooperation, even when there is conflict and disagreement.

Clinical assessment

From these theoretical foundations, I propose a two-step theory of *belonging uncoupled* that embraces the identifications and internalizations around levels of intersubjectivity. Clinically, I ask questions to assess both partners in a coupled relationship. Is his or her identification with the other partner in a two-person dyad, which uses the attachment brain? Or is the identification more with the *team* as a shared experiential state, using our complex neocortical brain level within a multi- intersubjective system?

On a team multi-level, we make the affective playing field more complex to include an observing and interactive function (see Reis 2010), which can then engage reflective capacities and a theory of mind. You shift the essential question—who are you to *me*?—to its converse—who am I to *you*? Attachment brain processes emphasize the *me*, with the self as separate *and* simultaneously different from the other.

With Jack and Jill, their early identificatory process used predominantly the *attachment* system. They remain negatively attached. Any communication from the other creates danger. Both their anxious attachment styles result in constant vigilance and paranoia. They mirror one another's threat stances, so their brains and nervous systems are always in a defensive reaction of fight mode, hanging onto a dangerous negative bond of attachment.

I have found it useful to assess a couple, whether separating or working together in therapy, using this belonging frame. *How* does this couple belong to one another? Or do they? Have the winds of indifference blown away any motivation to belong to one another? Do both partners have both feet out of the door? Or, more typically, one partner has one or both feet *out of* the door while the other stands shockingly still *at* the door.

I unbraid the dynamics embedded in their transferences to one another and to me. This helps outline their attachment styles and preferred defenses. Are there intimacy absences? Longings? Terrors? What kind of brain level characterizes their relating? A less conscious midbrain where their amygdala is the primary emotion regulator? Or a more conscious intersubjective system engaging executive functions and theory of mind? In this process, you can frame the goal of a couples' treatment as a progression from reactive self-regulatory affective triggers to mutual regulatory teamwork and from lower and midbrain regions to higher cortical levels of brain functioning, which privileges rational observation and critical thinking. And, ultimately, can they earn security together in a co-created space?

Conclusion

With this proposed theory of *belonging uncoupled*, we can expand a dyadic perspective into a complex intersubjective one. It is possible to develop and to earn a secure functioning relationship whether that relationship is coupled *or un*coupled. In either relationship state, a couple can develop and find Rumi's field.

References

Arnsten, A. F. T. (1998). The biology of being frazzled. *Science*, *280*, 1711–1712.

Aron, L. (2006). Analytic impasse and the third: clinical implications of intersubjectivity theory. *International Journal of Psychoanalysis*, *87*, 349–368.

Aron, L., & Benjamin, J. (1999, April). Intersubjectivity and the struggle to think. Paper presented at Spring Meeting, Division 39 of the American Psychological Association, New York.

Atwood, G. E., & Stolorow, R. D. (2014). *Structures of subjectivity: explorations in psychoanalytic phenomenology and contextualism* (2nd ed.). New York: Routledge. Originally published 1984.

Beebe, B., & Lachmann, F. (1994). Representation and internalization in infancy: three principles of salience. *Psychoanalytic Psychology*, *11*, 127–165.

Beebe, B., Lachmann, F., Markese, S., & Bahrick, L. (2012). On the origins of attachment and internal working models: Paper 1. A dyadic systems approach. *International Journal of Relational Perspectives*, *22*(2), 253–272.

Benjamin, J. (2000). Response to commentaries by Mitchell and by Butler. *Studies in Gender and Sexuality*, *1*(3), 291–308.

Benjamin, J. (2004). Beyond doer and done to: an intersubjective view of thirdness. *Psychoanalytic Quarterly*, *73*, 5–46.

Birnbaum, G. E., Orr, I., Mikulincer, M., & Florian, V. (1997). When marriage breaks up: does attachment style contribute to coping and mental health? *Journal of Social and Personal Relationships*, *14*(5), 643–654.

Boston Change Process Study Group (BCPSG). (2007). The foundational level of psychodynamic meaning implicit process in relation to conflict defense and the dynamic unconscious. *International Journal of Psychoanalysis*, *88*, 843–860.

Bowlby, J. (1982). Attachment and loss. *Attachment* (Vol. 1). New York: Basic Books. Originally published 1969.

Boyd, R., & Richerson, P. J. (2005). *The origin and evolution of cultures*. New York: Oxford University Press.

Bretherton, I., & Munholland, K. A. (1999). Internal working models in attachment relationships: a construct revisited. In J. Cassidy & P. R. Shaver (Eds.), *Handbook of attachment: theory, research, and clinical applications* (pp. 89–111). New York: Guilford Press.

Cortina, M., & Liotti, G. (2010). Attachment is about safety and protection, intersubjectivity is about sharing and social understanding: the relationships between attachment and intersubjectivity. *Psychoanalytic Psychology*, *27*(4), 410–441.

Decety, J., Jackson, P. L., Sommerville, J. A., Chaminade, T., & Meltzoff, A. M. (2004). The neural basis of cooperation and competition. *NeuroImage*, *23*, 744–751.

Fonagy, P. (2001). *Attachment theory and psychoanalysis*. New York: Other Press.

Fonagy, P., Gergely, G., Jurist, E. L., & Target, M. (2004). *Affect regulation, mentalization, and the development of the self*. New York: Other Press.

Fonagy, P., & Target, M. (2008). Attachment, trauma and psychoanalysis: where psychoanalysis meets neuroscience. In E. L. Jurist, A. Slade, & S. Bergner (Eds.), *Mind to mind: infant research, neuroscience and psychoanalysis* (pp. 15–49). New York: Other Press.

Freud, A. (1993). *The ego and mechanisms of defense*. London: Karnac Books. Originally published 1936.

Freud, S. (1959). Inhibitions, symptoms and anxiety. In J. Strachey (Ed. & Trans.), *The complete psychological works of Sigmund Freud* (Vol. 20, pp. 77–174). London: Hogarth. Originally published 1926.

Gergely, G., & Unoka, Z. (2008). Attachment and mentalization in humans: the development of the affective self. In E. L. Jurist, A. Slade, & S. Bergner (Eds.), *Mind to mind: infant research, neuroscience and psychoanalysis* (pp. 50–67). New York: Other Press.

Ghent, E. (1990). Masochism, submission, surrender: masochism as a perversion of surrender. *Contemporary Psychoanalysis*, *26*(1), 108–136.

Gottman, J. M., & Silver, N. (2015). *The seven principles for making marriage work* (rev. ed.). New York: Harmony.

Kernberg, O. F. (1975). *Borderline conditions and pathological narcissism*. New York: Jason Aronson.

Levy, K. N., Meehan, K. B., Kelly, K. M., Reynoso, J. S., Weber, M., Clarkin, J. F., & Kernberg, O. F. (2006). Change in attachment patterns and reflective function in a randomized control trial of transference-focused psychotherapy for borderline personality disorder. *Journal of Consulting and Clinical Psychology*, *74*(6), 1027–1040. doi:10.1037/0022-006X.74.6.1027

Lyons-Ruth, K. (1999). The two-person unconscious: intersubjective dialogue, enactive relational representation, and the emergence of new forms of relational organization. *Psychoanalytic Inquiry*, *19*, 576–617.

Main, M., & Goldwyn, R. (1984–98). *Adult attachment scoring and classification system*. Unpublished manuscript, University of California, Berkeley.

Main, M., Kaplan, N., & Cassidy, J. (1985). Security in infancy, childhood, and adulthood: a move to the level of representation. *Monographs of the Society for Research in Child Development*, *50*(1/2), 66–104.

Marvin, R. S., & Britner, P. A. (1999). Normative development: the ontogeny of attachment. In J. Cassidy & P. R. Shaver (Eds.), *Handbook of attachment: theory, research, and clinical applications* (pp. 44–67). New York: Guilford Press.

Porges, S. W. (2011). *The polyvagal theory: neurophysiological foundations of emotions, attachment, communication, and self-regulation*. New York: W. W Norton.

Reis, B. (2010). A human family: commentary on paper by Elisabeth Fivaz- Depeursinge, Chloe Lavanchy-Scaiola, and Nicole Favez. *Psychoanalytic Dialogues*, *20*(2), 151–157.

Richerson, P. J., & Boyd, R. (2005). *Not by genes alone*. Chicago: University of Chicago Press.

Rumi, M. J. (2004). A great wagon. In *The essential Rumi* (New Expanded Edition) (C. Barks, Trans.). New York: Harper One Press.

Schore, A. N. (1994). *Affect regulation and the origin of the self: the neurobiology of emotional development*. Hillsdale: Erlbaum.

Siegel, D. J. (1999). *The developing mind: toward a neurobiology of interpersonal experience*. New York: Guilford Press.

Siegel, D. J. (2007). *The mindful brain: reflection and attunement in the cultivation of well-being*. New York: W. W. Norton.

Stern, D. (2004). *The present moment in psychotherapy*. New York: W. W. Norton.

Tatkin, S. (2011). *Wired for love: how understanding your partner's brain and attachment style can help you defuse conflict and build a secure relationship*. Oakland: New Harbinger.

Tavormina, E. M. R. (2017). *How is attunement, disruption, and repair experienced by the therapist in an attachment-focused approach to psychotherapy?* (PhD dissertation, University of British Columbia). doi:10.14288/1.0357179

Tomasello, M., Carpenter, M., Call, J., Behne, T., & Henrike, M. (2005). Understanding and sharing intentions: the origins of cultural cognition. *Behavioral and Brain Sciences*, *28*, 675–735.

Trevarthen, C. (1998). The concept and foundations of infant intersubjectivity. In S. Braten (Ed.), *Intersubjective communication and emotion in early ontogeny* (pp. 15–46). Cambridge, MA: Cambridge University Press.

Tronick, E. (1989). Emotions and emotional communication in infants. *American Psychologist*, *44*, 112–119.

12 Belonging to an awakening

The analytic function of witnessing applied to the climate crisis

Elizabeth Allured

Abraham Maslow rated our need to belong, or affiliate, with a community as among our most primary needs (Maslow, 1943). It ranked third, after the absolute need for physiological care (food, oxygen, etc.) and the need for safety from external threats. In Maslow's hierarchy, "belonging" existed alongside "love," and it is easy to imagine these two needs overlapping.

With the advent of the Interpersonal School, psychoanalysis recognized the great psychological impact of belonging to a cultural group, whether by chance of birth or by personal choice. Within the psychoanalytic community itself, analysts find groups to affiliate with based on training institutes, working styles, or networking connections. These groups are a type of "analytic culture" that can support personal and professional growth. But these groups have rarely focused upon larger socio-political realities.

Our analytic communities have typically steered away from political involvement, in part due to the historical call for neutrality early in our discipline. However, recently, since the Guantanamo Bay scandal (Boulanger, 2008) and the 2016 presidential election (Lee, 2017), analysts have affiliated to bear witness to human tragedy and imminent threats, to call out societal truths that are difficult to bear alone. One could say that, very occasionally, severe threats to life and health have brought analysts out of their office comfort zones and into the larger world. Individual clinicians, such as Robert Lifton, have undertaken consciousness-raising missions to benefit society as a whole rather than only the patient sitting across the room. Lifton (2017), a psychoanalyst, went to Hiroshima in the 1960s to bear witness to the past and ongoing suffering of survivors of nuclear bombing. He is now attempting to raise awareness of the climate crisis with the publishing of his latest book, *The Climate Swerve*.

Lifton (2017) refers to those attempting to raise awareness of socially accepted unethical behavior as "witnessing professionals." These professionals bring the ghosts out of the closet, exposing the unspoken horrors of government-sanctioned policies and procedures. Certainly, we would want to know if our government's policies were contributing to infanticide and wide-scale human suffering. Or would we?

It is difficult enough to uncover the traumas of our patients, perpetrated by absent others in the distant past. Yet this is typical trauma work in psychoanalysis: uncovering, acknowledging, witnessing, grieving, moving through, integrating, moving beyond. Through our training analyses, we learn to tolerate the intense emotions stirred up in this process, to "follow the affect," as I was taught, rather than run from it. However, giving serious thought to the climate crisis and getting past defensive denial, numbing, and disavowal ultimately exposes our own contribution, and the contribution of our government's policies, to this devastating, life-threatening problem. In addition to feelings of helplessness, anger, grief, and annihilation anxiety, both guilt and shame can come into play. My carbon-consumptive actions lead to feelings of guilt; my materialistic, self-centric nature leads to shame.

The climate crisis and social justice

The climate crisis is the penultimate social justice issue: while people in richer countries deal with global warming by turning up the air conditioning, people in poorer countries (who have contributed significantly less to the problem) swelter and sometimes die in their homes or unsheltered, unable to afford the air conditioning units or the electricity that further contribute to the problem outside. Many people in the US are engaged in a massive exercise of disavowal, rationalizing that "we can't make a difference" or "the government needs to intervene." Meanwhile, migrants leave climate-change-parched farmlands in Central America and die heading north or are turned away at our border, "othered" by some of the news media.

I believe the analytic community has seen the environmental crisis as "not our problem" (not in the realm of analytic focus), even though Harold Searles raised the red flag in his 1972 paper on the crucial role of unconscious factors in the crisis (Searles, 1972). The traditional analytic stance, with a focus on the personal and interpersonal, has typically avoided our crucial psychological and physical relationship with the more-than-human, including our ecosystem and its many living and nonliving components.

How can analytic clinicians help raise awareness (in themselves and others) about our currently dysfunctional relationship with the "natural" world? Can we call this out as dysfunctional, since we are quite literally sawing off the branch of life that we depend on? Can the traditional analytic functions of witnessing together, containing affect, and alleviating isolation shift feelings of paralysis into awakening and empowerment?

Many years ago, I could not find an analyst to process my environmental concerns. My own analyst, who had been quite helpful with many interpersonal and intrapsychic issues, did not see this as the territory of psychoanalysis. Rather, it was the responsibility of governments. My search did not yield an environmentally aware analyst in the New York area, so I jumped at the opportunity to meet weekly online with a colleague in Toronto, Anthony Wilson, who had presented a paper on this topic at an international conference where I had also shared a paper. We met initially to discuss our work and our understanding of the importance of the environmental crisis. As the meetings continued, Anthony advised that I read some books that gave a thorough scientific overview of the crisis as it was unfolding. We then processed my emotional reactions to confronting the full bore of the crisis: massive species extinction, sickened and acidified oceans, planetary deforestation, baked-in tipping points for Arctic ice melt, changes in the deep ocean currents that stabilize weather, the rapidly evolving extreme weather that has led to human deaths and migrations, and the agnotology campaign to hide all of these truths (and their fossil fuel and agribusiness origins) from the public. The magnitude of the burgeoning crisis that was building full bore across the Earth seemed almost overwhelmingly massive. At times I felt like I was sitting in a driverless car, trying to read the owner's manual while hurtling toward a crash. Complicating the problem was the fact that during my everyday life, I felt surrounded by other driverless cars whose passengers were oblivious to the oncoming crashes ahead. But my colleague Anthony supported my efforts to uncover this story and to understand my own ambivalent relation to the more-than-human. The ecosystem was beautiful but frightening; it was nurturing but destructive; it was dependable but unpredictable. Questions began to emerge: Am I safe living in a coastal town with roads that flood during hurricanes? How many years before the road out of town floods regularly during typical storms? Riding the commuter rail into New York City during a minor storm, my anxiety grew as I glanced out of the window and noticed the waters of Long Island Sound lapping a few feet below the tracks. What will happen to these tracks as storm surges grow with more extreme weather? How will our food supply be affected as areas of farmland are flooded, dried, or burned? This has already occurred in Russia and Central America, among others (Semple, 2019; Climate Change Post, 2019), but for now there are enough trading agricultural partners to share foodstuffs. For now. But the future is predicted to have simultaneous food shortages in many regions as the climate becomes much less stable.

Anthony shared that he and his wife were taking a course in emergency first aid, anticipating that having this sort of skill could be very useful in a changing world approaching or enduring a societal breakdown. He shared that he was concerned about the birth of his first grandchild into a world that was clearly going to involve great suffering in her lifetime. He was obviously taking things to another level. I traveled to Toronto for a conference, where Anthony and I were on a panel together along with Susan Bodnar, and stayed with Anthony and his wife, noticing that they used public transportation or bicycle rather than owning a car. Their vegetarian diet was simple but tasty and healthy. Anthony had books and journals about the other-than-human world in his home office waiting room. The home atmosphere had a feeling of calm yet thoughtful acceptance of a serious situation. Anthony and his wife were clearly holding the environmental crisis in mind most of the time. I, on the other hand, mentally journeyed there during Thursday videoconferences with Anthony but typically retreated back to the "normal" world in between times. Compartmentalization held traumatic knowing at bay, much as the traumatized child "forgets" about their trauma when they can.

The psychological dependency upon Anthony became clear to me when, upon his leaving for a six-week summer vacation, I felt angry. This paralleled my former dependency upon my analyst and the resulting anger during his four-week August vacation. The Thursday of Anthony's return, I "forgot" our videoconferencing appointment in a classic enactment. We needed to process my anger before I could once again become dependent upon the weekly videoconferences to contain my knowing and affect about the climate crisis. Learning about devastating storms, climate instability, massive species die-offs, and the lack of governmental plans to address any of this can be traumatic in itself. It seems similar to experiencing a childhood in a dysfunctional home and coming to realize that one's parents do not have one's well-being in mind and actually don't care whether one lives or dies. This is certainly how the majority of national governments have been acting in the midst of climate crisis. DeMocker compares the situation to a party of drunken adolescents whose parents continue to provide more and more alcohol (DeMocker, 2018). In his paper, "States of Emergency: Trauma and Climate Change" (White, 2015), White refers to climate change as "perhaps even the greatest trauma," since it ultimately foreshadows the possible or likely extinction of our human species. Our typical dissociation of the current climate emergency is a hallmark of traumatic symptomatology. My work with Anthony was softening my defenses around the anger, shock, and annihilation anxieties that often suffuse learning about this. I had thought that the recent Paris Agreements on the climate were sufficient to prevent the climate from approaching multiple dangerous cascading interrelated changes. But the more I read the science and the consensus about our current emissions trajectories, the less hopeful I felt. Anthony could validate my perception about this, could tolerate the sadness and the seriousness of the current moment in time. As the months went by, seeing Anthony contain all of this helped move my knowing from the edges of consciousness toward the center.

I dusted off my old bicycle and started riding down the hill into town sometimes instead of using my car. I began sharing car rides with friends instead of taking separate cars to meet in places out of town. Things fell away, and a greater sense of peace took its place most of the time. Listening to the birds in the morning while doing morning stretching became preferable to hearing the morning news report. Reading the daily newspaper, however, was still essential most of the time. Added to the regular news was an online digest of environmental news, further expanding my vocabulary and understanding of the complex interrelated events occurring unseen by most.

Still, Anthony's breaks to visit family or take vacations for weeks at a time continued to stress me. It was with relief that I turned to another colleague to form another dyad. Belonging to this twosome was even more productive in certain ways.

Wendy Greenspun had been my first family therapy supervisor twenty-five years ago, a kind and professional mentor who had offered her time pro bono to share her prodigious skills with a newcomer in the field. She had attended my first professional paper on the topic of psychoanalysis and environmentalism a dozen years later, but we had not kept in touch. When she appeared at Lifton's book-signing event for *The Climate Swerve* in New York City last year, we reconnected around this topic and met a few weeks later in the city to catch up on our professional lives. I somewhat hesitantly shared that I hoped to eventually teach a course on ecopsychoanalysis. It was a "dream" course, one that incubated like plans for a dream house on a shelf in my mind. Wendy was enthused about the course idea and suggested the course might be considered at her institute in Manhattan. We decided to videoconference weekly, on Tuesdays, to develop plans for this.

Whereas Wendy had been my teacher in the realm of family systems theory, she became my student in the domain of climate psychology. As Anthony had done for me, I recommended books and papers for her to read, and she processed her thoughts and feelings about these in our weekly videoconferences. Like myself, she had initially felt optimistic about "solutions" for this crisis, but upon reading about the dire situation we now face, she shifted to feeling overwhelmed, angry, and at times helpless. Wendy shared that her daughter, graduating from college, felt that there was no hope for the survival of humans due to catastrophic climate events coming in this century. I shared that my son, who works in the area of astrophysics, said that the current theory of Venus being a "dead" planet was that naturally occurring greenhouse gases had raised the Venutian temperature so much that life itself had been extinguished there, essentially killed by a runaway greenhouse effect. Wendy found herself getting angry with people who had no sense of responsibility for their actions that could harm the environment, or people who did not want to become informed about the situation. With an analytic focus, we came to understand how this not-wanting-to-know and not-wanting-to-change is a defensive position that both of us could identify with at various times. We recognized that if we didn't belong to our dyad, we simply could not contain the information or feelings that were engendered by it. We studied Katherine Hayhoe's work (Yale Program on Climate Change Communications, 2018) on effective climate change communication. In yet another inversion of roles (Wendy as instructor for a topic I was still teaching her about), the dyad moved forward.

The fledgling four-student course met at Wendy's office, and all four clinicians expressed gratitude at finding a place to discuss and share reactions to the burgeoning environmental crisis. Wendy and I described our own process of awakening to the full extent of the traumatic destruction playing out largely unsung in the media at the time. We described the purpose of the course as not only increasing the psychoanalytic perspective on the problem but also encouraging connections with analytic colleagues in grappling with the emotional and cognitive complexities of the environmental situation. If one of the problems in the current crisis was inadequate spaces of containment, then encouraging containment among colleagues seemed part of the solution. Especially if these colleagues could then serve this same function with their patients.

After traversing analytic territory about this crisis from Searles through Bion's attacks on linking (Bion, 1959) and theory on trauma and dissociation, the class explored Klein's paranoid-schizoid position versus the depressive position of mourning and grief in facing this topic. At the end of the last class, students expressed concern that the course's holding environment had become so important that there was a need for follow-up sessions. Much like in an analysis, when new material breaks through consciousness and begs for integration, the environmental knowing that was so difficult to tolerate individually could be held by belonging to a group of like-minded seekers. No one wanted it to bury the knowing again.

Wendy and I arranged monthly follow-up sessions, and the former students again verbalized that without belonging to the follow-up group, they would not have been able to persevere in keeping the crisis in mind and moving ahead with environmental actions, such as planning out teaching a course or suggesting sustainable actions at their institutes. The sessions became a way of not only containing environmental affects but also supporting environmental actions that individuals had come up with subsequent to taking our course.

Meanwhile, as my work with Anthony and Wendy continued, I was asked to help form a new group: a North American chapter of the Climate Psychology Alliance, a UK-based organization with the purpose of "making connections between depth psychology and climate change" (Climate Psychology Alliance, 2019). The UK is significantly ahead of the US in its actions taken to mitigate the climate crisis, and the UK clinicians who reached out to me seemed quite advanced in their thinking compared to most of my analytic colleagues here. They had put out a text of many analytic perspectives on this crisis (Weintrobe, 2013), and they were holding events to teach about it. Belonging to this CPA network further increased my "normalizing" of holding the crisis in mind and seeing the dissociation of it as a sort of "malignant normality" that is a pervasive part of US culture at large. An analytic colleague once said to me, "Why worry about it? The only thing that's going to change anything is the election." One could have said the same thing about the Vietnam War in the early 1960s. However, as censorship of journalism was breached and consciousness was raised about the deaths of innocents during that war, people took to the streets to demand change. I have broken through the censorship here. The innocents are already dying, mostly in the less visible southern hemisphere but sometimes in Caribbean islands and even in Paradise, California. The fossil fuel companies have actively promoted doubt, confusion, and uncertainty regarding the human role in greenhouse gas emissions and have been hiding the collateral damage and expected outcome for decades (Mann and Toles, 2016; Bowen, 2009). The oil companies have withheld the truth, and the collateral damage, for decades. But the truth is now exposed, if we can bear to look for it and bear to take it in.

Two weeks ago, Wendy and I were discussants while one of our former ecopsychoanalysis students read her brilliant and comprehensive paper, "Thinking Catastrophic Thoughts: Psychoanalysis on a Warming Planet" (Kassouf, 2019). Kassouf labeled what she saw as the analytic community's "anenvironmental stance" and offered that getting beyond this had the potential for mental health benefits: "the malignant aspects of this (anenvironmental) orientation prevent us from a more full experience of aliveness, weakening our grasp on reality" (p. 4).

Promoting Kassouf's work was another role reversal, as her paper (with around a hundred citations) was clearly more well-researched and theoretically nuanced than any paper I had written. The dozens of analysts in attendance for her presentation gave me hope that perhaps a tide was turning in the avoidance of this topic among the professional community.

In the early history of psychoanalysis, groups of interested persons affiliated to share papers and discuss analytic topics. Often, a training analyst would later become a colleague; a writing mentor might become a supervisor. When Ferenczi could not find an analyst to help him explore his early parental relations, he turned to mutual analysis. There was little professional structure, as the knowledge base and clinical community were in a germinal phase. Ecopsychoanalysis is also in a germinal phase. Harold Searles planted the seed in the 1960s and 1970s (Searles, 1960; 1972), and five decades later, it has begun to sprout in the analytic community.

My work with Wendy and Anthony has components of mutual analysis, differing in that each of us has already undergone an analysis of our human relations. The trickiest of transferential struggles and defensive operations are therefore enlightened by past work and familiarity with our own go-to self-states.

Before belonging to these dyads, I often felt marginalized by my interest in understanding the psychological aspects of the nonhuman environment. As Searles noted in 1972, the psychoanalyst who showed too much interest in the nonhuman environment and its crisis would be seen as either having autistic characteristics, having annihilation anxiety, or being suicidally depressed. Thus the need for affiliation with professionals to validate each other's knowledge and feelings related to this crisis, to hold dissociation, numbing, and paralyzing fear at bay.

In his essay, "Climate Change in a Perverse Culture," Hoggett (2013) reminds us that we are ambivalent, and not rational, beings at the core, living with potential for overwhelm from a myriad of feelings ranging from terror to rage. He makes the point that the climate problem is located within the culture rather than in the seemingly isolated behaviors of individuals. There is also the problem of individual economic interest. I have written about this more fully in another paper, detailing the *economic cost* of living conscientiously when others are not (Allured, 2019). To this must be added the role of corporate self-interest in the climate crisis. When fossil fuel companies are focused on short-term profits while possibly accelerating millions of deaths, hundreds of thousands of individuals acquiesce by including (*Exxon Mobil and Shell Oil*) oil stocks in their retirement portfolios. It is likely that most people are feeling helpless in, and ambivalent about, stopping a process that is benefiting them economically, personally, in the short term. If all of us pulled our stock out of fossil fuel companies, they would fail, and renewable energy would possibly be developed more quickly. Likewise, if all of us adopted a vegetarian diet, greenhouse gases would steeply decline. If all of us bought used electric or hybrid cars instead of new gas-powered ones, greenhouse gases would fall. If all of us grew some of our vegetables and fruits, greenhouse gases would decline. If all of us had solar panels on our roofs for electricity production and hot water heating, greenhouse gases would decline. (These are not difficult actions to take. I took them years ago.) There are social factors holding many of us back, and belonging to dyads or groups can mitigate these social pressures, as Randall

(Randall & Brown, 2015) has written about in her group work aiming towards carbon footprint reduction.

Hoggett (2013) cites Steiner in seeing perverse climate change denial as a way of not coming to terms with the very real losses inherent in being human. This is related to our dependent position as regards other people, the biosphere, and all of the nonhuman world, which we are born into and eventually return to as elemental biomass. This dependent participation and eventual death can be felt as a narcissistic injury that must be kept an unthought known. Searles (1960) used a parallel metaphor to describe this denial of dependency on the Earth by describing his work with patients of a Southern background, who only after long periods of psychoanalysis could bear to explore their dependence in childhood upon African-American caretakers, whose love provided them at that time with their major source of nurturance.

Tate has recently described the state of mind of Western peoples as "trance-like" concerning the accelerating global climate emergency (Tate, 2018). Most of us are not still in denial of the problem, yet many, especially those whose lives are not immediately threatened by the prospect of rising seas, droughts, or floods from precipitation, appear to act as if climate change is not occurring in their part of the world. It is occurring to "other people" and will happen "in the future." In reality, it is occurring now in New York (stronger hurricanes, colder winters, hotter summers, floods), California (droughts, wildfires, heat waves), Texas (stronger hurricanes, floods, tornadoes), and most other places in North America. I have written about the metaphorical stance of most people as "sleeping through Pearl Harbor" (Allured, 2017). The climate noise is now so pervasive that many have shifted into defensive postures such as reactionary consumerism, behaviors or substances to self-medicate, hedonism, and displacement/projection of vulnerability onto refugees in a caravan in Mexico who are escaping bad environments (who must be walled off/othered).

Belonging to my dyads and groups of witnessing professionals helps hold all of this in mind and more. Each of us, in our own way, is expanding the boundaries of what can be known, and done, about this societal emergency. Each is an activist in our own way. We each need support in this work. Hearing others describe their efforts, and feeling recognition for my own, mitigates against helpless, avoidant defenses. If these colleagues can work so diligently, perhaps I can, also. If they can feel despair at times, my own has a place too. It is appropriate. Many simultaneous losses need recognition in this, the sixth great extinction in Earth's history (Kolbert, 2014).

In addition to losses, there is great potential for a crucial aspect of consciousness to re-emerge: living in conscious community with the more-than-human. Our Westernized technology-focused lives have often decreased our awareness of the many living beings surrounding us at any moment and our ultimate dependence upon this intersubjective web of life. Our associations with living closer to the Earth may involve hardships and deprivations endured by our ancestors or those in "developing world" countries. However, their way of life usually preserved an ecosystem stable enough to provide basic needs for their progeny. If we work hard enough to promote societal change and sustainable agriculture, we may yet usher in an era of renewable-technology-assisted living that provides basic needs for all but forgoes lifestyle amenities such as unlimited air travel, a meat-heavy diet, and products from all around the world to which we have come to feel entitled.

In the cold of winter, tapping my backyard maple tree and seeing the steady dripping of sap into the bucket reassures me that life persists when only bare tree limbs are visible. It also reminds me that a constant flow of life-giving fluids suffuses these trees and most living things and that my conscious participation in this inflow and outflow of life is, at a very elemental level, a joyous and life-affirming act.

One of the organizers of a conference on the theme of "Belonging" shared how he was very affected recently upon returning to the beaches of his native Greece. The fish that used to fill the waters there when he was a boy are now gone. These experiences of environmental losses, I believe, are like dreams that typically never find a listener. They sit, like unmetabolized traumas, when we have no one to witness them with us. The shock, grief, anger, and sadness is too great to fully hold alone. This memory of the beach was shared in a classroom setting when I was teaching about the subject of ecopsychoanalysis. The group heard it, and others spoke briefly about losses of this sort. The more we can be witnesses for each other, in dyads or groups, the larger our consciousness can stretch, into the world of the nonhuman and the great catastrophe that is occurring there. It is also actually occurring in the human family too, in many people whose lives have been lost due to extreme weather events. I move among embracing this knowing, compartmentalizing it, avoiding knowing, and wanting to know more.

References

Allured, E. (2017). *Sleeping through Pearl Harbor: how our psychology, our government, and special interests are fostering ecocide, and how to tolerate awareness and act.* Unpublished manuscript.

Allured, E. (2019). The tragedy of the Earth's commons: psychoanalytic perspectives on climate change and the law. In A. Harris & M. Plinio (Eds.), Psychoanalysis, law, and society (pp. 41–55). New York: Routledge.

Bion, A. (1959). Attacks on linking. *International Journal of Psycho-analysis, 40*(5–6), 308–315.

Boulanger, G. (2008). Witnesses to reality: working psychodynamically with survivors of terror. *Psychoanalytic Dialogues, 18*(5), 638–657.

Bowen, M. (2009). *Censoring science.* London: Penguin Books.

Climate Change Post. (2019). Climate Change Russia. Retrieved from www.climatechangepost.com/russia/agriculture-and-horticulture/ 5/1/2019

Climate Psychology Alliance. (2019). Retrieved from www.climatepsychologyalliance.org/

DeMocker, M. (2018). *The parent's guide to climate revolution.* Novato: New World Library.

Hoggett, P. (2013). Climate change in a perverse culture. In S. Weintrobe (Ed.), *Engaging with climate change, psychoanalytic and interdisciplinary perspectives* (pp. 56–71). New York: Routledge.

Kassouf, S. (2019, April 12). *Thinking catastrophic thoughts: psychoanalysis on a warming planet*. Paper presented to the National Psychological Association for Psychoanalysis, New York.

Kolbert, E. (2014). *The sixth extinction: an unnatural history*. New York: Henry Holt.

Lee, B. (2017). *The dangerous case of Donald Trump*. New York: St. Martin's Press.

Lifton, R. (2017). *The climate swerve*. New York: New Press.

Mann, M., & Toles, T. (2016). *The Madhouse Effect*. New York: Columbia.

Maslow, A. (1943). A preface to motivation theory. *Psychosomatic Medicine*, *5*, 85–92.

Randall, R., & Brown, A. (2015). *In time for tomorrow? The carbon conversations handbook*. Stirling: Surefoot Effect.

Searles, H. (1960). *The nonhuman environment*. New York: International Universities Press.

Searles, H. (1972). Unconscious processes in relation to the environmental crisis. *Psychoanalytic Review*, *59*(3), 361–374.

Semple, K. (2019, April 13). Central American farmers head to US, fleeing climate change. *New York Times*. Retrieved from www.nytimes.com/2019/04/13/world/americas/coffee-climate-change-migration.html

Tate, A. (2018, January 30). Personal communication.

Weintrobe, S. (Ed.). (2013). *Engaging with climate change: psychoanalytic and interdisciplinary perspectives*. Hove: Routledge.

White, B. (2015). States of emergency: trauma and climate change. *Ecopsychology*, *7*(4) 192–197.

Yale Program on Climate Change Communication. (2018). Katherine Hayhoe. Retrieved from https://climatecommunication.yale.edu/about/people-partners/katharine-hayhoe/ 6/4/2018

Part 4

Belonging and mindfulness

13 Where does a discussion of Buddhism belong in psychoanalysis?

Robert Besner

Similarities between psychoanalysis and Buddhism have been noted and written about since Fromm, Suzuki, and De Martino published *Psychoanalysis and Zen Buddhism* in 1960. Recently there has been a revival of such writings, including *Thoughts Without a Thinker* by Mark Epstein (1995), Jeremy Safran's (2003) edited volume *Psychoanalysis and Buddhism*, Robert Langan's (2005) *Minding What Matters*, and Eltschlinger's (2010) "Dharmakīrti." More specific comparisons have included works on Wilfred Bion (e.g. Pelled, 2008; Cooper, 2016; Zhang, 2019); on Lacan (e.g. Webb & Sells, 1995; Moncayo, 2012); and on Stern (Molino, Carnevali, & Giannandrea, 2014). I wish to elaborate on some of these commonalities as well as highlight some important distinctions between the two traditions.

This chapter explores two essential threads of Buddhism and their relationship with aspects of the psychoanalytic models offered by Daniel Stern, Jacques Lacan, and Wilfred Bion. The first of these core Buddhist constructs, Beginner's Mind (Suzuki, 1970), refers to an open, gentle psychic posture. The second construct, the obverse of Beginner's Mind, is the dualistic fixation (Rangjung, 2019b), characterized by our minds' grasping and fixation upon arising mental contents. A construct closely related to grasping and fixation is "ego-clinging" (Rangjung, 2019a). Ego here connotes *das Ich*, the "I", the self as subject, and not a psychic apparatus or structure. Ego-clinging imputes adherence to the notion of a personal self. In the dualistic fixation, we create a reflexive subjective awareness and experience ourselves as distinct from the rest of reality.

In Buddhist understanding, the absence of Beginner's Mind and the corresponding expression of our habitual dualistic posture, taken together, generate psychological suffering. In this posture we create ourselves as separate from the rest and attribute substantiality to our subjective experience. We become naturally compelled to protect and defend our "selves" from the slings and arrows of life. We become increasingly concerned with preserving our psychic space, and so build up successive protective layers. Our psychic space becomes self-referenced and constricted, and our capacities for empathy and compassion atrophy. Conversely, the appearance of Beginner's Mind and the diminution of the dualistic fixation are pathways to liberation from this suffering inherent in the human situation.

Buddhism, through its meditation practices, offers us an alternative to our conventional mode of experiencing, one characterized by openness to and immersion in arising experience at each instant. This quality of mind is one in which each new moment bursts upon us, emerges before us in fullness and freshness, its contours and textures palpable. Beginner's Mind refers to being attuned to the evanescence of each instant without hope or expectation preloading the experiential moment. How does this bedrock feature of Buddhism interface with psychoanalysis?

One psychoanalytic contribution evocative of Beginner's Mind is Daniel Stern's articulation of the Present Moment. Stern (2004) wrote, "The present moment is the felt experience of what happens during a short stretch of consciousness" (p. 32). Unfolding with mounting intensity over only a few seconds, it then trails off into the next moment. Stern finds the foundation of subjective experience in the micro-moments of interaction that underlie the telling of the narrative. He further suggests that these two classes of events, the present moment and the narrative, have a potentially contradictory nature. This is because there is a distinction between the present moment of experience and how it is later reshaped by words.

The inherent contradiction is that "the present moment, while lived, cannot be seized by language, which reconstitutes it after the fact" (p. 8). The present moment is *the experiential referent* that language builds upon. "It is hard to grasp and tends to remain subliminal because we so often jump out of the present ongoing experience to take the reflexive, objectified third person viewpoint" (p. 33). Further, we take the reflection of the previous moment as an objective moment when it is a totally new instantaneous construction that will itself be objectified in turn. To the extent to which we rely on a person's narrative reconstruction in or out of treatment, we are at risk of losing the person's actual experience to their retelling of it. While the narrative construction is meaningful in itself, it is a different class of events.

Another psychoanalytic contribution to this discussion lies in the work of Wilfred Bion (1967), who expanded the notion of Freud's evenly suspended attention into his notion of "without memory or desire." Bion emphasized a quality of openness to experience. Facing our patients' or our own mental productions without memory, desire, or understanding creates a posture open to the freshness of experience, with the capacity to tolerate it instead of the compulsion to prematurely foreclose on it. He exhorts us to "resist any attempt to cling to what we know" in favor of tolerating unformed experience until it resolves itself into a pattern. He wrote: "patience should be retained without irritable reaching after fact and reason until a pattern evolves" (1970, pp. 123–124).

An instance of psychoanalytic thought that bears on both the question of Beginner's Mind and the problem of the dualistic fixation comes from Jacques Lacan. In naming the symbolic, imaginary, and real registers of psychic experience, Lacan offers another possibility of exploring the question of foreclosing upon our emergent process of being. It is the register of the imaginary that is salient here. The imaginary is the realm of all imagined representation, epitomized in the reflection of one's image in the mirror. For Lacan, the infant, from its earliest moments of self-consciousness, perceives in the mirror or in its mother's eyes a reflection of itself. It is with this reflected, and therefore alienated, entity that it identifies. The individual is forever in this way caught up in identification with their reflected mirror image. Forgetting that this is an alienated image, one literally takes the way they represent themselves to themselves (Lacan, 1988; 1977)

Lacan developed his position based on his understanding of Freud's 1914/1959 essay "On Narcissism," where the ego is considered as a love object more than as an agency or substructure of any kind (Richardson, 1985). Lacan suggested that, in Freud's theory, narcissism structures all of our relations with the external world. He wrote that all objects are structured around "the wandering shadow of one's ego. Therefore all objects have a fundamentally egomorphic character" (Lacan, 1988, p. 165).

The same can be said for consciousness: as an object of itself, as soon as it is grasped by reflexive awareness, it, too, is relegated to the register of the imaginary and given as egomorphic. We love it; we identify with it; we are married to it; we take no distance from it. We can see in Stern's loss of the present moment to the retelling of it in the narrative, and in Lacan's description of the imaginary, echoes of the Buddhist model of grasping and fixation and the loss of Beginner's Mind to a reflexive, reconstructed version of experiencing.

As the Present Moment becomes more alive and accessible to awareness, our experience may shift away from being located in a substantial self to which an attribute "belongs" to one in which our experience of ourselves, of our very being, is constituted in our raw experience, not narratively constructed, but immediate. It is not so much that "I am seeing" something, but instead that through this act of seeing I am created as I am at that moment. Through an act of seeing, I am created as seeing in that moment. Through an act of hearing, the hearing is creating me as hearing at that instant; the act of thinking is creating me as thinking; as I think, I am. Those experiences are not only attributes of a centralized self; they actually create us in their happening. To the extent to which we grasp and fixate upon these arising mental events, we are creating a reified, narrative self.

In these psychoanalytic examples, we can see Stern, Bion, and Lacan, each in his own way, approximating the idea of consciousness fixating on its own objects to create an egomorphic, reflexive subjectivity, with the ensuing loss of freshness in the moment and the alienating sense of separateness it creates in us all. To become attuned to Stern's Present Moment or to be in Bion's "never-ending getting to know," "without memory, desire, or understanding," requires equanimity and forbearance, both formidable developmental achievements in themselves in both psychoanalytic and Buddhist idioms. Both are evocative of Beginner's Mind. Similarly, Lacan's description of a fundamentally alienated psychic posture captures the flavor of the dualistic fixation.

Regarding the Buddhist model, however, sometimes these factors can be taken for the sum total of meditative effects when they lie in a spectrum of possible constructive outcomes. Buddhism is more than the system of subjective psychology it includes; it can be a path to mystical, even subjectless, experience. How can that aspect of Buddhism be excluded from the conversation? What links are there between psychoanalytic thinking and the further reaches of Buddhism? Do these further reaches belong in a discussion of psychoanalysis, and if so, where?

The dualistic fixation is our tendency towards grasping and fixation upon our objects of consciousness, the contents of our emergent mental process. The resultant state of reflexive, self-conscious subjectivity is analogous to the loss of Stern's Present Moment or to living in a world of reflected images populating Lacan's register of the imaginary. The openness to and immersion in arising experience characteristic of Beginner's Mind is progressive. Where does it ultimately progress to? From the point of view of Buddhist practice, it is ironic to ask this question—the answer is to right here in the present moment. To impose a direction or goal upon it is antithetical to practice. All we need to do is to be right here without an extraneous goal.

Buddhism understands our habitual mode of grasping and fixation on mental contents as ignorant in two senses. In the first instance, it may refer to conventional lack of knowledge or dissociative processes. Beyond this, in the second case it connotes ignorance or bewilderment about an underlying reality of pristine mind characterized by non-dual lucidity, brilliance, and compassion. Awareness, and the mind that arises with it, is seen at each instant of arising to have dual potentialities: either to rest in its pristine non-dual state or to initiate a cascade of instantaneous events culminating in a moment of reflexive self-conscious awareness. Awareness, deviating from its pristine state, is seen to progressively harden around any arising mental objects, including thoughts and sensations, which it grasps. This is a model of progressive mental articulation of any incipient object of awareness into an ultimate co-mingling with, and creation of, our reflexive subjectivity as reified and apart from the rest of creation (Guenther, 1977; Rab-Jampa, Dudjom, & Khyentse, 1978).

Despite the evolution in psychoanalysis from its focus on a unitary self to an understanding of subjective experience as composed of patterned, multiple transient self states, in our conventional understanding, this experience of a reflexively perceived substantial self is largely taken for granted. From within a self-conscious perspective, and in the absence of direct realization of pristine mind, it seems impossible to distinguish the figure of our reflexive, self-conscious reality from its ground in pristine mind. All we see is our self-consciousness. Our conventional experience of a substantial self seems to serve us well in navigating our being in the world. Yet it comes packaged with a problem: Our reflexive experience endures endless sources of psychic pain. How can we work with this recurrent sense of dissatisfaction?

For Buddhism, this quality of dissatisfaction associated with reflexive self-consciousness remains the focal issue—its first Noble Truth. In our conventional experience, both psychotherapies and meditation can help ameliorate this struggle by, as Freud described, replacing neurotic misery with normal human unhappiness. But how do we bridge the compelling felt experience of a substantial self with the potential experience of pristine mind offered by Buddhism, and what does the cessation of the act of creating self look like? What is there in the absence of grasping and fixation, and what is its place in the body of psychoanalysis? Does it even belong?

Again, both Lacan's and Bion's works are suggestive of milestones along the path to liberation from the dualistic fixation. From their rich imaginations they offer psychoanalytic renderings of the background state of consciousness out of which they see arising our conventional experience of self and world. In Lacan it is the register of the real that is salient here. Lacan (1988) imagines the register of the real as including that which is in its raw state, not yet given as egomorphic, imagined representation. He regarded the "imago" as the proper object of study of psychology; the real was foreclosed from analytic experience. Although he saw the alienation imposed by reflected images as problematic, he did not seem to think it possible to directly experience the state that exists before imaged geomorphic misconstruals come to dominate our perceptual consciousness (1988, p. 166).

Lacan (1988) referred to the real as lacking in all possible mediation, as something which, when faced with, all words cease and all categories fail. He seemed to struggle with this state, which he could imagine but not directly experience. He despaired of the real being accessible and concluded that it could only be supposed (p. 164). A further characteristic of the real for Lacan is that it is "the object of anxiety par excellence" (p. 73). It is impossible to transfer the imagined self to the register of the real because in this transposition is incurred the loss of the reflective image. He did not think it possible to experience this state. For Lacan, the appearance to consciousness of the real brings with it a fear of dissolution of the self-image and a sense of dread (p. 164).

Bion, in his notion of "O," as contrasted with his "K," which assumes a conventional self-conscious thinking subject based in reflexive awareness, explored new possibilities within psychoanalytic thought. Yet his model seems ambivalent in the same sense as Lacan's. Where in some moments he attributes to the experience of O qualities of the unknowable, or ultimate truth, he also sees it as both ominous and turbulent, threatening a loss of anchorage in everyday "narrative security" (Jacobus, 2005, p. 227). Bion would speak of "an intense catastrophic emotional explosion, O," (Bion, 1970, p. 12), which could only be known through its after-effects (Jacobus, 2005, p. 251n).

Grotstein (2000, p. 128), in a discussion of Bion, refers to O as "nameless dread." He wrote:

> I believe that we are born into "O" (or the Real, in Lacan's terminology), and that hopefully are rescued under the beneficent canopy of the organizing and mediating "filters" of the paranoid-schizoid and depressive position (sequentially, alternately, and in parallel). Randomness (chaos) is, with mother's reverie, transformed into phantasies and then into symbolic meaning ...

Here, O is seen as an immature, chaotic, disruptive state, a threat that needs to be mediated and tamed. It appears here that immature, primitive psychological states get confused with pristine cognition as consensually validated by generations of accomplished meditators. Grotstein's model, as a model of emergence from primitive psychological states, makes sense. But it seems not to fit as well as a model of the absolute.

Lacan, and Bion along with his commentators mentioned here, present what appear to be confused models of the absolute. They seem to conflate mystical union with a state still referenced to self. For these authors, while self-reference is attenuated or relegated to primitive states, it remains the ultimate reference point. Writing in this area seems to follow Freud in his inclination to see realization, enlightenment, or Nirvana as the ultimate manifestation of the death instinct, with no positive form.

From a Buddhist point of view, the Absolute *is* absolute. It rests outside of the realm of discursive thought. This quality of pristine mind, or emptiness (Sanskrit: *sunyata*), is literally inconceivable. It cannot be grasped as an object of reflexive cognition. How can we work with it conceptually? We can't. There are no reference points. It is not subject to narrative construction. Once it is fixated upon and grasped at, it is lost. This goes to the most subtle levels of practice: From *The Rain of Wisdom*, on Enlightenment: "even mystical experiences of all kinds fall within samsara" (life characterized by recurrent experience of (rebirth in) unpleasant mental states) "as long as they confirm the experiencer or solidify his experience, even in the most subtle way" (Trungpa, 1999, p. 347).

How do you discuss, or even consider, a state in which you are not there? Only clarity is there; only brilliance. There are no contents. You are not present, but neither are you absent; any self, any hardening of reflexive consciousness or even subtle flickering of arising mind, is quieted. There is quiescence.

A Buddhist rendering of this experience is as follows:

> (It) is non-dual awareness that transcends intellect; it is non-conceptual, lucid, like all-pervading space. Though manifesting boundless compassion, it is devoid of self-nature. It is like the reflection of the moon on the lake's surface. It is lucid and undefinable, without center of circumference, unstained, undefiled, and free from fear or desires. Like the dream of a mute it is inexpressible.
>
> (Namgyal, 1986, p. 95)

Intellectual analysis by itself, even down to its finest details, still does not eliminate the solidification of self or of the self-referenced state of being. Bion's writings, like Lacan's, seem to veer between approaching an idea of emptiness and then, by inserting a subject, reverting to self-referenced intellectual imaginings of it or finding it inaccessible. Analogous paradoxical threads in some corners of contemporary Buddhism in the west seem to conflate the investigation of subjective experience as developed in western psychology with the Buddhist project of liberation from the dualistic fixation. It appears that in two generations over the past forty or fifty years, concurrent with the transplantation of Buddhist teachings to the west and their adoption by western psychology, there has been a psychologization of Buddhism in the nature of the material being deconstructed.

What is the nature of this psychologization? In Buddhism, the personal psychology of any mind moment is not the only essential element. The actual process of mind arising to a fulminating experience of self-consciousness is also vital to consider; this process is applicable to and independent of any specific contents. The Abhidharma, an outline of Buddhist psychology, is a compendium of multiple elements of mind. It includes both the stages of construction of a self-conscious reflexive moment of awareness and the range of contents denoting the specific character of that moment. These contents are mental attitudes, postures, or emotional states classified as wholesome, neutral, or unwholesome according to their emotional valence. The fundamental Buddhist meditation technique of "letting go" of arising thoughts, of relinquishing mental formations, implicitly encompasses both of these features—the process and the contents. Psychologization occurs when the focus is shifted exclusively towards subjective contents and away from the actual process of arising of mind. This shift tends to reinforce the reification of self, our tendency towards "ego-clinging."

Some individuals in treatment may benefit from such structuralization and reinforcement of their sense of self (Engler, 1984, pp. 39–41). For them, this is the most compassionate course of treatment. Generally, in the presence of a self, the therapeutic process of "working through"—the relinquishment of ego-clinging, of fixation upon particular features of the self—may indeed relieve suffering and perhaps result in improved functioning and well-being. It may even induce a shift towards open psychic space. Yet Chogyam Trungpa Rinpoche, a Tibetan Buddhist teacher, spoke of the intention of Buddhist practice not particularly being improved personality, since personality resides in the realm of reflexive subjectivity, of grasping and fixation upon our selves (personal communication). Even successful treatment, with all its benefits, resides in the realm of subjectivity and is therefore only a partial representation of the Buddhist path. What, then, becomes of the essential Buddhist project of liberation from the dualistic fixation?

Filmmaker David Cherniak, in a 2011 film named *Dharma Rising*, documents the voices of several senior western Buddhist teachers of this generation, leaders who are one or two generations removed from the Buddhist emissaries who emerged from traditional Buddhist cultures. Their voices also appear contradictory. Some seem concerned about this shift in focus in contemporary western Buddhism. Others appear to justify the shift as a natural evolution of a tradition in a new setting. Perhaps from an understandable wish to bring to others the benefits of both western psychology and Buddhism, they are seemingly unconcerned with what might be lost in historical Buddhism's distinctiveness.

Psychoanalytic theories are inherently about subjective experience and require the presence of a subject—actually, two—in the room. How do we reconcile this when there is no subject, as in the far reaches of Buddhist practice? What is the middle way? Cooper (2016), in a thoughtful discussion suggestive of Buddhism's venerable Heart Sutra, analogizes Bion's K and O with Buddhism's registers of relative and absolute emptiness. He writes: "Radical nondualism includes both the continuity and discontinuity" (p. 527). Cooper discusses a continuum of experience ("realizational continuity") of interpenetrated K and O in psychoanalysis and of conventional experiencing and radical non-dualism in Buddhism. He argues against three hazards of making a rigid distinction between K and O or between conventional self-referenced experience and realization: "The problems include the tendency to bifurcate and compartmentalize K and O as unrelated; to form a biased and limited view of Bion's position as exclusively negative and nihilistic; the tendency to overvalue or idealize intuited O" (pp. 527–528).

Yet it seems it may still be useful to tread lightly in attempts to present a blended model of psychoanalytic and Buddhist thought. Hsuan Tsang (660/1973), in a traditional Buddhist text, addresses "those who misunderstood or make nothing of the doctrine of the two Sunyatas or voids [relative and absolute emptiness] in order that they might acquire a correct understanding of it" (p. 1). What is Hsuan Tsang referring to in "the two Sunyatas"? The first case, relative emptiness, refers to apprehension of an insubstantial self. It occurs in a framework still embedded in self-referenced experience and therefore seems amenable to the psychoanalytic domain. The second instance, absolute emptiness, alludes to an ultimate relinquishment of grasping at, even non-appearance of, arising mental contents, however subtle. It refers to cessation of and liberation from this activity to ultimate realization. It is subjectless and seems outside the domain of psychoanalysis. The interpenetrated mode of relative and absolute experiencing can be fragile and easily, insidiously disrupted. Even accomplished Buddhist teachers, in their subjectivities, may be susceptible to ordinary human frailties. A dialogue between two subjectivities, however attenuated, is still affected by the exigencies of selfhood.

Closing thoughts

Psychoanalytic exploration of the inherently reflexive nature of subjective life and Buddhist relinquishment of the grasping and fixation at arising mental contents are overlapping yet distinct projects. In our lived experience, engaged in the world, both clinical psychoanalysis and Buddhist meditation can help us both to remain open-hearted and to exercise intellect in a manner not characterized by the compulsion towards grasping and fixation. They may allow us to live in a space where symbols and meanings arise to be grasped at, yet not deaden our openness to the present moment. In the relative register of our conventional subjective experience, the imprint of one system on the other is compelling.

Yet once we move to the register of the absolute the transposition is not so facile. The relationship between the subjectively based project of psychoanalysis and the ultimate quiescence of arising reflexive mental contents in the further reaches of Buddhism is complex, with apparent differences in understanding in psychoanalysis and Buddhism of the term absolute, or ultimate, reality. What might be lost if we frame even esoteric Buddhism in terms of a reflexive subject essential to the psychoanalytic project? When psychoanalysis employs the language of absolute reality borrowed from Buddhism in the context of reflexive, subjective, or intersubjective experience, it may contribute to slippage in meaning and to confusion in the conversation between the two domains.

References

Bion, W. R. (1967). Notes on memory and desire. *Psychoanalytic Forum*, *2*(3), 272–280.

Bion, W. R. (1970). *Attention and interpretation*. London: Tavistock. Reprinted London: Karnac, 1984.

Cherniak, D. (Producer & Director). (2011). *Dharma rising* [Motion picture]. Toronto, Canada: David Cherniak Productions.

Cooper, P. (2016). Zen musings on Bion's "O" and "K". *Psychoanalytic Review*, *103*(4), 515–538.

Eltschinger, V. (2010). Dharmakīrti. *Revue Internationale de Philosophie*, *3*(253), 397–440.

Engler, J. (1984). Therapeutic aims in psychotherapy and meditation: developmental stages in the representation of the self. *Journal of Transpersonal Psychology*, *16*(1), 25–61.

Epstein, M. (1995). *Thoughts without a thinker: psychotherapy from a Buddhist perspective*. New York: Basic Books.

Freud, S. (1959). On narcissism: an introduction. In J. Strachey (Ed. and Trans.), *The standard edition of the complete psychological works of Sigmund Freud* (vol. 14, pp. 73–102). London: Hogarth Press. Originally published 1914.

Fromm, E., Suzuki, D.T., & DeMartino, R. (1960). *Psychoanalysis and Zen Buddhism*. London: Ruskin House.

Grotstein, J. (2000). Bion's transformations in "O" and the concept of the transcendent position. In F. Borgogno, F. Merciai, & P. Bion Talamo (Eds.), *W. R. Bion between past and future* (pp. 121–145). London: Karnac.

Guenther, H. V. (1977). *Tibetan Buddhism in western perspective*. Emeryville: Dharma. Originally published 1956.

Hsuan T. (1973). *Cheng wei-shu lun: doctrine of mere consciousness* (Wei-tat, Trans.). Hong Kong: Cheng Wei-shih Lun. Original work c.660.

Jacobus, M. (2005). *Psychoanalysis in the wake of Klein*. Oxford: Oxford University Press.

Lacan, J. (1977). *Ecrits: a selection* (A. Sheridan, Trans.). New York: W. W. Norton.

Lacan, J. (1988). *The seminar of Jacques Lacan*. In J. A. Millier (Ed.) & S. Tomaselli (Trans.), *Book II: the ego in Freud's theory and in the technique of psychoanalysis (1954–1955)*. New York: W. W. Norton. Originally published 1978.

Langan, R. (2005). *Minding what matters*. Boston: Wisdom.

Molino, A., Carnevali, R., & Giannandrea, A. (Eds.). (2014). *Crossroads in psychoanalysis, Buddhism, and mindfulness: the Word and the breath*. Lanham: Jason Aronson.

Moncayo, R. (2012). *The signifier pointing at the moon: psychoanalysis and Zen Buddhism*. London: Karnac.

Namgyal, T. (1986). *Mahamudra: the quintessence of mind and meditation* (L. Lhalunpa, Trans.). Boston: Shambhala. Original work 16th century.

Nandala Translation Committee (Ed. & Trans.). (1975). *The heart sutra*. Boulder: Shambhala.

Pelled, E. (2008). Learning from experience in Bion's concept of reverie and Buddhist meditation: a comparative study. *International Journal of Psychoanalysis*, *88*(6), 1507–1526.

Rab-jam-pa, L., Dudjom, R., and Khyentse, R. (1978). *The four-themed precious garland: an introduction to Dzogchen* (A. Berzin, Ed.). Dharamsala: Library of Tibetan Works and Archives. Original work 14th century.

Rangjung, Y. (2019a). Ego-clinging. *Wikipedia*. Retrieved from https://en.wikipedia.org/w/index.php?title=Rangjung_Yeshe_Wiki&oldid=929324993

Rangjung, Y. (2019b). The dualistic fixation. *Wikipedia*. Retrieved from https://en.wikipedia.org/w/index.php?title=Rangjung_Yeshe_Wiki&oldid=929324993

Richardson, W. J. (1985). Lacanian theory. In A. Rothstein (Ed.), *Models of the mind: their relationships to clinical work* (pp. 101–111). New York: International Universities Press.

Safran, J. (2003). *Psychoanalysis and Buddhism: an unfolding dialogue*. Boston: Wisdom.

Stern, D. N. (2004). *The present moment in psychotherapy and everyday life*. New York: W. W. Norton.

Suzuki, S. (1970). *Zen mind, beginner's mind*. New York: Weatherhill.

Trungpa, C. (1999). *The rain of wisdom* (Nalanda Translation Committee, Trans.). Boulder: Shambhala.

Trungpa, C. (2018). Karma, compassion, and the dark age. In C. R. Gimian (Ed.), *The future is open: good Karma, bad Karma, and beyond Karma* (pp. 3–14). Boulder: Shambhala.

Webb, R., & Sells, M. (1995) Lacan and Bion: psychoanalysis and the mystical language of "unsaying". *Theory and Psychology*, *5*(2), 195–215.

Zhang, Y. (2019). Wilfred Bion's annotations in the way of Zen: an investigation into his practical encounters with Buddhist ideas. *Psychoanalysis and History*, *21*(3), 331–355.

14 On being and belonging

Sara L. Weber

At the moment of conception, cells separated from the great ocean of existence—manifested by our mothers and fathers—combine to create a new form. After myriad multiplications, these cells form discrete body parts and functions. Each of us is then born, a unique human being. Development continues. We grow up, learn to walk, talk, go to school; perhaps we marry, find a career, age gracefully or otherwise. Each phase seems to leave connections behind and create new ones. Always, belonging to couples, families, or groups re-establishes a vital sense of connection, sparing us from unbearable disconnection, sparing us from nothingness and the anxiety of constant change. Ultimately, we die and turn back into what? Earth, dust, nothing, or is it everything?

Myriad feelings and identifications mark oneself as belonging or not belonging. Any self-representation perpetuates the problem of self vs. other. This dualism captures individuals, groups, races, ideologies, and countries over and over again. We are doomed to be "in" or "out." Tinges of discomfort inevitably arise from these dilemmas of belonging. Being "in" too often means burying some part of oneself, some sense of authenticity. Self-representations often feel false or claustrophobic or too static. Who is that "self" represented in a curriculum vitae, or even in a short biography? Yet being "out" may be experienced as painful rejection. Inclusion and exclusion inevitably lead to protective measures that fuel endless cycles of micro- and macro-aggression. We reject parts of ourselves and overwork other parts. We create allies and enemies, people who are like us and people who aren't, people who believe the way we do and people who disagree. Defending boundaries between insiders and outsiders too often entails coldness, misunderstanding, hatefulness, and, at times, explosive violence. Our world today is in a particularly virulent phase of these dilemmas.

Can a person belong or not belong without the experience becoming toxic in little and big ways? What are we longing for? Might we *"be longing"* for reunion? What is the ultimate aim of the longing for reunion? Could it be a balance between the safety of union and the freedom of separateness?

When I was in elementary school—maybe in third or fourth grade—we learned to write our addresses. Mine began: Sara Lee Weber. "Sara Lee" was the English transliteration of my Hebrew name. I belonged to the Jewish people. In fact, my name is a combination of two of the matriarchs of the Jewish people—Sara and

Leah. I was also told the name meant "weeping princess." I felt imbued with the pride, burden, and embarrassment of these identifications. It really did feel like it was "me." But I was only ten years old at the time—already defined with minimal regard for my own experience. Even my tears were defined in a way that lost their connection to why I was crying at any given moment. Something wasn't quite right.

The next part of writing the address was my last name, Weber, which identified me as part of a lineage of weavers. My grandfather had given his trade rather than his last name when questioned at Ellis Island. So we lost our familial lineage but had a newfound connection to the labor movement. Years later, to my great dismay, my father disavowed the labor movement. Thus, disrespect entered the field of belonging.

And what happened to my mother's side of the family? They were a warm and lively, if neurotic, bunch. I felt much closer to them than to my father's side—yet they didn't even get a mention.

Below my name came my street address, 13-11 Morlot Avenue. On the line below came the town created by unimaginative real estate developers: Fair Lawn, New Jersey, a suburban neighborhood of discreet houses surrounded by lawns that functioned as "keep out" signs. Even then I found all of this alienating, diminishing, stifling, claustrophobic—deadening.

Somehow, my lively friends in our pod of desks decided not to stop there. We added USA, then North America, then Earth (where the borders of countries disappear), then Solar System, then Milky Way, then Space. With each expansive address I felt increasingly open and free. I was no longer the little embarrassed, ambivalent Jewish girl. My "self," my self-representations, and my "self-consciousness" were gone. My friends and I were giggling with delight. Breathing was easy, unconfined by subtle predefinitions. Somehow, I felt more accepting and accepted, not at all diminished, but part of something grand—belonging to nothing and everything, momentarily abiding in the wholesome interplay between the finite and the infinite (Kierkegaarde, 1980).

As kids we hit upon a profound truth: Releasing the tight hold of one's attachment to self-representations, the hold of what one belongs to and what belongs to one, feels more wholesome than clinging to one's self, one's possessions, and the groups one identifies with. Letting go of dualisms of any sort creates a deeper sense of belonging—of being part of everything. Undefined empty vast spaciousness is pregnant with the possibility to experience more fully being and belonging. This is the experience pointed to by the *Heart Sutra* (Soeng, 2010), which dissolves the dualism of Form and Emptiness. It says: "Form is emptiness, Emptiness is form."

Relevant here are Buddhism's insights on non-duality—in particular, the insubstantiality of self and the serenity of the vast spaciousness of awareness. Often called "no-self," it is akin to the experience of the psychoanalytic concept of "true-self." I offer these thoughts from my understanding and experience of Buddhism, limited though it surely is. Buddhism offers an expansive, compassionate open awareness from which to view all that arises in our hearts/minds and the hearts/minds of our patients, friends, and family members. It is not meant to diminish or replace any of the insights of psychoanalysis, but it holds them in spaciousness. If anything, it restates what we already know in a fresh way, supports and expands the horizons, perhaps even simplifies and clarifies what we can know of our confusion and suffering with equanimity.

The Buddhist term for the insight of non-duality and "no-self" is *shunyata*, which has been commonly, and somewhat confusingly, translated as "emptiness." The Buddhist scholar Mu Soeng (2010) tells us that the word *shunyata* is composed of *shunya*, which means "empty," and *ta*, which means "belonging to." Thus *shunyata* means "belonging to emptiness." What could that mean? The root of the word *shunya* also means "to swell up" and "an uninhabited place," something like a bubble. My "self" is one such bubble. Individuals, dyads, groups, even thoughts and feelings are all bubbles, fragile and unsubstantial. We love to make bubbles, but if you try to catch one, it pops.

Many years ago I was at Mind Life Conference XXII when Wolf Singer of the Max Planck Institute was talking with the Dalai Lama. He burst into tears as he described how he had spent his life looking for the building blocks of existence only to discover that each particle he discovered was empty—comprised of vibration and vast space. Here is how Soeng (2010) describes what the scientist sees when he looks through an electron microscope at the particles people are made of:

> The electron-scanning microscope, with the power to magnify several thousand times, takes us down into a realm that has the look of the sea about it. In the kingdom of the corpuscles, there is transfiguration and there is samsara, the endless round of birth and death. Every passing second, some 2½ million red cells are born: every second, the same number die. The typical cell lives about 110 days, then become tired and decrepit. There are no lingering deaths here, for when a cell loses its vital force, it somehow attracts the attention of macrophage.
>
> As the magnification increases, the flesh begins to dissolve. Muscle fiber now takes on a fully crystalline aspect. We can see that it is made of long, spiral molecules in orderly array. And all of these molecules are swaying like wheat in the wind, connected with one another and held in place by invisible waves that pulse many trillions of times a second.
>
> What are the molecules made of? As we move closer, we see atoms, the tiny shadowy balls dancing around their fixed position with their partners in perfect rhythms. And now we focus on one of the atoms, its interior is lightly veiled by a cloud of electrons. We come closer, increasing the magnification. The shell dissolves and we look on the inside to find … nothing.
>
> Somewhere within that emptiness, we know is a nucleus. We scan the space, and there it is, a tiny dot. At last, we have discovered something hard and solid, a reference point. But no! As we move closer to the nucleus, it too begins to dissolve. It too is nothing more than an oscillating field, waves of rhythm. Inside the nucleus are other organized fields: protons, neutron, even smaller "particles." Each of these, upon our approach, also dissolve into pure rhythm.
>
> (Soeng, 2010, pp. 37–39)

What is true of the cells of our bodies is also true of each of us: We are manifestations of life, yet unsubstantial. At the heart of everything—as T. S. Elliot (1941) commented—there is only the dance. There are no *substantial* objects, no *substantial* self or group of beings, but only processes. These processes are continuously arising into form and passing away according to the laws of cause and effect. Contemplation of "self" and of any object, word, entity, or experience reveals the impossibility for words and concepts adequately to describe even our mundane reality.

These insights can be gleaned from simply watching your own body/mind. In the practice of Insight Meditation (Vipassana or Mindfulness), one observes the arising and passing of all sensations, thoughts, feelings, perceptions, concepts, and experiences—everything that comes and goes in mind. One discovers that "I, me, and mine" have no permanent, solid, inherent, cohesive existence but are comprised of a constantly changing series of self-states that arise and pass away. The self-concept becomes elusive—made up of shifting fragments of experience selected from whatever happens to arise in our body-mind. If you watch the show without selecting, without judgment, without clinging to wants or pushing away aversions, what remains is constantly changing, unstable, and affected by things we think of as external to ourselves. Concrete appearances are merely customary and do not exist in the way we imagine. In the words of the Dalai Lama, the "seemingly solid, concrete, independent, self-instituting 'I' under its own power that appears does not actually exist at all" (Gyatso, 1984, p. 70). We begin to see that we are not what we observe, but essentially an observing function. Bare awareness grounds us and brings us into a lively connection to unfolding life.

In the enigmatic *Verses From the Center: A Buddhist View of the Sublime*, Batchelor (2000) attributes Nagarjuna, the second-century Buddhist monk and philosopher, as the original author of a series of verses, also attributed to Lao Tsu, that—like Zen Koans—forcibly challenge our entrenched ideas about ourselves and the world in order to provoke the experience of "the terrifying and fascinating emptiness that quivers beneath the threshold of common sense" (p. 3). Therein lies the sublime. For him, "emptiness" is the experience of letting go of fixed ideas and surrendering to the freedom of what is. It is:

> ... an empty vessel
> That may be drawn from
> Without ever needing to be filled.
> It is bottomless, the very progenitor of all things in the world.
>
> (Tsu, 1934)

"Recognizing mental and physical processes as 'empty' of self was, for the Buddha, the way to dispel the confusion that lies at the origin of anguish, for such confusion configures a sense of self as a fixed and opaque thing that feels disconnected from the dynamic, contingent and fluid processes of life" (p. 8).

As such, "Emptiness is a metaphor for authenticity" (p. 9). Authenticity is a way of living that avoids succumbing to any form of dualism, neither to nihilism nor eternalism, nor to the essentialism of permanent self vs. self just as illusion. Everything is, but cannot be pinned down.

David Hinton, a poet and translator, points out that the pictograms of ancient Chinese poetry do not indicate a point of view. There is no I, no me, no mine. "Classical Chinese leaves out subjects and most other grammatical material ... (The) absent subject resides in the empty space (between the pictograms)" (Hinton, 2016, p. 30). So one might interpret the subject to be I, or you, or he, or she, or we, or one. Each would create a different meaning and all are possible. The language is a series of images, "ideograms [having] maintained their nature as visual art where an imagined thing is experienced as both noun and verb simultaneously— as alive" (p. 31). Essentially, the ancient Chinese language allows holding one closer to the raw experience that arises from what he calls the "existence tissue," the web of existence. In fact, as we are simply another manifestation of existence, of life, our experiences are nothing other than "the existence-tissue experiencing itself" (p. 30). We belong to the life force.

How might we apply these Buddhist ideas clinically and personally?

The wisdom of *shunyata* warns us not to identify with passing feelings or attributions. Labels such as "narcissistic" or "abusive" or "sociopathic" or "co-dependent," or even "my pain" or "my illness," distance us from direct experience. Psychoanalysis takes a sophisticated look at the ways people distance themselves. Buddhism simplifies the list, noting that people simply try to avoid unpleasant experiences and cling to pleasant ones. Hurt, sadness, loneliness, or any sort of negative experience can be diverted into a theory or -ism. Clear and direct awareness arises from equanimity.

For example, a young man who has struggled with alcoholism and with difficult relationships characterized by convoluted communications finds it intolerable to feel anger towards, or any subjective disagreement with, his partner. Too ashamed, "bad" and so unentitled to be angry, he feels alone, precarious. His thinking becomes angrily disorganized. When this painful experience of separateness arises, he eventually begins to blame himself—it's all because he is an "alcoholic." For him, the label groups people who do an especially poor job of relating to others because they are "co-dependent" and manipulative. Together therapeutically, we work our way to identifying the initial distress in a non-judgmental way. We find a simple subjective experience, like sadness or fear or a need to be recognized or the pain of being misunderstood. Somehow through this process, he is not defined or identified by the feeling. He feels saner, calmer, and closer to his partner. He is momentarily aware that he can be angry and not act on it, that he can identify his unpleasant feeling and that both he and his loved one can have different subjective experiences without breaking their bond. He is no longer alone. Free of the stickiness of these feelings, he moves on and the distress lets go.

An experience I had illustrates the power of radically letting go of a fixed self: Years ago, a group of people threw me a party in appreciation for some work I had done. The party was lovely, but I did not feel appreciated. Disconcerted, I only felt depressed, cynical, angry, and ashamed. I mentioned this problem to Ajahn Sucitto, a beloved Buddhist teacher. He suggested I appreciate appreciation—let go of it having anything to do with me. Miraculously, appreciation arose. I found myself joyfully and playfully writing a sentence of what I appreciated about each of the people at the party. More typical psychoanalytic insights regarding my struggles to be appreciated also arose in a clear and unfettered way. Letting go of "ego" makes good states better and unpleasant, painful states less difficult.

How might these ideas apply to people who have been so deeply traumatized as to dissociate from the feelings and perhaps even the cognitive knowledge of these traumas, so leaving them feeling only partially alive, lonely, and broken? These patients present with damaged minds/hearts/bodies. Unbearable trauma creates a concrete wall that prevents free immersion in the ongoing nature of experience and more over connection to self and others.

Another clinical example:

As a teenager learning to drive, Joan was practicing driving with her mother when their car was hit by a drunk driver. Her mother died a few days later from her injuries. Joan pulled through after lying unconscious for several days. When she woke in the hospital, she called for her mommy and her father told her that Mommy had died. She became distraught—screaming "NO!" Her father, confused, worried, and unable to bear any more emotional pain himself, insisted she stop. She did so immediately—stopped in the midst of denial. Following the tragedy, her father became increasingly emotionally withdrawn. If her only remaining parent could not bear the loss, how could she? Joan became disconnected from her feelings and from her self—all alone in the world—no mother—no father. Anguish lay in wait at every turn.

Joan, now a grown woman—a lawyer for accident victims—tried many different therapists before arriving at my office. In the first meeting she related her story in a matter-of-fact way, with the complaint that she didn't feel fully alive, had been unable to concentrate, felt disconnected from others, and had been on antidepressants for many years. Following that session, she spent the next several years of therapy wordlessly crying. What was she crying about? I sat without knowing. She became angry if I asked any questions—feeling that I had broken her mind. She could not, in fact, remember what she had been thinking about before my "interruption." Painfully, she consistently interrupted herself—stopping herself from the experiences she could not bear. Our objective was to allow her mind and feelings to arise and be known without question. I had to provide a quiet, non-judgmental, non-reactive, non-intellectualized presence for Joan to find her own mind. I also had to fully understand how profound her hurt was and not react to her anger towards me or to her rejection of my mind. The concept of narcissism is of no use in such a state.

In spite of the gulf within her and between us, there were areas of emotional resonance that ran deep. As I sat quiet and uncertain, my eyes would tear up. Aware that I was "with" her, over time she spoke a bit more. The first thing I understood was that Joan was in mourning for her mind/self that had been damaged by the terrifying accident and the abrupt interruption of mourning. She was not yet mourning the loss of her mother or experiencing the trauma of the accident itself. Eventually we discovered that she often felt that her mother had not died, but had abandoned her because she had caused the accident. She was guilty and angry with herself, her mother and her father—bad, unlovable, profoundly alone, and sad. She had rejected the importance, value, and goodness of everyone, including herself. She had to be perfect: to manage everything for herself from a general state of detachment (Bromberg, 1998). All alone—no mother, no father, no therapist—she was holding onto a grandiose self-representation for dear life. She had rejected/ejected/detached from those to whom she had once felt connected.

Having found a way that allowed her traumatized mind to be known and the depth of her pain accepted, the pattern of her reactions to interruptions became slightly more fluid. She began to be able to re-find her thoughts when she was interrupted. As she did, I began to talk a bit more, suggesting ideas, such as compassionate ways of viewing herself and others. Slowly she began to take me in. She was surprised to find that my ideas—new ideas—were with her when she wasn't in session. Loving memories of her mother and father began to arise (although they continued to be mixed with angry ones, as her new states mixed with the old defensive ones). One day she woke in terror from a dream that touched upon the truth of her traumatic loss. Although the terror of the accident and loss was beginning to arise, there was still a sense of their being unbearable. When she began actually to mourn her mother, the tears flowed and flowed and I comforted her. Now she was less alone and somewhat more fluidly living.

Clearly with this kind of trauma, there is a slow careful road to travel before direct experience of the dissociated can be borne. But spaciousness, patience, compassion, equanimity, and a profound tolerance for uncertainty create the possibilities. Both psychoanalysis and Buddhism recommend that the therapist needs fully to accept the mind and feelings of the patient. This is the state of *shunyata*, or emptiness. If one is part of the vast ocean of life, all sorts of things, painful and otherwise, will pass through. Not taking these feelings too personally, yet knowing them fully and clearly, offers relief from angst.

Freud (1912/1958) advised patients and therapists to adopt evenly suspended attention, allowing one's mind to run free, unfettered, uncensored by expectation and presuppositions. He recommended the therapist pay "impartial attention to everything there is to observe" (pp. 111–112). Buddhism trains and practices this state of mind in which one is unfettered by rigid concepts and free of hope and fear. As with physicality, in quantum theory, mental content is also seen to be a fluctuating illusion, mediated more or less by our biased senses and individual or group identifications. The capacity for unformed awareness is the healing, if somewhat terrifying, gift.

When one discovers emptiness/spaciousness, one feels more light-hearted, flexible, and at ease. Think back to the little vignette about my address. Were one to look at oneself from "space" rather than from close up, there might be more tolerance for knowing the unpleasant. It is the space between self-states (Bromberg, 1998) and the spaciousness of the entirety of non-impinging, non-judgmental, non-reactive space.

Also relevant is our relationship to the "problem." Constant demands to prematurely repair oneself don't work for most forms of suffering because they embody rejection of the problem. Openness, curiosity, and tolerance for the suffering help to find a path through the suffering via the release of efforts at clinging and aversion. The process is one of looking deeply as opposed to looking for solutions.

Buddhism and the principle of emptiness do not result in a complete freedom from the events that cause suffering in life: sickness, loss, old age, death. Bhikkhu Nyanasobhano (2002, p. 45) says:

> Sages, too, endure the same mundane circumstances as we—they fall sick, suffer injuries, meet with unwelcome changes—but their wisdom sees past the incidental to the universal, to the certainty of change that is best coped with by equanimity. Wisdom does not alter the world; it lets the sage transcend the world. Anxious pain strikes only those who cannot understand the impermanence of all these desired and feared states, and who cannot extricate themselves from the profitless flux of desire and aversion.

Identifications and feelings, when held too tightly, lead to distancing oneself from authentic experience and a fully realized sense of belonging. "Indra's net" is a metaphor that opens understanding to how *shunyata* ("emptiness") offers us a radical sense of belonging. Rather than focusing on the vastness of space within and without, it directs us to another aspect of *shunyata*. That is: everything exists because everything else does. Everything exists and dies because of the cause and effect created by everything else. Everything is both cause and effect.

> Indra's net is a wonderful net which has been hung by some cunning artificer in such a manner that it stretches out infinitely in all directions. In accordance with the extravagant tastes of deities, the artificer has hung a single glittering jewel in each "eye" of the net, and since the net itself is infinite in dimension, the jewels are infinite in number. There hang the jewels, glittering "like" stars in the first magnitude, a wonderful sight to behold. If we now arbitrarily select one of these jewels for inspection and look closely at it, we will discover that in its polished surface there are reflected *all* the other jewels in the net, infinite in number. Not only that, but each of the jewels reflected in this one jewel is also reflecting all the other jewels, so that there is an infinite reflecting process occurring.
>
> (Cook, 1977, p. 2)

Like Indra's net, Thich Nhat Hanh (1988/2009) defines *shunyata* as "Interbeing." Everything is connected. Imagine each of us—each tree, each raccoon, each cockroach, each political party, Donald Trump, each molecule, atom, mountain, planet, you name it—is a miraculous form that reflects and is interwoven with all other forms that arise into and out of existence. For Thich Nhat Hanh, the responsibility inherent in this aspect of *shunyata* is a guiding principle. Everything you do matters. Getting angry or greedy, killing, treating others badly, all affect the existence tissue, now and in the future. He created the *Order of Interbeing* in the mid-1960s when the Vietnam War and its inherent hatred, violence, and divisiveness were escalating around him. He felt that it was crucial that each person do their part to live with compassion and equanimity so as not to feed the existence tissue with hate and violence of any sort.

David Hinton (2016), remember, calls it the "existence tissue." In fact, at the quantum level, particles are "entangled" with each other—even at great distances from one another. The metaphor and the science weave aspects of *shunyata* together: the fluidity of subjectivity, the vastness of space and time, and the delicate interconnection of all that arises in space/time. We are part of the existence tissue, vast and vital, buzzing with life, mystery, uncertainty, dangers, and possibility. Can we recognize ourselves as living jewels that arise from and pass back into the existence tissue of Indra's net? Jewels that appear and belong in the great web of existence? Can we recognize a belonging without blind loyalty to anything but awareness? And if we do, will we paradoxically feel whole and connected to ourselves and others?

Finally, here is a little Zen Koan-like practice from Alexandre Jollien (2018), a philosopher who suffers from a serious disability.

> "The Buddha is not the Buddha, that is why I call him the Buddha."
> "Disability is not disability, that is why I call it disability."
> We can put many different concepts into this pattern, such as:
> "Back pain is not back pain, that is why I call it back pain."
> "My partner is not my partner, that is why I call him my partner."
> "Sara is not Sara, that is why I call her Sara."
> Try this last one using your own name.
>
> (pp. 297–298)

Jollien explains: "What is powerful in this formula—what is magical in it—is that it never helps to dwell on our wounds but not to deny them either" (p. 298). It also helps one detach from egotistical and idealizing fixations—or from fixed ideas about oneself or anyone else. Words cannot trap the ineffable. Reality is more varied, dense, and fresh than our fixed ideas. Living with the uncertainty of flow embodies a sense of belonging enfolded by freedom.

References

Batchelor, S. (2000). *Verses from the center: a Buddhist vision of the sublime.* New York: Riverhead Books.

Bromberg, P. M. (1998). *Standing the spaces: essays on clinical process, trauma and dissociation.* Hillsdale: Analytic Press.

Cook, F. H. (1977). *Hua-Yen Buddhism: the jewel net of Indra.* University Park: Penn State University Press.

Eliot, T. S. (1941). *Burnt Norton.* London: Faber and Faber.

Freud, S. (1958). Recommendations to physicians practicing psycho-analysis. In J. Strachey, Ed. & Trans., *Standard edition of the complete psychological works of Sigmund Freud* (Vol. 12, pp. 97–108). London: Hogarth. Originally published 1912.

Gyatso, T. (1984). *Kindness, clarity, and insight.* Ithaca: Snow Lion.

Hanh, T. N. (2009). *The heart of understanding: commentaries on the Prajnaparamita Heart Sutra*. Berkeley: Parallax Press. Originally published 1988.

Hinton, D. (2016). *Existence*. Boulder: Shambhala.

Jollien, A. (2018). Our daily practice. In M. Ricard, C, André, & A. Jollien, *In search of wisdom: a monk, a philosopher and a psychiatrist on what matters most* (pp. 295–313). Boulder: Sounds True.

Kierkegaarde, S. (1980). The forms of this sickness (despair). In H. Hong & E. Hong (Eds. & Trans.), *The sickness unto death* (pp. 29–35). Princeton: Princeton University Press. Originally published 1849.

Nyanasobhano, B. (2002). *Longing for certainty: reflections on the Buddhist life*. Somerville: Wisdom.

Soeng, M. (2010). *The heart of the universe: exploring the Heart Sutra*. Somerville: Wisdom.

Tsu, L. (1934). The Tao te Ching (A. Wiley, Trans.) (Verse 4, n.p.). Originally published c.1417.Retrieved from www.Wengu/wg/wengu.php?1+Daodajing

Part 5

Belonging and self-organization

15 (Not) belonging in one's own skin

Stumbling into the space between obsessions

Mark B. Borg, Jr. and Daniel Berry

Homing in on collaboration

Over the course of some seven years, five psychoanalytical professionals serially collaborated in the development of a theory and a set of therapeutic practices with the goal of putting the theory into practical application by publishing a self-help book. "In life," writes the Boston Change Process Study Group (2019) on the subject of *engagement*, "there are special relationships with others that shape who we are and who we become" (p. 540). The following is an account of one such transformative engagement, examined as it developed in fits and starts in the course of collaborating and falling apart and, after a pause, is reconfigured successfully and analyzed as the means by which Owen, who originated the project, used it as a means of defending himself against belonging to, being cared for by, and owning his own project. Simultaneously we will see how Owen ironically used the collaboration for the opposite purpose: it became a means for him to caretake others by inviting them to contribute to the project and themselves to experience a sense of belonging. The unfolding of the story reveals how, with insight and persistence, Owen and his final collaborators were able to work through the conflicts that each brought into, and played out in, the project, as well as how Owen used his obsessive-compulsive engagement with the project and its other players to work through his own conflict about being center stage in his own life.

The threat of life as it is

Searles's (1979) sweeping assertion that humans are natural born therapists (or "caretakers") so captured Owen's imagination that he put together a manuscript for a self-help book for compulsive caregivers in a few months. However, emotional and interpersonal entanglements that he unwittingly created while refining the manuscript took years to unravel. Owen's own caretaking compulsion was largely responsible for the most complicated of these entanglements, acted out with a colleague whom he invited to collaborate on the book project. Ultimately, Owen was forced to hire a lawyer to protect his stake in the project when that colleague attempted a legal claim that she was more responsible for the manuscript's development than Owen was. Owen's susceptibility to such a claim was aggravated by his tendency to downplay his merit as a writer, and it was abetted by his ambivalence and even apprehension about what might happen if the book were successful. This ambivalence delayed his recognition of the urgent need to take legal action to protect himself from his colleague-become-adversary. Ironically, despite her attempt to railroad credit for the project away from Owen, her commitment to actually participating in it had long since dwindled and even appeared retrospectively to have been opportunistic and capricious all along.

Once the lawyers had resolved the legal issues, Owen signed with a highly regarded literary agent who referred him to a suitable editor and began looking for a publisher. Before many weeks had passed, the agent was all but assuring Owen that his manuscript was probably not going to collect dust on a shelf.

This turn of events gave Owen a brief moment of calm. For some four years, his hours between seeing patients had for the most part been absorbed by writing this book—and not only in front of his computer; he was almost constantly writing and rewriting on his mobile phone even while walking down the street. Now his busy-ness seemed about to pay off—and Owen nearly panicked: Without work on the book to occupy his attention, how was Owen going to cope with having so much time alone with Owen?

Well, the idea was intolerable, and Owen didn't tolerate it. He grabbed his Blackberry and frantically began sketching out ideas for a follow-up to the first book, while at the same time casting about in his mind for names of associates whom he might be able to involve in this new project. Driven though he was to write, Owen was even more driven to avoid being at the center of his own life and consciousness. The brief interval between working on the two books marked the beginning of Owen's confrontation with his inability to assent to living in a space *between* obsessions.

The obsessive-compulsive routine

Our obsessions with people, places, and things are often driven by anxiety related to a deep-seated fear that we're *not okay*. In response, we take up behaviors or projects to distract us from the unease we feel about simply being in our lives as they are. While those distractions deliver fleeting relief, they soon leave us faced once again with the reality that we are still who we were and where we were when we started our latest dash toward distraction. In other words, we remain face to face with our anxiety. But it's even worse than that: the repetition of the pattern produces diminishing returns, which increases both the anxiety and the speed at which we seek relief. Moreover, constantly repeating this cycle stands in the way of finding genuine solutions to whatever is disturbing us, making the space between obsessions all but impossible to find and even harder to accept as a place we might actually live life.

As might be expected of a solid transference enactment (Boston Change Process Study Group, 2013; Hirsch, 1998; Levenson, 1991; 2009), Owen's deciding to write a book about compulsive caretaking brought him face to face with that exact compulsion in himself.

Of course, the good news about such an enactment is also the bad news: it works. It *does* relieve our *awareness* of anxiety by dissociating from how scary it is to live in our own lives as they really are. But, stepping back for a moment, in Owen's case, what, exactly, was wrong with his life as it really was? Dozens of his articles have appeared in peer-reviewed journals, and he has presented at conferences all over the world. In addition, his reputation as a clinician matches his standing as an academic. So where's the "wrong" part?

The answer to this question shakes down into four parts:

1. Compulsive routines dissociate us not just from awareness of our anxiety but from virtually *any* genuine feeling and need.
2. Such dissociation blocks our ability to enter into any kind of genuine, reciprocal relationship.
3. Relationships that lack reciprocity create feelings of exploitation and resentment toward those around us because (we tell ourselves) we're doing all the "hard work" in our relationships.
4. Pushback against this routine brings on sudden feelings of anger and fear—sometimes even panic.

Bitten in the backside

Owen and Madeline worked at a community mental health center in New York City. Madeline was in her early fifties and was embarking on a second career as a psychotherapist after writing and producing theater in New York for over two decades. Owen had crashed and burned at the end of a drug-fueled attempt at punk-rock stardom on the West Coast in the 1980s. He turned his life around, largely through a twelve-step program, completed a PhD in clinical psychology, and relocated to New York to take a staff position at the clinic.

Madeline and Owen hit it off immediately. In addition to their clinical work, they shared an interest in writing: Owen's papers had already begun to be published in academic journals while he was still in training, while Madeline continued working in theater as a writing consultant. They shared coffee breaks as well as thoughts and feelings about pretty much anything else. In addition, both had histories of involvement with romantic partners who required exaggerated amounts of attention, which aligned well with the caretaking compulsions each tended to exercise on others who came into their orbits—romantically or otherwise.

As they grew closer, Owen began targeting Madeline with his caretaking compulsion because of her pattern of infatuation with men who invariably "needed her more than she needed them," as well as her wanting a shoulder to cry on at the end of her serial attempts at romance.

Madeline had become fairly well known in the theater scene after an Off-Off-Broadway production on which she had consulted became an international success. However, her reputation devolved into that of an opportunist and parasite when she demanded a contract granting her royalties from all future productions of the piece, even though she had worked as a consultant without contract and only on the play's maiden production. Despite her limited role in the production, she repeatedly took producers and other associates to court and repeatedly won.

In the course of their acquaintanceship, Madeline shared with Owen a not entirely candid account of these events. Then one day Madeline's then-current romantic interest, Stanley, announced that he was leaving Madeline for a younger woman. Stanley styled himself an expert in New Age spirituality, which fascinated Madeline—or, at any rate, she affected that it did. The fact that Stanley otherwise had little visible means of support didn't seem to inhibit her buying into the relationship: She willingly picked up the tab for expensive restaurants, pricey theater tickets, and vacations in Asia and South America. Then, when Stanley dumped her, Madeline angrily accused him of exploiting her and abusing their relationship and threatened to take him to court. They compromised by going to couples' therapy. That ended; however, to Madeline's demanding that Stanley pay her back for his share of their expensive lifestyle, Stanley's unfazed response was, "How you spent your money was always your decision."

Being in close proximity to someone going through a life crisis was all Owen needed for his caretaking compulsion to kick in. As Stanley had been Madeline's project, Owen made Madeline his project. Whenever Madeline signaled the need for it, Owen was there to listen, to be supportive, and even to act as Madeline's escort to performances, professional events, and gallery shows.

At first, this arrangement seemed to work: Owen liked feeling needed and helpful, and he continually assured Madeline that he genuinely enjoyed her company. And, to give her her due, Madeline wasn't shy about expressing her appreciation for Owen's "being there for me." Reflecting on this time period later, however, Owen said he never quite shook the feeling that their relationship wasn't truly reciprocal even before their feelings began to sour.

"Well, one day," Owen recalled:

> I found out that my misgivings weren't misplaced: Stanley called Madeline out of the blue, full of apologies for "how wrong he'd been." It came out that he'd been dumped by his young flame. Without missing a beat, Madeline took Stanley back, no questions asked. And also without missing a beat, she basically dropped our friendship.

As a result of Madeline's sudden flip, relations between her and Owen became awkward and cool for a period of weeks, although out of collegial necessity, they ultimately resumed a friendly working relationship. When they graduated from psychoanalytic training, Owen almost immediately needed to find professional office space because he was already establishing a strong professional reputation and a steady practice. Madeline also needed office space, but since she wasn't interested in working full time as a therapist, she suggested to Owen that she might "help him out" by sharing his office for a few hours a week. Caretaker that he was, Owen agreed to Madeline's suggestion, thus relieving her of the trouble and expense of establishing an office of her own.

After a few years, Stanley again left Madeline for a younger woman. Now closer to sixty than fifty, Madeline had a harder time coping than previously. Again, she turned to Owen, and again, Owen became her rescuer. This time, however, Owen had a plan for preventing her from dumping him again quite so easily: he asked Madeline to join him in developing a writing project that (he hoped) would engage her enough to cement her commitment to their relationship. Madeline jumped at the idea. "I know!" she said. "Let's write a self-help book!"

"Great idea!" Owen exclaimed. "I've been working on an idea for a self-help book for years, and you're the perfect person to help me make something out of it!"

They began meeting weekly, sketching out a book that they fantasized would become "the next big thing" in self-help. However, after a few months, Madeline began to complain that the project demanded more time than she was able to commit, and also to protest that she wasn't really academically oriented anyway. As time passed, her misgivings grew and she started showing up late for their meetings or cancelling at the last minute. Unspoken resentments piled up on both sides and the project came to a standstill. Though he didn't admit it to himself, Owen felt that Madeline was dumping him and the writing project in much the same way she had dumped him when Stanley reappeared in her life. For her part, Madeline had begun to voice suspicion that Owen had involved her in the project only to trade on her reputation as a writer as well as suggesting that his personal interest in her was not altogether sincere. Both felt misused and angry.

In order to save the project without actually analyzing their feelings, Owen suggested bringing in a third collaborator to get the work back on track. Madeline initially liked the idea, although she required a lot of reassurance that Owen's motives were honorable and professional. Ultimately she agreed to Owen's inviting Leonard, a former colleague, to join the project.

For a time, the work seemed to progress, but after a couple of months, Madeline started criticizing the book's thesis while again accusing Owen of using her reputation to bolster the prestige of his own ideas. She was also put off by Leonard, whom she called "a pretentious blowhard," arguing that "his silly diagrams don't really add anything" to the book. Weekly meetings increasingly degenerated into arguments so heated that the project once again hit a wall.

Still unwilling to throw in the towel, Owen hired a consultant to help sort things out. The consultant suggested that, for the group to trust one another, they had to be able to validate each partner's contribution. However, Madeline's deteriorating commitment had already taken her to the point of no return: She announced that she was leaving the project, but she demanded rights to 20 percent of proceeds from the book, plus 10 percent of any derivative work.

"For what, Madeline?" Owen exclaimed. "For weeks you've argued with almost everything about the book while still claiming it wasn't really your thing, and now—this?"

"Ah, come on, Owen," she retorted. "Writing a self-help book was my idea! What would have come of it if you hadn't pulled me in? I know you think you were 'helping me' after Stanley left, but you actually *owe* me! You're lucky I'm not demanding a third!"

Years of legal wrangling ensued without either Owen or Madeline realizing that by acting as Madeline's caretaker, Owen had not only made himself scapegoat for Stanley's betrayal but also created an interpersonal situation that doomed their working relationship. In the end, Owen's giving Madeline co-authorship also gave her a leg to stand on when she made her legal claim against him, even though she was no longer interested in the book.

"How could I not have seen this coming?" Owen later asked a colleague. "This is exactly what she did with that theater production: She made herself rich off somebody else's work! I even got the payback for the way Stanley played her!"

Avoiding center stage

Not being center stage is an entré into a dynamic founded upon *Not-Me* experience (Sullivan, 1953)—a treacherous inner landscape in which, by intensely dissociated design (Bromberg, 1998; 2013), Owen continued the traumatizing weight and intensity of a role he learned as a small child and brought into adulthood: Contorting himself and his desires in order to help others "get well" and using that caretaking role as a place to hide from his own anxiety around being "seen" in his own life. Though Owen was experienced as an academic writer, that portfolio wasn't particularly useful for producing a book written in a "popular" style—or, at least, it wasn't a good medium for subduing his caretaking compulsion whose purpose was to deflect the spotlight from himself and onto his colleagues. This was part of the incentive for inviting Madeline's participation. But he also took the disastrous step of inviting her into co-authorship as well.

As the volatility of the situation increased, Leonard, already wise to Madeline's personal and professional history, shrewdly exited the project, pleading that he had no stomach for legal entanglements with Madeline.

Once the smoke from the legal battles cleared, Owen, still believing in the project, revised his thesis and invited two different colleagues, Martin and Philip, to join as collaborators. This, however, came after he had spent some months with his own analyst working through his obsessive-compulsive caretaking routine (Borg, Brenner, & Berry, 2015; 2018). This cleared the way for a genuine partnership with his new colleagues—an actual *engagement* (Boston Change Process Study Group, 2019). But that didn't just happen magically: In psychoanalysis, Owen had come to see that if working with his new collaborators was to be successful, he was going to have to at least try to defuse his caretaking compulsion by being honest with Martin and Philip about what had gone wrong with Madeline and about his tendency to downplay the value of his own work.

Owen initiated this disclosure by telling Martin and Philip about his acting out—and enacted—behavior. He shared how his mother and father, barely twenty years old when he was born, were driven by their anxiety to look to Owen for validation of their parenting while blaming each other for being caught in a situation for which they were woefully unprepared. Before long, they'd come to hate each other. Also before long, Owen figured out that something was badly wrong between his mother and father and began to look for ways to distract them from their anger and himself from his own unease.

> I could see they were unhappy, and it was scary for me. So I spent a lot of time and energy looking for ways to make them feel better. And, well, as an adult, I've done a lot of the same thing: I've kept my mind off my own fears by acting as if others' messed up ways of thinking and acting were perfectly okay, perfectly normal.

Owen went on to describe how this played out with Madeline and Leonard in earlier phases of the book project, comparing it to the experience of "alcoholics who get sober feeling grateful they'd gotten so badly beat up that they knew they had to quit drinking or die. I was forced to see how destructive my 'helping' was! But the bonus was realizing how liberating it can be to get beaten up so badly!"

Telling Martin and Philip this story opened the door to a type of collaborative engagement that was totally new to Owen. And, as it turned out, both Martin and Philip had their own histories of compulsive caretaking to share with Owen.

The ugly breakup of Martin's parents' marriage left his mother with seething anger, severe depression, and a well-developed conception of herself as victim. For Martin, this added up to a childhood in which he felt compelled to try to meet his mother's emotional needs while ignoring his own.

Philip's mother and father were so self-absorbed that they were essentially oblivious to their children's needs. Their neglect left Philip vulnerable to years of "Lord of the Flies"–style abuse at the hands of his four older siblings. At the same time, their mother and father demanded that their children repress any indication that their own needs were not being met.

The act of revealing their respective histories unexpectedly created a shared sense of belonging, intimacy, and engagement among Owen, Martin, and Philip that illustrates Benjamin's (2017) insight into the necessity of "encounter(ing) in the other some specific version of (the) desire for self-affirmation through knowing and being known. Mutuality is necessary insofar as the self needs to give as much as it needs to receive" (p. 12). Allowing mutual reliance on others is the epitome of belonging that, at the same time, risks triggering anxiety and dissociative defenses (Bromberg, 2009; Mitchell, 2002; Sullivan, 1953). Borg, Brenner, and Berry (2018) refer to this balance of giving and receiving as necessary for what they describe as "relationship sanity."

Owen's experience with Madeline forced him to confront his practice of involving co-authors to divert attention from himself. Fortunately, Martin and Philip were not only excited about the book but were also equipped by their own experiences to support Owen's thesis. Together, they were challenged to engage in a process in which each's subjectivity would be linked in a dynamic system that included chaotic and untidy aspects likely to generate unexpected shifts in the system's organization (Aron, 1996). This challenged Owen's habit of propping up others to avoid engagement and to avoid or manage group chaos. However, this also limited the transformational potential of such situations, hence the repetitive obsessive-compulsive dynamic of his professional collaborations before Martin and Philip came into the picture.

Occasionally, Owen's unease would prompt him to return to his accustomed practice of referring to himself and his collaborators as "only props" in a bid to distance himself from his bouts of anxiety about the work. But the cat was out of the bag: Martin and Philip, already wise to this tendency in Owen, didn't hesitate to call him on it, interrupt their work, and practice accountability in real time by sharing self-disclosure of feelings of anxiety, vulnerability, or anything else disturbing their process. Predictably, this generated discomfort early in their relationship, but it ultimately created a space in which each felt gratified by their shared ownership of the work as well as by their having nurtured a space of mutual creative interdependence.

"Sometimes I felt so uneasy that I couldn't resist downplaying my actual importance to the project," Owen admitted. "Revealing to another person that I felt so vulnerable was one of the hardest things I've ever done. But saying it out loud to the two guys I was working with was a total game-changer."

Owen's writing and caretaking compulsions had taken another even more costly toll on his life: it curtailed his availability for his wife and children and for his friends, and it even brought to the fore his unresolved caretaking issues that had distanced him from his mother and father. Coming to terms with how his feelings of vulnerability drove his caretaking freed him actually to deliberately step away from his compulsion. This made living *in* the space between obsessions and *with* his loved ones exciting in ways he'd never known were possible.

Between obsessions

Throughout his years of writing, both commercially and academically, Owen's obsession operated as a defense against authentic engagement with his environment (i.e., other people), but it also filled a void and give him a sense of purpose. Born in reaction to his parents' ineffective care when he was a small child, Owen's obsessive routines defended him against being overwhelmed by the anxiety of feeling isolated and having to fend for himself. It also defended him, inadvertently, against feeling, taking in, and making use of what others in his life—including his family—had to give. Because of this, and with only a hint of conscious awareness when he began the project, the book and the project gave Owen a sense of belonging that was missing in his life. Ironically, he exposed his dysfunctional ambivalence through his writing projects by:

- Inviting others to participate while questioning the value of their contributions.
- Camouflaging his role as primary author while overplaying the roles played by others.
- Advocating for a collaborative process while limiting the participation of others in creative aspects of their work.

By the final iteration of the project, enough pain and disappointment had infiltrated his defenses that Owen began to "see pretty clearly what I've been up to" and to have it verified by feedback from Martin and Philip. This acted as a chink in his armor that allowed Owen to work through his anxiety and defenses and the enactments expressing them, thereby enabling him to claim his own place as primary author while gratefully accepting others' contributions. Bringing this out in the open promoted growth for all three authors individually and as a team.

Change for Owen and his team was created through a process akin to what Levenson (1972) describes as *working through*: "the ability to be trapped, immersed, and participating in the system and then work (their) way out" (p. 174). This is how Owen and his colleagues used enactment as an ongoing source of growth. Becoming embedded in, and gradually emerging from, their enactment allowed all three to articulate the nature and depth of longstanding areas of conflict. Working through these enactments increased their ability to address and remedy conflict and crisis as they were occurring. Thus enactment improved their awareness of patterns of unattended or dissociated thinking, feeling, relating, and behaving.

Is writing books an obsession? In Owen's case, it may look like it in some ways, but his desire to do so collaboratively is also a marker of the need to engage with others, to be acknowledged, and to be creative as much as it may indicate ambition. Put another way, Owen's process was not only a defense against connection but was also a call for help that was met by others similarly conflicted who were willing to work through issues related to belonging. Motivating elements for the team, then, included creativity, feeling part of a group, and a shared need to persist and to share dreams. Even the unflattering profile of Madeline's involvement perhaps suggests an incipient desire on her part to be useful to someone other than exploitative men.

Of course, each player in the project brought a personal set of conflicts and desires, some of which proved useful to the project in the longer term while others were not. Whatever the case, engagement was a challenge each faced as individuals in interaction with each other, with the group, and with the larger project, supporting the notion that "in the absence of engagement, more flexible, complex and integrated forms of relatedness may fail to emerge" (Boston Change Process Study Group, 2019, p. 546).

The challenge faced by the three collaborators who completed the project was to balance anxieties enacted in obsessive and compulsive work dynamics with an increasing ability to accept and use those anxieties and conflicts productively as part of their work process. They accomplished this by consciously constructing a *space between obsessions* in which anxieties, obsessions, and older dissociated conflicts were consciously experienced and used by the group as a means of valuing of one another and the project. Stern (2010) observed that:

> There must be a way that behavior of the other has more value because of who they are to us, in reality or imagination. We must love, hate, respect,

fear, admire, be attached to, or be dependent on (i.e., be in important relationship with them). Their presence, then, has special value (conscious or unconscious).

(p. 143)

Despite the special value that each gave to the other and to the project, conflict naturally continued. However, ongoing engagement changed the project from a system in which each member resolved his conflicts individually as best he might into a place where conflict was entertained and contained in a way that gave each participant a sense of belonging and ownership as both individuals and collaborators.

References

Aron, L. (1996). *A meeting of minds*. New York: Routledge.

Benjamin, J. (2017). *Beyond doer and done to: recognition theory, intersubjectivity and the third*. London: Routledge.

Borg, Jr., M. B., Brenner, G. H., & Berry, J. D. (2015). *Irrelationship: how we use dysfunctional relationships to hide from intimacy*. Las Vegas: Central Recovery Press.

Borg, Jr., M. B., Brenner, G. H., & Berry, J. D. (2018). *Relationship sanity: the art of creating and maintaining healthy relationships*. Las Vegas: Central Recovery Press.

Boston Change Process Study Group. (2013). Enactment and the emergence of new relational organization. *Journal of the American Psychoanalytic Association, 61*, 727–749.

Boston Change Process Study Group. (2019). Engagement and the emergence of a charged other. *Contemporary Psychoanalysis, 54*, 540–559.

Bromberg, P. M. (1998). *Standing in the spaces: essays on clinical process, trauma, and dissociation*. Hillsdale: Analytic Press.

Bromberg, P. M. (2009). Multiple self-states, the relational mind, and dissociation: a psychoanalytic perspective. In P. F. Dell & J. A. O'Neil (Eds.), *Dissociation and the dissociative disorders: DSM-V and beyond* (pp. 637–652). New York: Routledge/Taylor & Francis.

Bromberg, P. M. (2013). Hidden in plain sight: thoughts on imagination and the lived unconscious. *Psychoanalytic Dialogues, 23*, 1–14.

Hirsch, I. (1998). The concept of enactment and theoretical convergence. *Psychoanalytic Quarterly, 67*, 78–101.

Levenson, E. (1972). *The fallacy of understanding*. New York: Basic Books.

Levenson, E. (1991). *The purloined self*. New York: Contemporary Psychoanalysis Books.

Levenson, E. (2009). The enigma of the transference. *Contemporary Psychoanalysis, 45*, 163–178.

Mitchell, S. (2002). *Can love last? The fate of romance over time*. New York: Norton.

Searles, H. (1979). *Countertransference and related subjects*. New York: International Universities Press.

Stern, D. N. (2010). *Forms of vitality*. New York: Oxford University Press.

Sullivan, H. S. (1953). *The interpersonal theory of psychiatry*. New York: Norton.

16 Confusion of belongings

Ms. F in search of true belonging

Laura C. Young

What does it feel like to truly belong in a relationship? You feel accepted as you really are. There are healthy conditions: you are responsible for your impact on others and vice versa (Benjamin, 2004). There can be negotiation between different perspectives, mutually recognized as valid (Benjamin, 1990). Ruptures can be survived and repaired (Kohut, 1971; 1977; Kohut, Goldberg, & Stepansky, 1984; Winnicott, 1969). Belonging feels false if you receive care only by developing a false self (Winnicott, 1960), censoring parts of yourself, and meeting unfair or impossible conditions. False belonging can sometimes be difficult to recognize, as it can appear good and real (Shengold, 2002) or perhaps seem like the only belonging that can be expected. True belonging can seem like an impossible, foolish fantasy.

What happens when true and false belonging get mixed up? Ms. F, a long-time analytic patient, consciously felt intense anxiety and confusion (Bion, 1959) about feeling awful when she believed that everything in her life was good (Slavin & Kriegman, 1998). Unconsciously, she knew that things felt bad and could not go on. For the confusion to dissipate and her anxiety to decrease, we had to become able to think (Bion, 1962). We had to engage in the painful process of recognizing the unfair and impossible conditions of false belonging and her false self (Winnicott, 1960). Only then might hope for the possibility of true belonging begin to grow.

I began to see Ms. F in therapy when she was an adolescent. It often felt impossible to think. My mind felt cloudy, and alpha function (i.e., the mental process in which raw sensory or emotional data is converted into meaningful, conscious thoughts; Bion, 1962) abandoned me. I felt like I wanted to shake my head to help me think more clearly. I mentioned wanting to shake the confusion away to Ms. F, who laughed and told me she felt that way a lot. Ms. F's anxieties seemed incomprehensible. She was afraid of fainting and vomiting. Mostly she was afraid that she would get anxious somewhere and need to leave but not be able to leave. She was afraid she could not continue to bear her anxiety. Her fears restricted her life, and she suffered terribly. She felt safe only at home. We could not find any meaning in her fears. It simply seemed to Ms. F that she could handle these situations just fine, if only she didn't have her anxiety.

I now believe that the confusion and difficulty thinking that Ms. F and I experienced throughout her analysis were connected to the pain of recognition that what had felt like true belonging with friends and family may have been harmful or false. Symptoms such as Ms. F's intense anxiety persist when this kind of realization is too painful to know consciously (Shengold, 2002). The following memory of Ms. F's regarding her "very good childhood" seems to illustrate the pain and impossibility of knowing. She recalls going to the Goodwill store, a second-hand store selling donated items, with her mother and feeling excited and delighted at being allowed to choose two toys. She is now aware that the toys were used and cost only fifty cents, but when she recalls this memory, she observes that she "didn't know that at the time." I believe this memory captures the difficulty of knowing due to the sadness of losing the illusion of goodness or perfection.

Ms. F's anxiety abruptly intensified just before her seventeenth birthday, and the suddenness of its onset added to the confusion between good and bad. It felt like everything was good and she truly belonged with her family and friends, and then anxiety appeared, stopping her from doing everything and interrupting her relationships. However, thinking of her anxiety instead as a signal that belonging based on a false self was no longer sustainable (Winnicott, 1960), then anxiety's interruption of Ms. F's life can be seen as providing her with time and space to identify and dismantle the conditions of false self-belonging and to explore the hope for belonging based on her true self. Ms. F has now been in therapy with me for over seven years, and much is different in her life and in our ability to think together. We are more aware of how, in Ms. F's family, she experienced love and acceptance while also absorbing her family's fears that the outside world is dangerous and people are harsh (Ignatieff, 1993; Klein, 1946). We recognize the high price Ms. F paid in terms of self-censorship to experience belonging with friends. I see Ms. F trying to see if she can truly belong in therapy: sharing vulnerable emotions and trusting me to take them seriously and risking telling me when I have upset her to see whether I can take responsibility for my actions (Winnicott, 1969).

Belonging in family

Ms. F grew up feeling a strong sense of belonging in her family. She felt that her mother loved her as she was, treated her feelings as valid, and did not force her to do anything she did not want to do. She believed that her mother did not receive this kind of acceptance in her own family of origin and tried her best to be a different kind of parent to Ms. F. This unconditional love and acceptance sounded wonderful. However, I puzzled over how it did not translate into the expectation that anyone outside of Ms. F's family would be understanding and take her feelings seriously.

Ms. F and I have begun to see that belonging in her family is complicated. For understandable reasons based on her own painful upbringing, Ms. F's mother has difficulty believing in a world where people can be accepting and treat one's emotions with respect, despite her wish to provide this safety to Ms. F in their rela-tionship. Ms. F has begun to notice how her mother expects people outside of the family to be judgmental. Slights are assumed to have malicious intent (Benjamin,

2004). People can be written off easily as all bad (Klein, 1946). There is little expectation that relationship ruptures could be followed by acknowledgment and repair (Kohut, 1971; 1977; Kohut, Goldberg, & Stepansky, 1984). I believe that some of Ms. F's confusing anxiety stems from this paradox. Consciously, Ms. F believes that people can be accepting and that she is a worthwhile person, and this is how she feels in her relationship with her mother. Unconsciously, she fears that the opposite is true—that people are harsh and that she will be found inferior, as her mother expects for herself.

Two experiences of Ms. F's illustrate this paradox. Recently, Ms. F's mother told her that when Ms. F was a child, she was allowed to walk the short distance to school with an older sibling. However, unbeknownst to Ms. F, her mother followed them, far enough behind not to be spotted but close enough to be vigilant for dangerous others who might harm her children (Klein, 1946). "But I didn't know that at the time!" Ms. F exclaimed (Shengold, 2002); however, I wonder what she felt and how this feeling impacted her sense of safety and belonging in the world outside her family.

Ms. F was mystified regarding why, while she feels free to show her emotions with her mother, who always conveyed that "it's ok to cry," it feels impossible to do so with other people. Gradually, she has become more able to experience painful feelings and cry with me, but it remains difficult. Years into her therapy, she recalled an incident that provided some understanding. As a young child, she had been out in public with her mother and started to cry. Her mother said, with agitation, "People are looking," trying to hush Ms. F. I think her mother's fears of others' judgments regarding expressing vulnerable emotions took over (Klein, 1946). Ms. F consciously felt that her emotions could be accepted in her relationship with her mother, but unconsciously, her sense that how she felt would be unacceptable to others grew.

In Ms. F's family, I wonder whether her false self developed early and in a tragic manner. Ms. F's mother desperately wanted and tried to provide Ms. F with the love and care that she felt she did not receive as a child from her own parents. Ms. F's mother's intentions were kind and loving, but I wonder if in trying to give Ms. F what she herself missed as a child, she was unable to attend to Ms. F's spontaneous gestures indicating what Ms. F actually needed and wanted (Winnicott, 1960), which seems to have been different at times from what she believes her mother wished for and needed as a child. In addition, it seems that her mother was not able to believe in what she was attempting to give Ms. F, which may have added to the feeling of falseness. This false self of Ms. F's feels old and ego-syntonic, and I think her developing intense anxiety was a signal that something felt wrong to her without her realizing it consciously.

Because Ms. F grew up feeling safe, loved, and accepted in her family, she is confused regarding why she experiences such severe anxiety (Slavin & Kriegman, 1998). It is difficult for her to feel entitled to her suffering and not to blame herself for it. It feels strange to her when I describe her as someone who has suffered. She views her anxiety as evidence of her personal failings, badness, or wrongness, leading to shame and self-criticism. It has helped us to think together about her symptoms as stemming not from discrete trauma, such as physical violence or sexual abuse, but from subtle, repeated, unconscious family relationship patterns resulting from intergenerational transmission of trauma.

Slavin and Kriegman (1998) describe the phenomenon in which a patient feels very bad but believes that "nothing bad" happened as arising out of what they call a "confusion of interests." This confusion of interests occurs when parents have good intentions to provide a child with what they think the child needs, but instead they attempt to provide what they would have wanted or needed as children. As the parent's intention is caring, the action and its impact seem good, and it is difficult to recognize the misattunement to the child's actual needs that has occurred. Therefore, belonging and connection can feel false, because the care received may be misaligned with the child's needs.

In therapy, I have attempted to attend to and reflect Ms F's unique experience, emotions, and needs (Kohut, 1971; 1977). However, it has also been important that I acknowledge my own at times conflicting needs and my sense of entitlement to take care of them (Slavin, 2013). Rather than deny my own needs and how they at times can harm Ms. F, I have tried to acknowledge my impact and to make repairs when possible. Perhaps this process leads to a form of belonging in which there is less pressure to be perfect—one that allows for a real, reciprocal connection in which it is possible to acknowledge the limits of caring.

At the beginning of therapy, Ms. F experienced her sense of belonging in her family as wonderfully unconditional. Over time, she has become troubled both by the seemingly unfair or impossible conditions of belonging in her family, and also by what appears to be insufficient conditionality. Two particular conditions have begun to feel untenable to Ms. F. First, family members are expected to sacrifice their own needs to take care of others without being asked. Second, family members are expected not to set boundaries by asking for something or expressing feeling bothered until they are extremely physically or emotionally impacted. Only when Ms. F started to experience severe anxiety did she become more able to tell her family directly what she needed from them. For other family members, setting boundaries becomes possible only when they are experiencing intense physical pain, exhaustion, or explosive anger. It is highly stressful to belong under these conditions.

Ms. F has also begun to question the acceptance and belonging she experiences in her family. She had shown some family members a YouTube video that she found touching and thought they might enjoy. They criticized the protagonist and mocked the vulnerable feelings he expressed. I understood this to be pre-emptive criticism, judging others as you anticipate being judged. Seeing how judgmental they could be toward a person outside of the family, especially a person expressing vulnerable emotions, Ms. F wondered how her family members might criticize her and her feelings if she were not part of the family.

Michael Ignatieff (1993) writes about the negative effects of a very strong sense of belonging in the context of violence arising out of increasing nationalism. However, Ignatieff's ideas seem relevant to "blood and belonging" in Ms. F's family as well. The family expectation that outsiders will be harsh, judgmental, and critical leads to fear as well as to pre-emptive attacks (Klein, 1946). The fear of attack from outside can also lead to tolerance of unsatisfying or harmful treatment from family, because family members are considered to be the only safe people, and outsiders are expected to be worse. A very high cost of belonging is accepted, which has begun to seem unacceptable to Ms. F over time.

I believe that the following anecdote illustrates how the fear of attack from the outside world present in Ms. F's family entered into her analysis with me. When Ms. F moved to three sessions a week several years ago, we discussed whether she would lie on the couch. This idea was terrifying. If she was lying down and could not see me, I could attack her, although she partly knew I would not. I think if she could not keep an eye on me, she would fear my harsh judgments about her. She needed to see me to ensure that she was accepted.

An unsettling absence of conditions placed on love and belonging in Ms. F's family has also troubled her and is illustrated in the following interaction. Ms. F has a keen interest in serial killers, and she was discussing a case with her mother in which the parent of the killer had turned him in to the authorities. "I could never do that," exclaimed her mother. "I'd help you bury the body!" This disturbed Ms. F, who told her mother that in the unlikely event that Ms. F committed murder, she should hold Ms. F accountable by having her face the legal consequences of her actions. Ms. F finds the logical conclusion of this lack of conditions in relationships highly problematic: If two people belong together, particularly in a romantic or family relationship, they should accept any kind of treatment from each other. She has observed her family members' relationships and found that some members tolerate treatment that they find dissatisfying or even emotionally abusive or neglectful. She is beginning to want a different kind of belonging and relationship for herself.

Belonging in friendships

As in family relationships, belonging in friendships has been complicated for Ms. F. In middle school, she made a new best friend who was popular and mean. This friend needed Ms. F terribly, as she feared being alone. She always wanted to be with Ms. F, to the point of being intrusive and dismissing Ms. F's requests for space. I think this felt like true belonging, as this friend's intrusiveness and need seemed like love. Her friend mocked Ms. F's vulnerabilities, trying to get others to join in. She compared Ms. F to herself, always unfavorably. Ms. F started hiding aspects of herself, especially insecurities. She did not mention crushes, as her friend would either try to date the person or shame Ms. F for her choice of romantic interest. She lied to get out of plans or to leave her friend to go home to avoid being coerced into doing things she did not want to do. She avoided conflict by not sharing her true feelings. She apologized after arguments, even when she felt she had done nothing wrong.

In this friendship, Ms. F developed a mostly conscious false self-presentation (Winnicott, 1960), hiding her vulnerability in order to avoid judgment or mocking. As a result, her friendships did not feel genuine or satisfying. She felt a sense of belonging based on a false self rather than feeling accepted for who she truly was. This false belonging also allowed Ms. F's belief that her true self would be rejected to remain unmodified. A condition of this false belonging was that Ms. F had to tolerate her friend treating her disrespectfully and was not entitled to hold her friend accountable for her behavior if Ms. F could understand its origins in the friend's own issues. In Ms. F's peer group, to show hurt feelings was considered a sign of weakness to be preyed upon. Hence, if she expressed being hurt, she opened herself up to retaliation (Winnicott, 1969) through mocking and dismissal of her emotions. This false belonging required suppressing her understandable responses to her friend's hurtful actions for fear of being blamed as if her painful feelings were the problem, not her friend's behavior.

Ms. F's fears and hopelessness about being accepted also prevented her from pursuing relationships where more genuine belonging based on her true self might have been possible. In high school, she got to know two seemingly thoughtful people with whom she got along well. Though they appeared to enjoy her company, they were not effusively affectionate to the point of intrusiveness like her best friend. It felt too scary for Ms. F to initiate plans or express her interest in deepening the friendships, perhaps because she could not be certain of being needed unconditionally as she was with her best friend. As an adolescent, Ms. F began a romantic relationship with a good friend of many years. When the relationship grew closer, she ended it, using a recent argument as an excuse. She may have become too afraid to continue the relationship given what she expected the conditions of belonging to be: that she would have to sacrifice her own needs for those of the other person. In these past relationships, there might have been potential for real belonging to grow, but Ms. F's fears that her true self (Winnicott, 1960) would not be accepted and that her needs would have to be submitted to those of the other felt too great, and it was impossible for her to pursue belonging further.

Belonging in therapy

Over the course of her analysis, I have observed shifts in Ms. F and in our relationship that seem to suggest greater hope for finding true belonging outside of her family. After Ms. F's anxiety intensified, she was frequently too anxious to leave her house, so I offered that she could have phone sessions if needed. I worried I was treating her like I did not believe her to be capable of surviving difficult emotions; however, it seemed better to have the sessions than not. In some phone sessions, she told me she might not be able to speak the whole time due to feeling anxious or sick. I said, "Okay, let's just begin; we'll see how you feel, and if you have to end the session early, that's what we'll do." She never needed to take me up on this; it seemed enough to offer. While I was simply trying to allow us to continue her therapy, I think I was also communicating something about safety and belonging. By saying that she could end the session if she needed to, I was expressing that I viewed her feelings and needs as valid and deserving of care (Kohut, 1971; 1977). Ms. F feared the dangers and harsh others of the outside world (Klein, 1946), so phone sessions may have allowed Ms. F to feel the security and belonging of home while reaching out into the world over the telephone to see if it was safe.

Gradually, Ms. F's need for phone sessions decreased, perhaps as she felt safer with me and in the outside world. In my office, she was at times afraid she would faint or vomit, or get anxious and need to leave, and that I would prevent this, even though she in part knew I would not. We made plans for what I would do if she vomited, felt faint, or actually fainted, though none of these outcomes ever happened. I think my office became a safer place where Ms. F trusted that her emotions and needs would be treated as valid (Kohut, 1971; 1977) and where she could feel that her true self was accepted and belonged (Winnicott, 1960).

In order for Ms. F to feel a sense of belonging in our relationship, my attempting to meet her needs for twinship, mirroring, and healthy idealization (Kohut, 1971; 1977; Kohut, Goldberg, & Stepansky, 1984) has been important. Ms. F has needed to feel that we were similar in order to feel safe, and over time she has also begun to see that we can be different in some ways without that difference leading to harsh judgment or posing a threat to our relationship. Ms. F has also needed mirroring of her emotions, and experiencing me treating her experience as valid, not dismissing or blaming her, has helped her feel more accepted and self-accepting and also helped to build her capacity for reflection (Bion, 1962). I think that Ms F's healthy idealizing of me, admiring some of my positive qualities while not needing to deny my sometimes negative impact on her, has also helped with feeling genuine belonging in our relationship. For example, Ms. F trusts me to set appropriate boundaries for myself. However, she also knows that I can unintentionally hurt her because my needs conflict with hers at times, but that when I do, I can acknowledge my harmful impact, take responsibility for it without excessive self-criticism or defensiveness (Winnicott, 1969), and attempt to repair ruptures in our relationship (Kohut, Goldberg, & Stepansky, 1984).

I think it has been important for Ms. F to gradually move from viewing me as being very similar to her, which was necessary to feel safe enough to share her true self and feel accepted by me, to recognizing that we can be different and have different, at times conflicting, needs (Benjamin, 1990; Slavin, 2013) without that threatening the belonging she experiences in our relationship. An example of this recognition of difference occurred when it became obvious to Ms. F that I had not seen the movie *101 Dalmatians*, a childhood favorite of hers. This difference disturbed her initially, and she wondered how drastically different our lives had been, even speculating that perhaps I had been raised in a cult with no exposure to television. I think Ms. F's grappling with the meaning of our difference represented the beginning of her growing sense that perhaps I could accept and care about her even if we were different and had differing needs.

Over time in Ms. F's analysis, our capacity for alpha function (Bion, 1962) has grown. I have observed a gradual increase in our ability to think, wonder about meanings, and connect Ms. F's experiences across situations and time. I think that we have both felt less confused and bewildered. At the beginning, our confusion seemed to be greater than a typical feeling in the early period of an analysis that things are complicated or that we do not yet understand what is happening. It felt like a true inability to think, a brain fog so thick that I would feel a physical urge to shake my head to try to get it to dissipate. I think that our increased capacity for alpha function can be seen in how sensory experiences became thinkable. For example, Ms. F's fears of physical symptoms such as vomiting or fainting were transformed into thoughts about how difficult it is for her to trust that she is capable or competent.

As Ms. F's ability to reflect on her own experience has increased significantly, her intense anxiety has decreased. It seems natural and understandable that she would unconsciously attempt not to think (Bion, 1959) when thinking could lead to the painful recognition that the belonging she experienced with family and friends contained many false and harmful aspects. When Ms. F started therapy, she was using cannabis daily, which significantly interfered with her thinking. She has stopped completely for over a year, although she sometimes wishes she could return to using cannabis and that it would "work" again, meaning that it would once again prevent her from experiencing the painful emotions related to her real situation. In the past, when she felt anxious, Ms. F would say, "I just don't want to do it," and no further thoughts would occur to her. Another idea that shut down our ability to reflect in the past was that Ms. F "would be fine if it weren't for my anxiety." It was difficult to make meaning out of this concrete view of her anxiety. Now, we can reflect on connections among symptoms, emotions, and relationships. For example, Ms. F has recently experienced an obsessive-compulsive symptom in which she is very disturbed by soap residue and does not trust her parents to clean soap off themselves or surfaces to her satisfaction. We have reflected that this symptom may be connected to other things she does not trust her parents to do, including taking care of their own and her emotional needs.

Recently, Ms. F has twice told me after the fact that something I said bothered her: once, that I had made an insensitive remark, once, a hurtful joke. This had not happened before in nearly six years. In the past, with friends and family, Ms. F had experienced varying reactions to saying that someone had upset her, including defensiveness, invalidation, excessive guilt and self-criticism, mocking and increasing the hurtful behavior, accusations regarding Ms. F's own behavior, dismissal of her feelings since she had raised the issue after some time had passed, apologies followed by no change in behavior, and the suggestion that she "shouldn't let it have power" over her, in essence blaming and shaming her for her inability to rid herself of her painful emotions. Many of these responses involved the other person not surviving in Winnicott's (1969) sense, instead either retaliating or being destroyed. Ms. F's understandable solution had been to remain silent when someone hurt her in order to preserve whatever conditional belonging she could experience in these relationships.

In my relationship with Ms. F, it was very important therefore for her to feel that she could tell me that I had bothered, hurt, or angered her, and that I could survive knowing about my destructive impact on her and acknowledge it without being destroyed or retaliating (Winnicott, 1969). Ms. F took a risk by telling me I had upset her, as, depending on my reaction, her nascent hope of a different kind of safety, acceptance, and belonging with others might have been destroyed. I tried to acknowledge the unintentionally hurtful impact of what I had said without becoming defensive, invalidating, or retaliatory. In the case of my insensitive remark, I could recall hearing its morbidity as it came out of my mouth and wincing; however, I had not realized how upsetting Ms. F would find it. In the case of my hurtful joke, I scoured my memory but could find no conscious awareness when I had made it that it had been related to a painful area of Ms. F's history. I asked about her internal reactions to my remarks. I tolerated the discomfort of knowing that I had hurt Ms. F in a previous session and had continued, unaware of my blunder. I felt some guilt about my missteps—enough to allow me to acknowledge them and to try to make repairs, but not so much as to feel excessively self-critical, which would lead to Ms. F feeling pressure to reassure me of my goodness. I expressed my intention to attempt not to make similar insensitive remarks or jokes again, which I felt would be relatively easy to do. Ms. F told me that it would still have felt like too much to request that I change my behavior. In sum, I felt I survived in a way that she had frequently not experienced before, hopefully contributing to an expanded sense of acceptance and belonging in our relationship.

I also spoke about making mistakes and my own human limits (Slavin, 2013). I expressed hope that Ms. F would continue to tell me in future when I said something hurtful and to remind me if I slipped and made a similar thoughtless remark or joke, despite my continued effort to avoid doing so. I felt heartened by Ms. F's ability to tell me I had upset her, and I am also aware of how Ms. F struggles with what, in these situations, was my side of the dilemma. Would I be accepted even though I had caused harm? Would I be forgiven, or would I be written off as all bad (Klein, 1946)? Ms. F fears that she will be given no leeway to unintentionally harm others, and that in order to belong, she will have to censor herself and never offend or hurt. This restricts her freedom to express her thoughts or make jokes and makes it difficult for her to feel genuine connection and belonging, as she cannot share much of herself for fear of destroying the relationship (Winnicott, 1969). It seemed reasonably easy for Ms. F to allow me to be human and to give me the opportunity to repair the ruptures in our relationship caused by my hurtful remark and joke (Kohut, Goldberg, & Stepansky, 1984). I hope this is evidence that Ms. F could be beginning to feel entitled to the same.

Recently, Ms. F observed in a session, "I think my mother parented me the way she would have wanted to be parented. I'm not sure it's exactly what I needed." She is becoming more aware of the previously described confusion of interests between herself and her mother (Slavin & Kriegman, 1998). Ms. F experienced love and care but perhaps not recognition as an individual. A recent example of this confusion of interests occurred when Ms. F thought she had found a lump in her breast. She made an appointment with her family doctor, and when her mother asked if she wanted her to accompany her to the appointment, Ms. F said, "No, I want to do it myself." She went to the appointment on her own, and when she came out of the doctor's office, she found her mother in the waiting room, saying, "You didn't think I'd let you go to something like this alone, did you?" Ms. F relayed how she had later told her sister about what happened, and they had both reflected on their mother's kindness and caring. When I observed that her mother had disregarded what Ms. F had explicitly said she wanted, leading to misrecognition of Ms. F's unique needs in my mind, Ms. F responded that this had not occurred to her.

It seems that true belonging in a relationship requires a move from paranoid-schizoid to depressive functioning (Klein, 1935; 1946) or from "doer-done to" relations (Benjamin, 2004) to mutual recognition (Benjamin, 1990). As Ms. F did not expect to be recognized for her unique subjectivity when she began therapy, it was difficult for her to fully recognize my subjectivity. A change in Ms. F gives me hope that her capacity to experience mutual recognition is growing. Ms. F takes public transit to my office. When she began therapy, she was frequently late, and she would not call to let me know. I would wait in my office, sometimes calling to check if she was on her way. Now, on the rare occasions when she is late, she always calls. I believe this indicates that Ms. F is more able to keep me in mind, to recognize that I will be wondering where she is and might like to know that she is running behind but will be there. I appreciate this recognition and thank her for calling.

The prerequisite for this increase in capacity for recognition of another's subjectivity seems to have been my attempting over time to recognize and reflect Ms. F's subjectivity (Kohut, 1971; 1977), as recognition of others cannot occur unless one has received this kind of recognition oneself. With her friends, Ms. F would consciously hide her subjectivity due to fears of judgment and mocking, so there was no chance for her perspective to be recognized. In her family, it seems likely that Ms. F's mother never received this kind of recognition of her own subjectivity and, according to Ms. F, did not even feel entitled to acknowledge her own needs and desires. In addition, it seems that her mother's wish to give Ms. F what she herself longed for and did not receive made it difficult for Ms. F's mother to recognize Ms. F's unique and somewhat different needs and wants. Benjamin (1990) writes that "the mother has to be able both to set clear boundaries for her child and to recognize the child's will, to both insist on her own independence and respect that of the child" (p. 39). Ms. F believes that her mother neither felt entitled to set clear boundaries for her children nor felt entitled to insist on her own independence, and this lack of entitlement to recognition probably interrupted the development of mutual recognition necessary for true belonging.

Conclusion

Ms. F is in a transition period with respect to belonging. She ended her relationship with her former best friend a few years ago, as she began to recognize that what had previously felt like belonging cost too much and was based on the creation of a false self (Winnicott, 1960). With other friends, it still feels too risky to show her true self and find out what kind of belonging may be possible. She still lives with her family and loves them deeply, but she is beginning to want different relationships than they have—relationships characterized by fewer unfair conditions and more healthy conditions (e.g., acceptance of emotions as valid and repair of relationship ruptures, Kohut, 1971; 1977; Kohut, Goldberg, & Stepansky, 1984; mutual recognition, Benjamin, 1990; 2004; acceptance of human limits, Slavin, 2013; mutual survival of destructive impact, Winnicott, 1969). The idea of moving out of her family's home is appealing for the first time. She would like to hope, as her family seems unable to do, that people can be trustworthy, not only harsh and dangerous (Ignatieff, 1993; Klein, 1935; 1946). She would like to have a caring, mutually respectful romantic relationship, though she still fears this will be impossible.

Ms. F desires belonging outside of her family, and its absence feels shameful. The old idea sometimes still looms that before her anxiety, she was "normal" and the false belonging she felt was good and real (Slavin & Kriegman, 1998; Winnicott, 1960). She had a caring family and friends, went out, and did things. She feels to blame for ruining the good by developing intense anxiety. However, I feel hopeful about this transition phase. Ms. F's intense, confusing anxiety has decreased, and we are now able to think more clearly together about her previously obscured fears regarding finding true belonging outside her family (Bion, 1959; 1962; Shengold, 2002). She has accomplished a great deal that she had been previously unable to do. Ms. F is involved in a necessary but painful process of recognizing and dismantling false belonging that costs too much, while not yet experiencing true belonging—sometimes not even believing this could be possible. I believe that as false belonging is recognized and questioned, there is space for true belonging to grow, and I see signs of this beginning to happen in our therapy relationship and in Ms. F's interactions in her family and in the outside world.

References

Benjamin, J. (1990). An outline of intersubjectivity: the development of recognition. *Psychoanalytic Psychology, 7S* (Supplement), 33–46.

Benjamin, J. (2004). Beyond doer and done to: an intersubjective view of thirdness. *Psychoanalytic Quarterly, 73*(1), 5–46.

Bion, W. R. (1959). Attacks on linking. *International Journal of Psycho-Analysis, 40*, 308–315.

Bion, W. R. (1962). The psycho-analytic study of thinking. *International Journal of Psycho-Analysis, 43*, 306–310.

Ignatieff, M. (1993). *Blood and belonging: journeys into the new nationalism.* New York: Farrar, Straus, and Giroux.

Klein, M. (1935). A contribution to the psychogenesis of manic-depressive states. *International Journal of Psycho-Analysis, 16*, 145–174.

Klein, M. (1946). Notes on some schizoid mechanisms. *International Journal of Psycho-Analysis, 27*, 99–110.

Kohut, H. (1971). *The analysis of self.* New York: International Universities Press.

Kohut, H. (1977). *The restoration of the self.* New York: International Universities Press.

Kohut, H., Goldberg, A., & Stepansky, P. E. (1984). *How does analysis cure?* Chicago: University of Chicago Press.

Shengold, L. (2002). "What do I know?" Perspectives on what must not be known when change means loss. *Psychoanalytic Quarterly, 71*(4), 699–724.

Slavin, M. O. (2013). Meaning, mortality, and the search for realness and reciprocity: an evolutionary/existential perspective on Hoffman's dialectical constructivism. *Psychoanalytic Dialogues, 23*(3), 296–314.

Slavin, M. O., & Kriegman, D. (1998). Why the analyst needs to change: toward a theory of conflict, negotiation, and mutual influence in the therapeutic process. *Psychoanalytic Dialogues, 8*(2), 247–284.

Winnicott, D. W. (1960). Ego distortion in terms of true and false self. In D. W. Winnicott (Ed.), *The maturational processes and the facilitating environment: studies in the theory of emotional development* (pp. 140–152). London: Karnac Books.

Winnicott, D. W. (1969). The use of an object. *International Journal of Psycho-Analysis, 50*, 711–716.

17 Belonging to, belonging with, and the right to privacy

Jenny Kahn Kaufmann

A fully formed person has the right to tell what they wish about themselves—no more and no less than they are comfortable telling. As they put themselves out there into the world—especially in the mental health world—people learn that the more they can say and the clearer they are about their personal history, the better they will be received. But at what point does a person say more than they want to, and at what point do they feel over-exposed and uncomfortable with how much has been said? Is speaking the "truth" a choice, or does it become a compulsion? In this paper I examine some of these questions—how much a person needs to say, how much they want to say—and I maintain that the ability to choose what one wishes to say—and to have the courage to hold back and not say more than one wants, despite group pressure—is a developmental achievement. It's my contention that not everyone feels that they have the right to tell as much or as little as they would like to say. While this may be related to many different factors, I believe the key factor that helps a person decide what feels comfortable is their sense of belonging. By this I mean the sense that people have of knowing where they come from and where and to whom they belong. I believe that the ability to choose what one wishes to say evolves from going through specific developmental steps of belonging to and then belonging with, and it is not something that can be taken for granted. I also believe that when people have not grown up with a sense of belonging, it is something we can offer to them in our psychoanalytic practice.

This experience was brought home to me in the summer of 2018 when I wrote a paper for the Halifax Conference on Belonging. I'd been very excited to write a paper about my own experience of growing up in a family that felt so focused on making money and achieving social status that my experience was of feeling that social and material comfort was a poor substitute for the feeling of belonging to a family. In many ways, I was so alone in my experience of growing up that I was overcome with the need to feel known and understood through my writing. I wrote a paper about my formative experiences entitled "Belonging to the Family or to the 1%?" Even though I liked the paper I'd written—and received good feedback about it—something very interesting happened to me after I'd written the paper. I began to feel worried about feeling overexposed, and I became concerned about how patients, supervisees, and students would feel if they were to know so much about me. Even though it had been important to me to write the paper, I began to feel—for the first time in my life—that I wasn't comfortable exposing myself in this particular way. And that feeling of wanting to protect my privacy was an entirely new feeling for me, and that really struck me as something important. Other people had always guarded their privacy, but for me, being known and feeling that my story had been witnessed had always been more important. But suddenly for the first time in my life I felt known and held enough by the people I was closest to—my husband, analyst, supervisor, and close friends—and that felt like enough. I didn't want to give the paper I'd written, but I realized I had an interesting and important paper I did want to give—on the feeling of belonging and how grounding that can be in terms of having the right to be discerning about what one chooses to share and what one wishes to hold back.

I've often wondered whether our "say all" mentality is an unfortunate byproduct of the analytic credo that came from Freud's fundamental rule, "Say all that comes to mind." It's not always in one's best interest—or even in the best interest of the analysis—to say everything that comes to mind. While it's good to learn to associate freely, it's important to keep one's eye on making meaning, and too many associations without understanding leaves a person in a floundering state. In addition, feeling you have the right to say whatever comes to mind without regard for the listener can lead to the all-too-familiar situation of narcissism run amok. With these ideas in mind, I was happy to find the following comment in a recent book by Thomas Ogden called *Reclaiming Unlived Life* (2016). Ogden writes:

> I do not adhere to Freud's (1912) "fundamental rule." I have found in my own experience and in the work of analysts who consult with me that the injunction to "say everything that comes to mind" compromises the patient's right to privacy, which is necessary for the freedom to dream in the session. So, rather than asking the patient to say everything that comes to mind, I tell the patient (sometimes explicitly, sometimes implicitly) that she is free to say whatever she wants to say and to keep to herself what she chooses—and that I will do the same.
>
> (p. 2)

My thesis is that in the beginning, when the baby is in the holding phase, the baby looks into the face of the mother and has the sense of being seen and the accompanying feeling of *belonging to* her. The baby forms an initial, core sense of self through the expressiveness of the mother, who shows the baby what she has seen and understood and reflects that back to her baby. The mother is responsive to the baby. She mirrors the baby's affect and expressions. She picks up when the baby is happy or sad or in distress—and on all sorts of other subtleties about the myriad states in between. When the mother functions as such an accurate mirror and reader of her baby, so good at validating all that the baby is feeling, then the baby is happy to be with this mother. The baby feels safe with this mother. And, most importantly, the baby feels they *belong* to this mother—and, by extension, the mother *belongs to* them.

As Winnicott (1953) wrote about in "Transitional Objects and Transitional Phenomena," this early sense of belonging continues through the use of transitional space and transitional objects that the baby creates—on their own initiative, but also with the help, support, and validating understanding from the mother. The baby carries on what was good with this mother because of the feeling of belonging. It's this basic sense of *belonging to* the mother (as well as to the totality of the family unit) that's so critical to the baby's core sense of identity, and it is part of what the baby draws from as they go on to become more of a separate, independent self.

When all goes well, the child moves somewhat fluidly from this early stage of *belonging to* the mother to being able to assert more of a boundary—albeit a permeable boundary—so that they can feel more separate and exist somewhat more independently from the mother (in gradual increments, of course). In the model I am proposing, the child starts to evolve from an early stage of *belonging to* to a later stage of *belonging with*. In the beginning, the child is totally dependent, and it's the mother's job to take care of her child. But in later stages of development, when the child starts to belong *with* the mother, the child is no longer a total dependent but a subject—an individual with their own separate perspective—a subject who takes their rightful place *with* the family, both as a member of that family and also as an individual in their own right. It's the mother's ability to survive—in a Winnicottian sense—that gives children the feeling they are worthwhile and will be accepted by the mother (and the rest of their clan), even if they choose to live in different ways than their parents.

But when the child is born to a narcissistic mother (primary caretaker) who is inattentive and self-preoccupied, bad at mirroring, and unable to keep the baby in mind, then the baby does not grow up with a basic, core sense of belonging. I contend that babies who don't grow up with a real sense of belonging to their mothers don't grow up with a strong, stable, coherent, cohesive sense of self either—so not only do they not feel they belong to their mothers, but, even more poignantly, they frequently don't feel as if they belong to themselves. These beings grow up without having an authentic sense of self. They don't feel as if they belong to the mother; they don't feel they belong to themselves; and as they develop, they struggle to find their place in the world. They have trouble putting out a clear vision of who they are (which can make it difficult for them to find a suitable partner), and they also have trouble figuring out where they belong in the world—what sort of work they should do, how they should live, eat, exercise, etc.

I've worked with many people who come into treatment without having a clear sense of belonging. They're unclear about where they come from and can't quite figure out where they wish to belong. It's not always easy to grasp how insecure these "lost" people are because they're good at hiding. They may present as good caretakers for others, and they may appear to be self-sufficient. I think of these patients as presenting with defensive omnipotence.

Patients who've grown up with narcissistic parents or other sorts of parents who've been unable to hold them through the stages of belonging to and belonging with can develop this stance of defensive omnipotence. In reaction to continual misattuned responsiveness, these patients split off their vulnerability and authentic affects that they anticipate will meet with parental disapproval. Instead, they aspire to achieve a defensive self-ideal that they hope will protect them from incurring parental criticism and rejection. In striving to actualize this ideal, they attempt as much as possible to be self-sufficient so as not to risk parental condemnation for seeming weak and needy. So they present in treatment as if they need very little or nothing from the analyst, and the analyst has to find ways to address this defensive stance so that the patient can begin to feel that they belong to and with the analyst.

Generally speaking, the beginning phases of treatment are about trying to find ways of reaching these patients in their defensive, walled-off places. It's hard to specify exactly how I do this—but I know I bring a personal sensitivity to this issue because I didn't grow up with a clear feeling of belonging, and I know that I looked for this feeling of belonging with every therapist I saw. Even though most of the therapists did not provide the feeling that I belonged to them, there is still a way in which I was taken in by different therapists that was life-saving for me. My personal sensitivity to being slighted—even in small ways—makes me try to ensure that patients feel taken in by me. I want people to feel as if they belong, and I know how much it hurts when there is a fundamental feeling of not belonging.

I think in the beginning there may be a sense of being merged. I listen from an empathic, subject-centered perspective, and I make it clear that I'm not going to ask or require this person to take care of me in any way. At this point in my career I am vigilant about this particular issue. In my experience, it's a fairly common occurrence for narcissistic patients to end up in caretaking roles for their analysts. We can speculate about reasons why this happens—and I do have some ideas about it—but that would be beyond the scope of this paper. Suffice to say that I do everything in my power to avoid putting the patient in the familiar role of caretaker. I communicate that the session belongs to them and our job is to work as well as we can together to ensure that their story is witnessed—by both of us. Slowly, the person starts to trust and depend on me and see me as someone who appreciates them for who they are.

This process tends to happen slowly and in gradual increments over extended periods of time. In early phases of treatment, the person is usually in a stage of object relating rather than object usage (Winnicott, 1971). As Winnicott wrote:

> In teaching, as in the feeding of a child, the capacity to use objects is taken for granted, but in our work it is necessary for us to be concerned with the development and establishment of the capacity to use objects and to recognize a patient's inability to use objects, where this is a fact.
>
> (p. 87)

The person sees me in terms of the old object, and they may test me, and it's important that I survive these tests by not collapsing or retaliating, and thus emerging for the patient as someone who is different from the old objects. This helps move the person along from object relating to object usage (Winnicott, 1971), but it's not always enough. It's also important to reach for latent parts of the person that haven't been developed but which I can see are there, waiting to be noticed. I've also found that as the person begins to feel more like their own person, they may also need to push away from me and assert their independence for a period of time. Sometimes this happens metaphorically, and sometimes it plays out more literally. The person may need to take some sort of break from treatment and be assured that there will still be a place for them once they decide to come back. In other cases, the person may need to find other ways of asserting their right to do things on their own terms, rather than on my terms.

Just as the baby goes from a feeling of belonging to to a place of belonging with, so does the adult patient who's been overshadowed by narcissistic parents move from a place of belonging *to* the therapist to a place of belonging *with* the therapist. As many people have noted (Aron, 1996; Pizer, 1992), the relationship is always asymmetrical, but the important thing is that once the patient feels that they *belong to* the therapist, *to* their own authentic self, and *with* the therapist, there is an important shift that can take place regarding the patient's feeling of having the right to privacy.

Clinical examples

In the following section of this paper I will take the reader through two different clinical processes, both with patients who were born to narcissistic mothers and struggled with the sense of not feeling that they belonged, though in very different ways. I will show how I broke through their defensive omnipotent stances and helped them feel as if they belonged to and with me and, from there, both of them were able to feel as if they had the right to their own sense of privacy.

Zora: spilling as a means of controlling the other

Zora did not have a good sense of belonging to her mother, and it was initially difficult to engage her in a therapeutic relationship. She never felt her mother was there for her and could never figure out which key would unlock her mother's heart. When she began three-times-a-week treatment with me and lay on the analytic couch, she looked at the lines on the Drury rug in my office and associated them with the bars on her baby crib. Her mother left her alone in that crib, and her grandpa used to tell her mother, "You have to pick that baby up." But Mom didn't pick her up, and Zora was left alone in the crib. As she grew older, she became the fiercely independent, defensively omnipotent middle child who didn't need attention from her mother. But Zora wasn't as self-sufficient as she imagined, and she ran into difficulties trying to navigate on her own, without any sense of how to get help from mentors. She read a lot and created a life filled with fictions, both in her portrayal of herself (to herself) as a fearless adventurer who lived abroad for twenty-five years and in her portrayal of herself to others. She created a CV that made her seem like the person she fancied herself to be, while maintaining awareness that the fiction she'd created didn't quite fit with the actual facts of her life. She felt like a fraud and worried about being found out.

I had to withstand a lot of coldness and rejection from her, but my counter-transference included identification with her aloneness and a drive to prove I would stick with her through thick and thin and could take her through the steps of creating a more authentic and "real" life. I imagined I was not going to be rejecting of her, even when she threw ice water at me (metaphorically), as her mother had literally done to her.

Zora had many "friends," but none of them were good friends, and I was struck by the lack of true intimacy between her and others. There was a way she would try to control interactions by "spilling"—which included telling people she didn't know well far too much about herself. She wasn't paying much attention to who the other people were or what was going on with them.

A pattern emerged where Zora would tell me about her most recent friend "conquest," accompanied by the phrase, "Jenny, this is the one. I can feel that this one is different—we have so much in common—this is the friendship that's going to work out." I had to brace myself—knowing that inevitably conflict would arise, and there would be a big eruption in the weeks or months that lay ahead.

Zora loved coming for sessions and felt I was appropriately attentive and attuned to her, but she noted I wasn't there for her in the evenings or weekends or in the middle of the night when she woke up with her heart pounding from a nightmare.

She didn't like the feeling of needing me so much—and particularly didn't like it when there was a break in her academic schedule, so that the only structure in her schedule was appointments with me. She didn't want me to feel burdened by the weight of her need for me, and she didn't want to feel the weight of her dependence on me.

So a pattern emerged where she would plan extended vacations during these times without checking in with me about them. And then we would fight about it: I would feel annoyed about the disruption from treatment, and she would feel fine. What was my problem and why was I so needy? On one of these occasions, Zora made plans to go to Rome for the summer. She let me know she'd be fine and she didn't need me. She'd be with a group of friends who'd look out for her and take good care of her. She'd lived with many of these people when she was younger and was excited about being reunited with so many people she'd known so many years ago. I had a bad feeling about this plan. I sensed she was being unrealistic about these people and their ability to look out for her. I refused to be pushed away so easily and kept saying I was not going to be uninvolved. I insisted she bring her computer so we could have sessions over Skype. And, as predicted, the problems and disappointments started almost immediately. What was different from her experiences with her mother when she was younger was that she was able to turn to me for help and I was able to be there for her.

We talked on Skype and she recognized the difficult situation she was in without blowing it up entirely. She accepted my help and felt gratitude for my continued presence in her life. In a Winnicottian sense, I survived her destruction of me as the old object—as the mother who didn't care and would stay uninvolved—and she was able to use me as a real object in her life. I had value for her because

I survived—in that I wouldn't allow her to push me away during her holiday. In the language of this paper, she then felt she belonged to me—because I was in touch with her previously unarticulated need to be supported. At the same time, I belonged to her—but she was in the process of working out a way of belonging *with* me, not to me.

During the years we'd worked together, I'd helped her navigate the hurdles of getting a college degree (a real one—not the imaginary one she'd invented for the CV), and she had done so well that she'd gone on to advanced studies. She was ready for a change, though, and wanted to join the Peace Corps. She'd wanted to join the Peace Corps since John F. Kennedy had established them in 1961, and now that she had the necessary academic credentials to be considered, her dream could become a reality. For Zora, the Peace Corps offered a perfect marriage of her love of travel and adventure and her more newly developed desire to give back to the world. Being in the Peace Corps in an undeveloped country was not easy, and many people dropped out. But Zora was resourceful: she made friends with people who lived there, and they were able to be good neighbors and to look out for her. She taught kids in an elementary school and coached a girls' soccer team. She stayed for the requisite two years, and though we talked a couple of times, for the most part she was able to keep her own counsel and rely on friends she made there.

After she finished her stay in the Peace Corps, Zora came for a session and was eager to tell me about something she'd handled very differently once she got back to the States. She'd bumped into an acquaintance from the neighborhood— someone she'd been friendly with in the past, but, as I well knew, whenever she'd visited with this person, she'd always felt awful afterwards. She always went in hopeful, and then felt so dismissed by the way that they treated her (or dismissed her in their lackadaisical approach to being a host) that she was in danger of either feeling awful about herself or, more likely, blowing up at them. So when she bumped into this neighbor on the street and she invited her to come over, Zora declined the invitation. This was a step forward for her. She didn't have to go along with a program that was guaranteed to fail her. In being able to decline, Zora was able to hold on to herself, to know that it wasn't something she wanted to do and it was okay to decline the invitation. Perhaps for the first time in her life, she had a solid feeling of belonging to herself and belonging with me. Rather than feeling compelled to go to the neighbor's home and say too much about herself in an effort to get them to attend to her, she was able to feel the right to her own privacy. She was able to keep her own counsel and politely decline the invitation.

Rose: when privacy is not a choice

Like Zora, Rose was another patient who didn't feel as if she belonged to her mother in a fundamental way, and she coped with it by living in the shadow of her narcissistic mother and being so private and non-disclosing about herself that she could be rendered invisible. Her need to be private about herself wasn't a choice—rather, it was an automatic "go-to" place that came out of a need to hide and a terror about being seen. When she had more of a sense of who she was, she began to feel as if she belonged to herself. In the treatment, she began to feel as if she belonged to me and I belonged to her. In addition, she came to feel that she belonged with me, and eventually I became the "go-to" place where she was able to become more vocal about what she wanted. She could also choose to keep some things to herself, but the difference was that not talking and guarding her privacy became a legitimate choice rather than the "go-to" place she went to automatically.

In terms of her history, Rose didn't really feel like she belonged to either of her parents. They were successful musicians, but they were immature. They weren't particularly connected to one another, and they weren't well equipped to be parents. They divorced when Rose was three years old.

Rose's mother was narcissistic, alcoholic, and hidden. She loved Rose, but she was self-preoccupied. Rose never felt kept in mind by her mother, so that was a way in which she didn't feel as if she really belonged to either of her parents. As an adult, she became a perfect caretaker for her mother.

In terms of my counter-transference, I really identified with Rose's story, as I had my own story that had intense areas of overlap and connection. I too had a parent who was unable to be the caretaker I needed, and, like Rose, I kept my own counsel and was hidden. I could really see myself in Rose, and she picked up on this and felt very connected to me. We could belong to—and eventually belong with—one another.

In earlier stages of the treatment, there was a sense of murkiness about her story that came from her own dissociation—and the same could be said of me. There were ways in which I was overly identified with Rose, so that we were murkily intertwined in our subjectivities. But as her history got clarified, she felt more and became less dissociated, and as I felt witnessed in my own treatment, I also became less dissociated, so eventually there was more of a sense of our being delineated and not merged.

As the treatment began to change and each of our lives came into sharper focus, I let Rose know that we shared similarities in our histories. The specifics of our similarities were never made explicit, but there was still a way in which our connection became solidified over many years of treatment, and there is a way in which Rose and I do belong *with* each other.

The more Rose understood about her history and the more she felt she belonged to herself and with me, the more she became free to make choices about what she wanted to say and what she wanted to keep to herself. One interesting change that took place: like her parents, Rose was also a musician. She had a near pitch-perfect voice and was genuinely talented. But she never achieved the degree of success that we both felt she should have. She felt she had to go along with what everyone wanted, and it put her in a place where she wasn't well looked after and didn't get the opportunities she should have gotten. I'd always thought that when she got better, her career would take off. But instead, what seemed to be happening was that she had more choices but didn't want to disrupt her life to perform to the extent that she would have to in order to become a big success. Her privacy and her quality of life really do matter to her. But at this point it's more of a conscious choice rather than an automatic "go-to" hiding place. Her ability to choose came out of a feeling of belonging, both to herself and with me, in a way she never could feel with her mother.

Conclusion

As the clinical processes with Zora and Rose illustrate, gradually enabling patients to relinquish the defensive omnipotent stance and open up to the analyst's recognition and support gives patients a sense of belonging to and with themselves and the analyst. And with this increased sense of belonging, patients then can assert their right to privacy and decide if, when, and to whom they want to share themselves. And what a significant assertion of agency this can be—that comes out of a greater sense of belonging!

References

Aron, L. (1996). *A meeting of minds: mutuality in psychoanalysis.* New York and London: Routledge.

Freud, S. (1958). Recommendations to physicians practicing psychoanalysis. In J. Strachey (Ed. & Trans.), *Standard edition of the complete psychological works of Sigmund Freud* (Vol. 12, pp. 109–120). London: Hogarth. Originally published 1912.

Greenberg, J. R. (1986). The problem of analytic neutrality. *Contemporary Psychoanalysis, 22,* 76–86.

Kaufmann, J. K. (2018). Rejection by a boyfriend: from idealizing transference to "real" partner. In R. C. Curtis (Ed.), *Psychoanalytic case studies from an interpersonal-relational perspective* (pp. 213–217). London and New York: Routledge.

Kaufmann, J. K. (2015). Modeling a therapeutic identity for a beginning therapist in supervision. In S. Tuber (Ed.), *Early encounters with children and adolescents: beginning psychodynamic therapists' first cases* (pp. 67–74). London and New York: Routledge.

Kaufmann, J. K., & Kaufmann, P. (2013). Witnessing: its essentialness in psychoanalytic treatment. In A Richards, L. Spira, & A. Lynch (Eds.), *Encounters with loneliness: only the lonely* (pp. 139–158). Astoria: IPBooks.

Kaufmann, J. K., & Kaufmann, P. (2018, March). *Emerging from the shadows of parental narcissism.* Paper presented at the William Alanson White Institute, New York.

Ogden, T. H. (2016). *Reclaiming unlived life: experiences in psychoanalysis.* London and New York: Routledge.

Pizer, S. A. (1992). The negotiation of paradox in the analytic process. *Psychoanalytic Dialogues, 2*(2), 215–240.

Winnicott, D. W. (1953). Transitional objects and transitional phenomena: a study of the first not-me possession. *International Journal of Psychoanalysis, 34,* 89–97.

Winnicott, D. W. (1971). The use of an object and relating through identifications. *Playing and reality.* London: Tavistock.

Part 6

Belonging, the psychoanalyst, and the psychoanalytic process

18 The analyst's peculiar paradox in the question of belonging

Michelle Flax and J. Gail White

We are dependent social animals from birth. Our need for close connection with others is not only a biological imperative but the basis of our psychological well-being throughout our lives. It is the wellness of this connectedness that carries us as we navigate the stormy waters of development through the years. And within this connectedness, there can be tensions relating to our sense of belonging that can be enacted in both our love and our work lives.

Anxieties of belonging and not belonging are particularly salient during early developmental stages. The first belonging anxiety concerns separation from the caretaker, and the second anxiety is realizing our exclusion from the parental couple. The psychic conflicts we encounter during the primal scene and the resulting oedipal phase of development stage the theatre of the tensions between the poles of belonging and not belonging. We have to learn to manage these anxieties and come to terms with our exclusion anxiety. We can either collapse into either/or psychological dichotomizing relating or metabolize the distressing affect and contradictions between belonging or not belonging and allow space for a third possibility. Carveth (2018) writes about this dialectical tension: 'we need to dialectically deconstruct the privileging of one pole of a binary opposition over the other and … strive toward the synthesis that negates and yet preserves and elevates both' (p. 232).

In all of us there is the ongoing struggle to both belong and at the same time to hold on to our individual self. On the one hand, we seek to belong, as there is a high price to pay for not belonging. On the other hand, belonging can compromise our personal freedom, our creative thinking and our authenticity. C. S. Lewis addressed the perils of 'belonging': 'And you will be drawn in, if you are drawn in, not by a desire for gain or ease but simply because at that moment, when the cup was so near your lips, you can not bear to be thrust back again into the cold outer world' (Lewis, 1944). To be thrust into the cold outer world gives one an uncomfortable 'outsider status' and revives the early struggles with the oedipal situation. We can go to great lengths to avoid this outcome, often at the expense of our own authenticity and personal freedom.

We look at how we, as psychoanalysts, play out the tensions of belonging and not belonging not only in our psychoanalytic professional affiliations but also in our clinical work. We believe that we have to balance the tension in this complicated place of both belonging and not belonging in our various psycho-analytic engagements, and that we can best do so from an 'optimally marginal' position.

As psychoanalysts, we know better than most that our inborn and developmental psychic frailties can lead us to difficult places. Despite our informed awareness of these primitive psychic processes, we cannot completely leave behind our own regressive longings. When it comes to those tensions about belonging, our narcissistic fault line can be exposed and we can enact our feelings rather than reflect upon them. The countertransference dangers around our sense of belonging are heightened if we see belonging or not belonging as this stark dichotomous choice – in the face of no third (no overarching holding environment), splitting results. In that compromised position, we lose the ability to hold the safety of the analytic frame. Rather, we can occupy the Hegelian 'both/and' space, avoiding the inside/outside thinking where the binary is maintained.

The analytic frame is what McLaughlin refers to as an 'optimal marginal' space (McLaughlin, 2001). This optimal marginal position, as McLaughlin describes it, is a position that enhances creativity by combining embeddedness with a certain distance from the centre or core of the field. This notion of 'optimal marginality' is instructive, as it describes a state of being both separate and attached. It bridges the borders, giving us a sense of belonging without engulfment or rejection. We can occupy a position that respects our quest to belong and at the same time be our own person with our own mind. An optimal marginal space becomes a safe place of creative thinking and a place to imagine alternatives that precludes the collapse of thinking into binary categories. Where binary was, dialectic can be.

Psychoanalysts, by definition, study the unconscious, that unruly realm that is often seen as threatening to the power of rationality and hence threatening to the larger social order. Starr and Aron (2013) argue that 'psychoanalysis is at its best, not when it is part of the mainstream, but when it is optimally marginal' (p. 335). Precisely because Freud and his followers were situated at the margins of their society and were using psychoanalytic concepts to study the culture, they were able to apply a psychoanalytic sensibility – what Reik referred to as 'listening with the third ear' (Reik, 1948). Marginality is a dynamic and dialectical process whereby the centre and the margins mutually influence and define each other (Bos, Park, & Pietikainen, 2005). In occupying these border spaces, we allow for a place of openness and free-flowing discourse.

Currently, while the ideas of psychoanalysis are thriving in the humanities and the social sciences, clinical psychoanalysis is seen as a marginalized profession in North America. Witness the independent status of our professional schools existing outside our universities, tucked away, so to speak, from the mainstream. Stepansky (2009) writes about how psychoanalysis struggles to survive in a post-analytic world of manualized therapy, psychopharmacology and managed care. Interestingly, we psychoanalysts have all self-selected to be part of this marginal group. At the same time, we can feel ourselves part of a superior exclusive group in relation to other schools of therapy. We thus hold a dual position of belonging and not belonging.

Many schools of psychoanalysis grew out of Freud's original model. The discipline splintered into various factions, each putting forward their own version of the practice of psychoanalysis and thereby enacting those belonging conflicts. In our professional affiliations we have 'insider status' or 'outsider status' (Simmel, 1971). Historically, the question of what school of psychoanalysis one belongs to has been a defining factor in psychoanalytic politics. As McDougall (1995) said: 'today we have sects rather than schools, doctrines rather than theories' (p. 233).

Inasmuch as we recognize our theoretical differences as clinicians, we can dismiss other points of view as doctrinaire and sectarian. We engage in exclusion politics as we drink the Kool-Aid of ideological conviction. Both within and across our institutes there is vehement adherence to ideologies that claim to have the 'right way' to think and practice psychoanalysis. This culminates in an 'us versus them' (black-and-white thinking), which can result in distressful countertransference enactments in our home institutes of analytic thought. The result is that psychoanalysts can feel they belong as an 'insider' or can be thrust out as an 'outsider'.

As analysts, we have always aspired to frankness and openness with our colleagues. We hoped this would be an outcome and added blessing of belonging to our profession, especially because of our particular training and understanding of the darker areas of being. We felt safe in the company of those in this noble profession. From the time of Freud, our learning has been based on the case study, that personal, vulnerable offering that we share with our colleagues. We have learned, however, that there are many analysts who feel unsafe in presenting clinical material. We can become more reluctant to risk vulnerability in presenting the surprise moments that emerge spontaneously from within the analyst, emanations from the joint unconscious work. When institutions cease to feel like safe places for like-minded professionals, it does our profession no good.

Too often, we disrespect our colleagues when their theoretical and clinical beliefs are different from our own. This can take the form of passionate power struggles, verging on uncompromising fundamentalism (McDougall, 1995). As McDougall (1995) notes, we can be 'intellectual terrorists' to our colleagues (p. 233). We often look up to the leaders of our psychoanalytic schools in an idealized way as if they are secular prophets. This lays the ground for in-fighting that can be vicious. Green (2005), in a paper entitled 'The Illusion of Common Ground and Mythical Pluralism', states:

> I myself was part of a group in which the decision to co-opt Hanna Segal led to the resignation of the group's organizer. I heard another American friend expressing his disgust at Melanie Klein's ideas. I still remember a bloody duel between Herbert Rosenfeld and Ralph Greenson in 1973 in which the latter tore the former to pieces, ... I myself still have an unhappy memory from the Amsterdam Congress of a discussion of Ted Jacobs's presentation ... the latter, angry, did not greet me for two years after the session. And who can forget the bitterness of the quarrels between Kohut and Kernberg ...
>
> (p. 628)

Managing the tensions with regard to being 'in' or 'out' when there is this level of hostile engagement can be a psychically difficult task both for those in the fray of it *and* for those observing the devastation. Kirsner (1999) reminds us that it is not only in large psychoanalytic politics that we see infighting but it is frequently seen in the day-to-day management of institutes, for example, in the formation of committees and the selection of faculty, supervisors and conference speakers. Many of us have felt the sting of being thrust out of the centre of our institute and have paid the price for defecting from the party line. As an example of intellectual terrorism, Utrilla Robles (2013) cites a particular leader within an unnamed psychoanalytic institute. To quote:

> She was described by everyone as very clever with an extraordinary power of seduction. Since she was endowed with great persuasion skills, her ideas were almost always accepted. At the same time she was manipulative, malicious, possessed exaggerated self-esteem, and she lied profusely … she could weave a fabric of terrible rumours that would cause people to be afraid of her … in the institution, she would create an atmosphere of distrust and persecution counterbalanced by excessive compliments … Despite the fact that the institutional environment became increasingly awful, the institution in question seemed to absorb her terrorism. We could say that the intellectual terrorism and the aggression to which she subjected her victims acted as an impediment to taking any action against her.
>
> (pp. 12–14)

This is an extreme example of what can happen when analysts play out their most primitive narcissistic dynamics in their communities. It is incumbent upon us all to be alert to these kinds of injustices that surround us in our home institutes. These kinds of dynamics, whether in their extreme or subtle forms, can lead to turmoil for constituent members, who may then attempt to avoid such turmoil by complying with a 'party line' or withdrawing from the fray. We also have to be alert to our willingness to be bystanders to such dynamics because of our fear of being cast out. Maintaining the frame of respectful civility is essential in our work and in our professional relationships.

Just as we need to be aware of our belonging countertransference manifestations in our institutes and societies, we have to be alert to how our belonging countertransference plays out in the clinical situation. In the clinic, we simultaneously live in two stories: that of an insider and that of an outsider. The nature of psychoanalytic treatment builds a bridge of attachment through empathy between ourselves and our patients. In connecting deeply with our patients to feel a sense of belonging in their inner world, we can often feel in our countertransference the wish to be more present in their external world. Yet, paradoxically, as psychoanalytic clinicians, we know that we both belong and don't belong in our patients' lives. We have an intimate space in the patient's psychic life, where a meaningful relationship develops. This private intimate world with our patients is limited by the safety of the analytic frame. Bringing that intimate space into the wider world has unconscious ramifications that we would do well to consider. Our analytic dyad is akin to the dyadic withdrawal from society that is similarly evidenced in secret love affairs. We occupy a central place in the patient's internal world, but we are peripheral in their social world. This is evident for us on the rare occasion when we enter into the social world of the patient for one reason or another. We are often in a dilemma about whether to attend a patient's wedding or their funeral. Dual relationships, while sometimes inevitable, stretch the comfort of the analytic frame.

Some extra-analytic moments may be unintended, but there are many occasions in which it is a playing out of our wish to belong that creates analytic dilemmas. In the clinic, we see the countertransference wish to break frame with patients. For example, we may be tempted to accept tickets we are offered to a private screening; perhaps it is a small way to be part of the patient's glamorous social world. Or we may be tempted to attend the wedding of a couple who have success-fully negotiated pre-wedding relationship difficulties in our office. These counter-transference enactments can remain unexplored if we do not acknowledge our own vulnerable quest to belong that drives us. The prospect of being cast out of the inner circle activates our primal scene fantasies where we feel the exclusion anxiety and loneliness of being left out of the intimacy of belonging. The younger generation beautifully capture this uncomfortable feeling with the term FOMO (fear of missing out). We have to respect and understand in ourselves this ancient, unconscious wish to belong in the centre of things and at the same time struggle to maintain healthy boundaries. If we do not, we are likely to have difficulty man-aging our affect and risk countertransference manifestations. The following case vignettes are illustrative of this dilemma.

Elizabeth is a 99-year-old educated cultured woman that I (J. Gail White) have seen for many years. Owing to the advancing vagaries of ageing, I began to make house calls three times a week. This past year, due to her growing dementia, her son assumed power of attorney. He then dictated our meeting times and became responsible for the payment of my account. Inadvertently, I was thrust into her social world and out of our shared intimate workspace. Earlier this year, her son cut back our session times to once a week from three times a week, telling his mother, 'There are other girls here you can talk to,' referring to her personal care workers, who barely speak her language. Her son's comment shook my profes-sional confidence. I was insulted, sad and thrust out of the close circle she and I had occupied together. Both of us were cast out of that closeness. I have belonged very dearly and it has been mutual.

My sense of belonging was now assailed. The paradox for me was that I was no longer in my patient's world and I was not out of it either. I existed on the per-iphery. In my anger at being undervalued by her son, and in facing the limits of her understanding imposed by the dementia, I noticed myself withdrawing from her. I was enacting the 'cast out' position assigned to me by her son. My counter-transference was looming large, and I struggled not to withdraw.

What helped me in my struggle was to recognize that my wish to belong as I previously had was contributing to my feeling wounded and my wish to withdraw.

This recognition helped me to neither agree with the son's diminishment of me and the meaning of our connection nor succumb to a wounded narcissistic ego. Presently, I am doing what I can to hold on to a more distant orbit relationship where we can creatively work with what has been left behind. I certainly feel Elizabeth's pleasure and relief in seeing me, and I feel the delicacy and complexity of her soul still in connection with me. We have made the best of the situation and attempt to maintain a sense of belonging in our now much more limited space.

Another example of countertransference belonging tension is illustrated by the following case. Some months ago, my (Michelle Flax) patient of many years was diagnosed with a fatal illness. We had a meaningful therapeutic connection, and he often spoke about what a difference I had made in his life. I was profoundly saddened when he was diagnosed, and then shocked at his death three months later. I heard about his far too early death by email from his wife, who let me know about his funeral the next day. It was clear to me right away that I wished to attend his funeral, and I made arrangements to do so.

When I walked into the funeral home, I was asked with whom I was affiliated. I was caught off guard. I avoided the question and said merely, 'I knew him well' and proceeded to sit on my own at the back of the sanctuary. I was aware of the feeling that there was no place outside the consulting room for the intimate, private world we had and that I did not belong in the social acknowledgement of his death. I found myself questioning my wish to attend his funeral in the first place and felt awkward about being there. A question by Adelman (2013) came to mind: 'Without a patient, who is the analyst?' I considered slipping out of the funeral home but felt compelled to stay.

I was pleased that I stayed. As I heard my patient being eulogized, I fully recognized his embeddedness in his social world. At the same time, I felt the value of the world we shared. I sat quietly with his presence and said a private goodbye.

To collapse the question into whether or not I belonged at the funeral would take me away from the optimally marginal position of the quiet inner presence of being with my patient in thought and from finding a way of being comfortable with both belonging and not belonging in that poignant space.

The binarism of belonging or not belonging is troublesome and reductive. If we can manage the tensions that emanate from this position, we can move to a third possibility. The belonging countertransference feelings that are played out in our professional lives may be better managed if we can aspire to this third possibility, the 'optimal marginal position'. Within psychoanalysis as a whole, we can maintain optimal marginality by taking the position that no one school of psychoanalysis has the 'truth'. It is a position that respects pluralism, where we can acknowledge that psychoanalysis is one among many of the human sciences that seeks meaning. Voltaire reminds us to cherish those who seek the truth but to be beware of those who find it. This philosophy welcomes an open exchange of epistemological knowledge without resorting to personal attack and/or ideological rigidity.

Similarly, within institutes, optimal marginality allows for a truly comparative approach, where respectful relating among members predominates and ease of movement between institutional affiliations is encouraged. Keeping the frame in institutes, as we do with patients, involves members engaging in a truly democratic process so that roles are duly elected rather than appointed. In that way, all sub-groups with different theoretical beliefs from the larger group have representation and the dialectic is maintained among all theoretical positions.

And with patients in the clinic, optimal marginality, synonymous with the frame, guards against the collapse into countertransference enactments arising from longings to belong in the outside social world of the patient. It is the recognition of these longings that allows us to find the thoughtful middle position.

The word be-longing captures the human struggle to both 'be' our own person and to 'long for' essential social connectedness. As psychoanalysts, we hold this paradox in mind. Ideally, we dwell in the oscillating tension of belonging and not belonging without collapsing into the either/or polarity.

References

Adelman, A. J. (2013). The hand of fate: on mourning the death of a patient. In A. J. Adelman & K. L. Malawista (Eds.), *The therapist in mourning: f*rom the f*ar away nearby* (pp. 73–92). New York: Columbia University Press.

Bos. J., Park, D. W., & Pietikainen, P. (2005). Strategic self-marginalization: the case of psychoanalysis. *Journal of History and Behavioral Science, 41*(3), 207–224.

Carveth, D. L. (2018). *Psychoanalytic thinking: a dialectical critique of contemporary theory and practice.* Abingdon: Routledge.

Green, A. (2005). The illusion of common ground and mythical pluralism. *International Journal of Psychoanalysis, 86*(3), 627–632.

Hegel, G. W. F. (2013). *Hegel's aesthetics: a critical exposition (abridged)* (G. W. F. Hegel, Ed.). New York: Classics US. Originally published 1835.

Kirsner, D. (1999). Life among the analysts. *Free Associations, 7*(3), 416–436.

Lewis, C. S. (1944). *The inner ring.* Memorial lecture at King's College, University of London, London, UK.

McDougall, J. (1995). *The many faces of Eros: a psychoanalytic exploration of human sexuality.* New York and London: W. W. Norton.

McLaughlin, N. (2001). Optimal marginality: innovation and orthodoxy in Fromm's revision of psychoanalysis. *Sociological Quarterly, 42*(2), 271–288.

Reik, T. (1948). *Listening with the third ear: the inner experience of a psychoanalyst.* New York: Straus, Giroux.

Robles, M. (2013). *Fanaticism in psychoanalysis: upheavals in the psychoanalytical institutions.* London: Karnac.

Simmel, G. (1971). The stranger. In D. N. Levine (Ed.), *On individuality and social forms* (pp. 143–149). Chicago: University of Chicago Press. Originally published 1908.

Starr, K. E., & Aron, L. (2013). Deconstructing the psychotherapy/psychoanalysis binary: the case for optimal marginality. *Psychoanalytic Perspectives, 10*(2), 336–349.

Stepansky, P. E. (2009). *Psychoanalysis at the margins.* New York: Other Press.

19 Psychoanalysis and the disavowal of classism

John V. O'Leary

> Feelings about class are suffused with tensions: between ethical and economic evaluation; between status and worth; between judgements of moral luck and worth in terms of deserved and undeserved advantages and disadvantages; between acknowledgements of injustice and defensive rationalization and evasion; and between recognizing class as ethically problematic yet being able to do little or nothing about it.
>
> (Sayer, 2005, p. 225)

On a summer day in 1979 when I was notified of my acceptance into the William Alanson White Institute for psychoanalytic training, I did something I have never done before or since. Indeed, something I hardly imagined I would ever do. I went to the classic building at 20 West 74th Street, got down on my knees, and kissed the steps. I cared little who saw me. Like the proverbial nineteenth-century immigrant encountering the new soil of America, I was overwhelmed by gratitude and hope. I knew that the next four years would change my life. It would change me professionally, intellectually, and would catapult me into a new social status. Having lived the West Side Story of gangs, drugs, alcoholism, neglect, and working-class poverty, I felt among the chosen. Yes, I was helped along by a talent for sports, a dad who believed in education, and the unsparing discipline imposed by an extensive Catholic school education. Still, I knelt at this port of entry, hat in hand.

And how did these dreams play out, given that choice some thirty-nine years ago? My two previous careers were working in New York State clinics servicing seriously mentally ill patients and teaching a variety of different psychology courses as a full-time college professor for ten years. My tenure at White, with its diversity, its small and intimate classes, its old-world feel, suited me perfectly. I came to love the classes. With a few exceptions, I loved the supervision and learned much from my training analyst, especially once I was able to leave my first assigned analyst. And how has it been since? I did gain a great deal intellectually; discovered the power of the unconscious, the importance of childhood, the significance of dreams; learned how to be confident and at the same time humble in the analytic work; and learned how to tolerate ambiguity and uncertainty. I also became interested in writing and developed some of my closest friends while a candidate. The Institute has truly been a second home to me. It also counts that through my private practice I was able to send two children to private schools and college and leave them debt free at graduation. I am also proud that I never refused a patient because of money.

And what are the costs? Sometimes I wonder at being part of a movement that the rest of the world sees as anachronistic, a relic of the past. There also exists a long history of the natural-scientific critique of psychoanalysis, which has been canonized in every contemporary textbook of psychology (Teo, 2011). Then I remind myself of how much I love string theory, a unified theory of the universe, certainly odd, certainly idiosyncratic (Greene, 1999). For all the time it's been around and all the good math attached to it and its sweeping elegance, it has not been able to predict anything. Explain, yes; describe, yes; predict, no. Nonetheless, psychoanalysis, unlike my fascination with astronomy, has allowed me a career of helping people.

While the specifics may differ, I know that this journey is similar for many of you readers. Several of you came from immigrant and working-class homes. Some of you come from middle-class homes and are now well established within the upper-middle class with yearly incomes between $100,000 and $200,000. In terms of educational achievement (PhDs, postgraduate degrees—a significant variable tied to social class), you are easily among the top 1 percent.

My purpose in writing this chapter is to provide greater clarity around this important construct and to explain why we analysts have neglected it for so long. There are compelling reasons why we need to engage it from a clinical, moral, and social perspective. Finally, I also want to explore why we have been negligent around treating the poor.

Social class can be understood as a multi-determined (wealth, income, educational achievement, neighborhood, aspirational language), socially constructed hierarchical classification system whereby we assign power, prestige, deference, and privilege to people depending on how high up they are. While existing on a continuum, it has become increasingly popular to divide American society into five social classes that roughly correspond to the Poor, the Working Class, the Lower-Middle Class, the Upper-Middle Class, and the Wealthy. This quantitative system underplays the role of subjective determinations of class belonging. It also diminishes more objective criteria such as the role of being born wealthy, years of education, housing, and patterns of behavior, although many of the latter are significantly correlated with income. "Classism" is the term that captures the evaluative, action component of social class. It is similar to the way "racism" captures the discriminatory element of race. **What seems crucial is that, historically, class has often served as a moral designation of a person's value or worth. It is therefore highly personal. We cannot afford a psychoanalysis that ignores it!**

The lower end of the top 20 percent is a salary of $117,000, one that includes professionals, college professors, mid-level executives, and highly trained mental health professionals (Reeves, 2017; Bui, 2014). We are not the millionaires or billionaires (top 1 percent), but we wield a lot of influence as members of the top 20 percent, not only financially but as thought leaders. Reeves, the Brookings Institute author of *Dream Hoarders*, argues that belonging to that class also shapes how we see our world. For example, we are more likely to hold the belief that we live in a meritocracy. If we moved up the status hierarchy and are a little more privileged, we earned it by dint of sacrifice and discipline. This may harden us to the plight of the working class and the middle class—who appear **not** as diligent and hard-working. It also has the effect of softening our critique regarding the increasing power and influence of the 1 percent.

As clinicians, we have traditionally disavowed social class (Ryan, 2017; Whitman-Raymond, 2009; Layton, Hollander, & Gutwell, 2006), despite what we know about our personal trajectories. "Class can also arouse feelings of embarrassment, guilt, envy, anger, contempt. It can be a source of great defensiveness, and inhibition, and also of solidarity and belonging" (Ryan, 2017). Class creates a dividedness within the person: a split between the conscious understanding of the injustice or unequal opportunities and an inner conviction of personal responsibility and self-blame (Ryan, 2017; Sennett & Cobb, 1972). And there is the issue of shame. Whitman-Raymond (2009) has done an excellent job of reminding us of the many places in the psychoanalytic dyad where the shame of difference can contaminate effective communication. For example, we may feel deeply ashamed of our envy of wealthier patients. Likewise, we can fail to empathize with patients who had to drop out of school or who had trouble with the law. Other reasons include our general tendency as Americans to see ourselves as part of that great middle class, that is, the historical myth that except for a few people at both extremes we are a nation of equals. This belief can facilitate our ignoring the plight of the poor and the excesses of the 1 percent, as well as blur the wide range of difference in the middle.

Clinical case

The patient I wish to discuss seems to have a viscerally negative effect on me that I believe is class generated. He is a white male, a Trump supporter—although he does not fully own this latter designation. He is, however, a committed devotee of Jordan Peterson, a self-fashioned conservative who gained fame attacking the Canadian government for conceding to the needs of its gay and transgender community. My patient's presenting problem was hoarding. In the first session, he showed me several pictures of his apartment with an overwhelming amount of clutter. I have had hoarders before, but generally they kept me at a distance from their messiness. The pictures he showed were very graphic. I took him on in part because he had been a student of mine many years ago when I was a college professor.

This patient, who is sixty-six, has a long history of stalking an old girlfriend. He has been issued summonses and Orders of Protection by the police for this behavior. He believes he is the father of a child she had, but the evidence for that is very circumstantial. The mother denies his paternity claims. The patient is extremely poor and earns less than $13,000 a year. He pays for treatment with Medicare but cannot afford the supplement. I see him on a once-a-week basis. The patient has a two-room apartment. He earns extra money by renting out one of the rooms. His tenant has complained of bedbugs. Recently, the tenant moved out, complaining he had been bitten by the bedbugs. My patient says he has had bedbugs before and knows how to get rid of them. I have expressed concerns about his bringing the bedbugs into my office.

This patient has yelled at me on a couple of occasions, the most recent for not remembering a fact about his alleged son. He claims to have told me that on one occasion he had seen his son coming out from school and followed him for about an hour. When I failed to remember the event, he accused me in an angry manner of going senile. I reacted defensively and told him he could not yell at me like that. To myself, I could not imagine forgetting an action like his following his son around the city, as it reminded me so powerfully of the stalking of his girlfriend of long standing. It turned out I was wrong. I was to discover that the patient had indeed told me this story several months before. It tallied with my notes on the day of the session in question. I admitted my failure to remember and said I would try to listen more closely. I said I had come to see that I had not been closely listening because I was so bothered by a lot of his behaviors. He, in turn, was moved by my apology and admitted he had a problem with losing control when he was angry. This admission was to figure importantly in later work on the pervasiveness of his anger.

My point in telling this story is not to discuss his treatment but to let the reader in on some distinctive countertransference that come up when treating members of a different social class. I think this patient got less than optimal treatment for a number of reasons. He dressed in a way that was distinctively working class. For example, he had a penchant for white tee shirts and pants pulled up a tad too high. Second, I was not used to working with people who had clashes with the police department. If you were in trouble with the police, something **had** to be terribly wrong. Third, his right-wing political leanings made me think he was stereotypical and black-and-white in his thinking. He was also likely to be a racist, although I have zero evidence for that. When he threatened to quit on the day of our fight, I was quick to think "good riddance." After all, I was being paid so little for seeing him. Problems with bedbugs are problems of the poor. The upper classes and the rich can afford expensive exterminators, and their premises are built in a way that prevents the rapid spread of these creatures. The problem itself disgusted me. I could go on. I think you get the point. We carry these biases without being conscious of them. None of us is consciously neglectful … but neglectful and sometimes hurtful we are, nonetheless.

Doing analytic therapy with the poor

Our colleagues in the counseling psychology community have written extensively about classism and its role in psychotherapy. It is part of a much more extensive program of dealing with diversity issues (Sue, 2019; Liu, Soleck, Geoff, et al., 2004; Thompson, Cole, & Nitzarim, 2012). They have been working in this field for nearly forty years. Hundreds of research programs have been launched. Educational and training programs whose goal is "cultural competence" have been launched. Several top universities like Columbia have been in the vanguard of this effort. There have been, in fact, recent efforts toward systematically integrating sociocultural issues with psychoanalytic theory (Tummala-Narra, 2015). However, there is a lack of empirical research examining the components of culturally informed psychoanalytic psychotherapy. Many of the psychoanalysts in Tummala-Narra and colleagues' (2018) study offered that they had a resistance to many of the features of cross-cultural training. New York psychoanalysts interviewed in this study said things like:

> Cultural competence is needed … to carve out a space for something that White people have not wanted to create room for … but it becomes commodified, and I think that it gets taught in ways that are not that helpful. So, I both am a proponent of it and a critic of it as reductionistic.
>
> (p. 48)

Or again, "It's not about learning that Japanese people do this, or people from Malaysia do that, or people from the West Indies think this way. It's not about homogenizing the whole culture" (p. 48). Another voice said:

> I am also very wary about cookbook assumptions about cultures, about the way people so readily say or think, "Hispanics have this value or assumption, … Caribbean Blacks have this kind of attitude, … South Asians have this kind of family structure, … Working class men have this stance toward women," and so forth. We are caught in a kind of bind here. We do need to know these general cultural accounts and differences and do need to take them into account in the ways we hear and interact with our patients. But at the same time, we need to be deeply skeptical about the ways these accounts lend themselves to stereotypes.
>
> (p. 50)

Perhaps psychoanalysis is largely a middle-class (even upper-middle-class) enterprise and perhaps that is the audience that it is ideally suited for. These analysands tend to be highly verbal, introspective, well educated, disciplined in their personal lives, and imaginative, with the power and ability to sneak away from work several times a week, and they can afford to pay fees that are commensurate with the long years of training that analysts typically bring. Is this a state of affairs that we should be ashamed about?

Furthermore, Smith (2005) has offered many reasons why middle- and upper-middle-class therapists may not want to work with the poor. These class-related attitudinal barriers organize themselves into four overlapping themes: (1) Poor people are faced with so many day-to-day problems that they have no use for what a psychoanalyst has to offer. What they need assistance with is identifying resources and practical problem-solving. (2) Your intervention will be paltry given what they are up against. This induces a sense of failure in the analyst. What analyst wants that? (3) Working in a poor community takes away the comfort of not knowing how poor people live. Those whose jobs bring them into immediate touch with the poor experience this harshness, squalor, and danger more directly. It is difficult and hard work. (4) Conventional psychological services are neither familiar to nor widely accepted in the cultures of many working-class communities. Even poor people who could benefit will not be likely to use them. They may feel more at home with the local minister.

Many arguments could be put forward to counter these beliefs, and Smith (2005) does exactly that in her compelling paper. There may be some truth to each of these assumptions. Perhaps the underlying question should be: what do we owe the poor? What is the just and honorable thing to do? Tolstoy says that all we need for evil to triumph (in this case, the poor to go under-treated) is for good men to do nothing. The ethical code for psychoanalysts has the following imperative: "The psychoanalyst is expected to treat patients and their families, students and colleagues with respect and care. Discrimination on the basis of age, disability, ethnicity, gender, race, religion, sexual orientation or socioeconomic status is ethically unacceptable" (apsa.org code of ethics, Section 2; Apsa.org, n.d.). Does the well-substantiated preference for working with the middle class constitute discrimination? I believe it does, although I do not believe it is conscious discrimination. I remember giving a paper about race and psychoanalysis in New Zealand and someone from the audience offered the following analogy, "I keep my store open for all comers. I never turn down a customer. They can choose to come or not to come. I will not go out of my way to pressure them." This attitude parallels the attitude of many of my colleagues. "If they can afford my fee and can accept the rules (frame), they are welcome." Surely this attitude is not deliberately classist or discriminatory. It might reflect a common presumption that the suffering of the poor is not of my making or the meritocratic posture that they are somehow choosing to remain poor through laziness or poor choices. At the other end, there is the argument that we as practitioners should focus our efforts where there is the greatest need, which is clearly in the direction of the working class and the poor.

Also, as psychoanalysts, do we have an ethical duty **not** to collude with the ideologies of our time related to individualism and class oppression? In practice, this means exploration of our own internalized political framework of ideas, which, left unchallenged, would probably be a reflection of the dominant ideology. Our unexamined unconscious biases would continue to influence our interpretations. Might we acknowledge a need to recognize the reality of institutional classism (Liu, 2002) and to see psychoanalytic therapy as a moral, political, and existential activity rather than a scientific, expert-led one?

Differences in the way rich and poor see their world

We already know that poor people experience more stress, are more likely to die an early death, are exposed to more physical danger, experience more divorces, and are generally less happy. They are also far more likely to have serious mental illnesses like depression and schizophrenia and are more likely to suffer from addictions. Whereas the country as a whole is dealing with an epidemic of obesity, it affects the poor, with all its collateral damage, in much greater numbers (Curtis, in press; Crosnoe & Dunifon, 2017). They are also less likely to engage mental health services. When in treatment, they drop out sooner (Liu, 2002; Liu, Ali, Soleck, et al., 2004).

Are rich and poor different in how they think about things, how they process their world? I spoke earlier of the stronger belief in meritocracy among the upper middle class and the wealthy. There is growing debate in the field as to whether we can with sufficient precision correlate specific beliefs—even character traits—with membership of different social classes. This is made difficult by the differing views among scholars as to how many social classes there are, as to the considerable differences between urban and rural communities, and as to which variables (e.g., income vs. wealth) should be used to define distinctive classes. There is also a fluidity to social class where it can change dramatically in the course of a lifetime. The picture is further complicated by the multiplicity of terms that can be seen as a function of class. Bourdieu's valuable introduction of terms like "social capital" (the network of powerful friendships you have) and "cultural capital" (intellectual and aesthetic skills) is an example in kind. We could also argue that the world is seldom experienced as something that includes pure identities; that is, intersectionality is the more common event. For example, one encounters someone who is black, poor, and female. We are less likely to encounter the homogeneous, categorically distinctive other. We are strongly indebted to Liu and colleagues (2004), who have provided the most rigorous description of the complexities of the concept and culture of social class.

Notwithstanding the definitional complexities of class, we have come to see that the wealthy and the poor in our country have some deep differences in the ways they see things, which in turn causes them to act differently—often in ways that make for profound misunderstandings and promote stereotypical kinds of thinking.

Current research (Kraus, Piff, Mendoza-Denton, et.al., 2012) has shown that lower social class is associated with a contextualist orientation toward understanding personal and social outcomes. This explanatory tendency is linked to viewing the world as less controllable. In other words, external circumstances play a much bigger role for the poor. We can see how social class differences lead to differences in the way individuals construe and interpret their social environments and the events that impact their lives.

A second consistent finding is the greater amount of empathy expressed by the poor. The rationale here is that the poor have more powerful authorities in their sphere of influence, such as landlords, bosses, and debtors. This makes for a higher payoff value for reading what is in the mind of others; that is, their mood, their compassion, and their anger.

Smith (2005) suggests that the poor may be both more dependent and more interdependent than the wealthy. Wealthy people simply hire those they need to perform certain tasks. When they remodel the house, for example, they bring in contractors and other experts that they pay for. The poor depend more on one another to help out. These findings also suggest that cultural context and its resulting mental habits allow people of higher classes to disconnect from others' concerns, suggest Stellar and colleagues (2012). You have to carefully attend to other people—to what they're thinking, feeling, and saying—if you are going to be compassionate. The wealthy don't have to do that as much, argue these authors, because the context of their lives allows them to disengage, to leave the scene. In other words, having more material goods, money, and free time makes it easier for wealthy people to buy their way out of problems and avoid certain communal social interactions or take a vacation when things get stressful.

Jensen (2012) has studied the culture of working and middle classes in urban and rural America and makes the very useful distinction between *belonging* vs. *becoming*. Within this "belonging" construct, working-class people are more likely to desire acceptance by those in their immediate surroundings—their families, those in the neighborhood, and their friends. They highly value these relationships and realize that separation (being seen as special in school, leaving friends and family behind to go off to college) creates ruptures to that sense of belonging and kinship. Becoming, on the other hand, describes a value that is highly endorsed in middle-class structures. It implies that everyone is striving to be the best they can be. It affirms individual self-determination even when that may set you against the needs of others. In Jensen's words, "the higher their status and the longer people have belonged to the American middle class, the more individuality, competition, the pursuit of public excellence, and having power over others figure significantly into what feels right" (p. 61). Jensen holds that psychotherapy frequently supports these more middle-class features, such as individualism, psychological mindedness, and ego strength.

Basil Bernstein (1971) has carried this concept over to styles of communication. When he compared the two classes, they differed greatly. The speech of working-class people has both less vocabulary and fewer ways of putting words together. Their language is often less exacting, with a more frequent use of non-verbal cues (meaningful glances; more variation of vocal tones, volume, and pace). These more restricted codes of the working class boil communication down to essential images and meanings trying to create a more intimate connection between the speaker and the listener. In contrast, the middle-class group used language to display their individual ability to think and argue and uncover differences within the group.

One psychological plus may be that people with power and influence have more freedom to be themselves without worrying about adjusting to others' expectations or wishes. A 2011 study by Kraus in the *Journal of Experimental Social Psychology*, for instance, found that people with more self-defined power were more likely than low-power people to report having a coherent self-view. Having influence and control is really freeing. High-power people stay authentically the same person no matter the context. But people who are relatively low-power change little aspects of themselves because having low power means having to adapt and fit into different contexts.

By paying more attention to class and class embeddedness, psychoanalysis would accomplish the following: First, we as analysts would engage people in their lived reality; that is, how much they can afford to pay in their actual circumstances. Second, we would become more attuned to the day-to-day insults and shaming that come about because of abrasions that occur on the edge of social class. In this past election, many totally missed how much suffering was going on for the working class. Third, we would be better attuned to subtle signs of class difference in the transference—as, for example, when an analyst introduces an original painting into their office. For some patients, this action might be as important as the experience of an analyst's pregnancy or heart condition—matters that have been extensively written about. Fourth, we would be better able to recognize class-induced trauma, such as when someone makes a long-term vow as a result of early poverty that they will never be poor again. Fifth, we might take more seriously why patients of color do not want to engage us even when we are inviting—they may feel we are not going to understand them. Our upper-middle-class mores may not be just shaming but irrelevant to their class-based interests and needs. Sixth, in stretching the boundaries of social class, we might look for ways that us analysts can better reach the poor. We may be able to return to a period like Freud's when the poor could receive analytic treatment, unlike today, when their options at public clinics are mostly medication and short-term cognitive behavioral treatment. On the other hand, I am proud of the tradition where many institutes provide low-cost analytic treatment for the poor. Seventh, it might become a tool for getting someone more politically or socially engaged. Isolation and lack of engagement are tied to many of the problems in living that we face. Eighth, it might open a more honest dialogue in the analytic community about money and fees—another subject we find it difficult to talk about. Ninth, we might become better attuned to those unconscious derivatives like eruptions of shame and humiliation that signal a transference-countertransference enactment. These derivatives were evident in the case history mentioned earlier. Finally, it might create a better understanding of our own class origins and how they may be affecting our view of the plights or successes of others.

Overall, we need to see social class—and our own class embeddedness—as some of the most powerful factors affecting how people feel about themselves, as well as gauge their reality in a social world. We need to learn how to work psychoanalytically in a manner that includes greater recognition of the social world without losing the complexities and nuances of more traditional psychoanalytic work.

References

Apsa.org. (n.d.). Code of Ethics. Principles and Standards of Ethics for Psychoanalysts, Section 2, Respect for Persons and Nondiscrimination.

Aron, L., & Starr, S. (2012). *A psychotherapy for the people: towards a progressive psychoanalysis*. New York: Routledge.

Bernstein, B. (1971). *Class, codes, and control: Vol. 1 theoretical studies towards a sociology of language*. London: Routledge.

Bourdieu, P. (1984). *Distinction: a social critique of the judgement of taste*. Cambridge, MA: Harvard University Press.

Bui, Q. (2014, May 5). Most Americans make it to the top 20% (at least for a while). *Planet Money: The Economy Explained*, NPR.

Crosnoe, R., & Dunifon, R. (2017). A developmental perspective on the link between parent's employment and children's obesity. *American Psychologist, 72*(5), 474–486.

Curtis, R. C. (in press). Distributive justice: the racial gap between the rich and poor, health, and education. In J. L. Chin, E Garcia, & A. Blume (Eds.), *The psychology of inequity*. Santa Barbara: Praeger Press.

Greene, B. (1999). *The elegant universe*. New York: W. W. Norton.

Jensen, B. (2012). *Reading classes: on culture and classism in America*. Ithaca: Cornell University Press.

Kraus, M. (2011). The power to be me: power elevates self-concept consistency and authority. *Journal of Experimental Social Psychology, 47*, 974–980.

Kraus, M., Piff, P., Mendoza-Denton, R., Rheinschmidf, M., & Keitner, D. (2012). Social class, solipsism, and contextualism: how the rich are different from the poor. *Psychological Review, 119*(3), 546–572.

Layton, L., Hollander, N., & Gutwell, S. (2006). *Psychoanalysis, class and politics: encounters in the clinical setting*. New York: Routledge.

Liu, W. (2002). The social class-related experiences of men: integrating theory and practice. *Professional Psychology: Research and Practice, 33*(1), 355–360.

Liu, W., Ali, R., Soleck, G., Hopps, J., Kwesi, D., & Pickett, T. (2004). Using social class in counseling psychology research. *Journal of Counseling Psychology, 51*(1), 3–18.

Reeves, R. (2017). *Dream hoarders: how the American upper middle class is leaving everyone else in the dust, why that is a problem, and what to do about it*. Washington, DC: Brookings Institution Press.

Ryan, J. (2017). *Class and psychoanalysis: landscapes of inequality*. New York: Routledge.

Sayer, A. (2005). *The moral significance of class*. Cambridge: Cambridge University Press.

Sennett, R., & Cobb, J. (1972). *The hidden injuries of class*. New York: W. W. Norton.

Smith, L. (2005). Psychotherapy, classism, and the poor. *American Psychologist, 60*(7), 687–696.

Stellar, J. E., Manzo, V. M., Krauss, M. W., & Keltner, D. (2012). Class and compassion: socio-economic factors predict responses to suffering. *Emotion, 12*, 444–459.

Sue, D. W. (2019). *Counseling the culturally diverse* (8th ed.). Hoboken: John Wiley.

Teo, T. (2011). Radical philosophical critique and critical thinking in psychology. *Journal of Theoretical and Philosophical Psychology, 31*(3), 193–199.

Thompson, M., Cole, O., & Nitzarim, R. (2012). Recognizing social class in the psychotherapy relationship: a grounded theory exploration of low-income clients. *Journal of Counseling Psychology, 58*(2), 208–221.

Tummala-Narra, P. (2015). Cultural competence as a core emphasis of psychoanalytic psychotherapy. *Psychoanalytic Psychology, 32*, 275–292.

Tummala-Narra, P., Claudius, M., Lentendre, P. J., Sarbre, E., Teran, V., & Villaba, W. (2018). Conceptualizations of cultural competence in psychotherapy. *Psychoanalytic Psychology, 35*, 46–59.

Whitman-Raymond, L. (2009). The influence of class in the therapeutic dyad. *Contemporary Psychoanalysis, 4*, 429–443.

20 To belong broadly or affiliate narrowly?

Psychoanalysis' pluralism problem

Brent Willock

August 11, 2017. Charlottesville, Virginia. A mob of angry white men marches determinedly down a dusky street. Torches held high, they holler angrily, "The Jews will not replace us!" This shocking video clip plays repeatedly on television news broadcasts over the next several weeks. Afterwards, it appears sporadically, continuing to assault many viewers' sensibilities.

For many, this vulgar vignette seemed too awful to be real. Surely this outrage could not be happening in a world that has supposedly evolved since the Third Reich. To these viewers, the repeating Charlottesville clips are like a bad dream, a recurrent nightmare.

What if we regarded these striking images as just that—as troubling oneiric outpourings? Where might that perspective lead us? Could it help us to further comprehend this deeply perturbing phenomenon?

Considering the menacing chanters' slogan as dream-like verbalization might permit us to take it not just as a frightening demand or a frightened threat. Their bitter slogan could also be perceived as a factual statement. Surely they are right. Jews will not replace those troubled men. No doubt they are correct. Jews have neither the desire nor the intention of displacing them.

Primary processes and defenses, like displacement and condensation, are central to dream formation (Freud, 1900/1953). Could those protesters' agitated chant involve such psychic operations? Might they have been displacing their anxiety and rage concerning other possible, more likely replacers onto Jews?

As multinational corporations continue relocating factories abroad in search of greater profits, poorly paid laborers in countries such as China, Mexico, and India might well be used to replace many of these anxious, angry men. Tireless robots possessing astounding artificial intelligence might also displace them to a devastating degree. Economic forecasters increasingly predict that most jobs will before long be taken over by these proliferating bots.

Might the Charlottesville mob be displacing angst and anger about their current, historical, and anticipated economic difficulties onto a scapegoat, the Jews, that happens to be so much more convenient than faraway foreign workers? This handy minority is much more capable of absorbing projected terror and pain than any bot ever could. Might their rage against Jews reflect a displacement of hostility that would otherwise have been directed at corporate decision-makers who abruptly close factories, relocating them without many or any second thoughts to countries with weaker pollution standards, cheaper labor, and other cost-saving factors?

Redirecting rage away from corporations also helps maintain the illusion that those who run the country's businesses are purely and simply good people, like benevolent parents whom we may not always comprehend very well but surely can trust unquestioningly. Such denial and displacement is a variation on Fairbairn's (1952) "moral defense" that children often deploy in order to keep on going in unloving homes. Believing they or some bullied scapegoat must be the bad entity—not their parents or corporations—these marchers may have been embracing a variation on the adage that it is better to be a sinner in a world governed by God than to be an innocent in a world run by Satan. They may feel it is less awful to be agitated thugs in a world ruled by loving parents, wise capitalists, and a magnificent deity than to be vulnerable beings trembling in a realm run by grossly flawed parents, an exploitative ruling class, and some demonic deity like the one portrayed in the Bible when God and Satan teamed up to carry out a sadistic experiment on poor old Job.

In exchange for their dazzling feats of displacement, members of the Charlottesville mob would acquire a potent sense of belonging to a dangerous assembly of self-righteous haters happily targeting a vulnerable group. Like other minorities, Jews are relatively safe to bully. Sheer numbers buttress the majority, propping up their faltering sense of profound insecurity in a rapidly changing world. Men who feel increasingly tormented by fears that they no longer have a secure place in the American socioeconomic dream can regain some feeling of power by collectively projecting their threatened selves into the handy Jewish community. These others can feel terrified instead of us. They can and will replace us in that regard, and so they should, the reasoning goes. Let them carry the horrific pain and anxiety that we cannot bear.

The marchers may dimly sense that those running the American economy have let them down, abandoning them without any concern for the impact of their actions on those lower down the socioeconomic ladder. They can overlook that inconvenient thought by focusing their attention on preferred heroes with proven talents for mobilizing manic masses. Hitler, for example, not only shared the Charlottesville gang's fondness for defensive displacement and genocide but also provided many good jobs that underpinned the righteous war effort. Surely he, or someone with similar talents, would never let Aryans down. Surely some Führer can be trusted to assist us in displacing all his and our hostility onto various minorities. That fearless leader will serve as a beacon of dark light, a loving father figure for his chosen race. Circle the wagons. Affiliate narrowly. Fight the good fight. Attack designated outgroups. "The Jews will not replace us!"

One route or many to the science and profession of psychoanalysis?

It seems like only yesterday that American psychologists launched a lawsuit against the American Psychoanalytic Association and other groups that had long collaborated to prevent them from becoming psychoanalysts and practicing their profession autonomously. In real time, it has been about four decades since that battle was fought and won. Back then, the ruling psychoanalytic class was almost entirely medical. They seemed to think: "Psychoanalytic psychologists will not replace us! They will not rob us of our patients, teaching positions, income, and ingroup prestige!"

A few psychologists had been permitted to train at some mainstream American psychoanalytic institutes before the lawsuit, but they had to accept the label of Research Psychoanalyst. They were not supposed to practice post-graduation unless supervised by a physician. They were expected to contribute to psycho-analysis through writing, teaching, and research. They had to understand and accept that they could never fully belong to the psychoanalytic establishment.

Ultimately, psychologists struggling against the oppressive status quo prevailed. Many now believe that the conservative psychoanalytic groups that fought against these progressive changes were actually saved by the psychologists. Increasingly, institutes were having serious problems attracting suitable psychiatrists willing to undergo lengthy, expensive, rigorous training to become analysts. The new gen-eration of psychiatrists was being taught to devalue analysis in favor of biological psychiatry. This new pedagogical direction was facilitated by the fact that one could make many times as much money prescribing medications as opposed to conducting psychoanalyses.

The influx of psychologists into the medical institutes enabled them to have enough candidates and graduates to keep operating. Psychologists no longer had to be segregated under the label of research (non)members. This feared integra-tion turned out to be a blessing for the conservative institutes, at least in some ways. Moving from a narrow definition of who could belong to a more inclu-sive understanding was not, after all, the dismal beginning of the end but, rather, merely the end of the beginning phase of American psychoanalysis.

Once the doors to the profession were opened to psychologists, it became pos-sible for members of other groups to apply for admittance and eventually belong. Social workers, marriage and family counsellors, and others could now be viewed as qualified applicants for training. Individuals from academia could also find routes to becoming fully qualified psychoanalysts. At last, the discipline was becoming the rich, multidisciplinary collective that Freud had envisioned.

Caste and class warfare

Despite these beneficial deconstrictions, many institutes continue to be divided into those members who truly belong and outsiders. These distinctions are no longer determined so much by one's disciplinary background as by one's orien-tation. Sexual orientation no longer matters so much, but clinico-theoretical perspective still does. At an ego psychological institute, for example, a few self psychologists, Kleinians, Bionians, relational psychoanalysts, and so forth may be tolerated, devalued, or embraced as exotics who may occasionally contribute something interesting and, therefore, of value, so long as they understand their particular place and do not seek to have much influence. (For a description of the contributions of these diverse psychoanalytic groups to the evolving discipline, see Mitchell & Black, 1995.)

In contrast to this continuing ingroup/outgroup mentality, I and some of my colleagues have advocated for a comparative-integrative psychoanalysis (Willock, 2007). Rather than valorizing any one privileged perspective, the comparative-integrative approach emphasizes dialogue between diverse viewpoints. In a comparative-integrative institute, one belongs to a stimulating conversation rather than to a rigid school of thought. Many of us believe that the comparative-integrative perspective needs to be enshrined at the core of an institute's philosophy, thereby permeating all the group's activities. The goal of this explicit commitment is to create a more comprehensive, valid, sophisticated, and useful discipline.

Kleinians will not replace us! Self psychologists will not replace us! Relational psychoanalysts will not replace us! Demonized new and not-so-new perspectives have historically often been feared, loathed, and excluded by the mainstream. For example, the doyen of American ego psychology, David Rapaport (1959/1967), proclaimed that "The 'theory' of object relations evolved by Melanie Klein and her followers is not an ego psychology but an id mythology" (p. 750n). Reflecting the common prejudice of his time and place, his stance would hardly encourage comparative investigation and would make integration virtually unthinkable. Rapaport's brilliant student, Roy Schafer (1976), opined authoritatively, in sync with his mentor, that "Klein and her so-called English school ... carried the reifications of metapsychology to a grotesque extreme" (p. 3).

Later, Schafer (1983) became a vigorous advocate for a more open-minded, comparative psychoanalytic viewpoint. He had come to realize that he had been "indoctrinated to consider Kleinian analysis ... as a mythology or demonology" and that "dutifully, I went even further" (1997, p. 427). In time, Schafer came to believe that Kleinians actually had their own ego psychology based on object relations. Without explicitly saying it, he (1994) began moving toward a comparative-integrative perspective, considering at least contemporary London Kleinians to be *Kleinian Freudians*, related to, integrated with, not alien from, traditional Freudians.

When idealized figures like Roy Schafer, Otto Kernberg, and Thomas Ogden started to publicly endorse Kleinian contributions, traditional Freudian contempt began to weaken. Today, Klein is widely considered cool, even though, appropriately, her school is regarded by many as a body of thought that contains both wheat and chaff, like all perspectives.

While Schafer's term, Kleinian Freudians, is comparative-integrative, he did not see himself that way. Or at least he did not see himself consistently that way. At IPA's Rome Congress, he (1990) declared: "I do not believe that common ground can be found." Instead, "It is best to regard the two approaches [Freudian and Kleinian] as incommensurable" (1994, p. 474).

Pondering why comparative analysis was so undeveloped, Schafer (1983) concluded that it was because analyzing the structure of thought in just one school is formidable. Analysts within an orientation cannot agree on basic assumptions, relationships between propositions, what constitutes evidence, the relationship between evidence and practice, and so forth. These problems are compounded when comparing different schools. He therefore settled for the notion that while it is important to pay attention to what different perspectives propose in order to guard against one's fictions becoming myths, one needs "a firm base, a consistent orientation, a defined culture of one's own in which to work" (1983, p. 285). From that point of view, comparative psychoanalysis, let alone comparative-integrative analysis, would not be a good place to commence training.

Schafer's beliefs about the enormous obstacles one would have to tackle and overcome to begin even a comparative approach to psychoanalysis sound daunting indeed. One can, however, approach the pluralism problem in less intimidating ways. A comparative-integrative perspective need not be overwhelming. It can be the opposite of intimidating.

Many feel comparative psychoanalysis is fine, even admirable, but they may balk at the idea of integration. How can we address this integration anxiety? If we consult the impressive US civil rights movement, we might learn that integration ultimately need not be as frightening as we may originally fear. In the psychoanalytic field, for starters, it could suffice to get all theoretical orientations into the same schoolhouse, much as happened via legislation in American schools. This basic step constitutes a first stage of integration. When this is accomplished, diverse psychoanalytic perspectives have the opportunity to hesitantly, or zestfully, become familiar with one another. This familiarity may increase over time and lead to something much more interesting than contempt. Just as white and black students often learn from each others' cultures, enriching their lives, so, too, can analytic subcultures benefit from each other. Through this process, each school of thought may gradually become broader, wiser, less narrow-minded and rigid.

Thanks to influential figures like Schafer, Freudians can increasingly regard Kleinians collegially as Kleinian Freudians rather than as devalued, despised aliens. Freudians and others may come, and they may already be regarding themselves as expanding into an ever broader identity under the umbrella of comparative-integrative psychoanalysis that includes those with special interest in other perspectives, such as British object relations, self psychology, and relational psychoanalysis. In this transition, some self psychologists, for example, are beginning to view themselves as relational self psychologists. Ultimately, most of these single or compound monikers may gradually wither away as more and more analysts began to understand themselves as comparative-integrative psychoanalysts.

Psychoanalysts who came of age under the auspices of some new orientation may increasingly be able, with a comparative-integrative outlook, to find treasures in older schools of thought that they may have been taught to regard with suspicion or hostility. In Schafer's words, after one has become an analyst "of one persuasion or another" (1983, p. 281), something peculiar happens.

There are important things you begin to see in your work that your teachers told you were not there or were not important; or else they never led you to expect to see them and so, when you do see them, they startle and dismay you ... You may for a time simply try to explain them away. At some point, however, you may face them directly and begin to raise some serious constructive questions about the tradition within which you work.

(p. 286)

"The Jews will not replace us!" One might see the Jews as having helped to usefully challenge and expand previous pagan religions, including their own. Christianity, in turn, may have contributed ideas capable of enriching pagan, Jewish, and other belief systems. At the same time, the best pagan traditions may continue to enliven Christian, Jewish, and other perspectives. The pagan habit of bringing evergreen trees indoors during the dark winter months continues to be a hit in many quarters. Openminded citizens can learn from diverse cultures, beliefs, and traditions, each with its numerous strengths and weaknesses. Comparative-integrative dialogue facilitates separating each group's wheat from its chaff, ultimately yielding more nutritious products.

The Kleinians ... the British object relations ... the self psychologists ... the relational psychoanalysts ... will not replace us! Hopefully these frightened, sometimes intimidating declarations will become less adamant, less frequent, and less self-destructive to our discipline. To a considerable extent, Kleinians have "replaced" (i.e., broadened) our narrow Freudian perspective, helping to enrich it into a Kleinian Freudian perspective. Self psychological and relational perspectives have also significantly "replaced" narrow Freudian Kleinian perspectives, nudging them toward a more comprehensive, scientifically respectable, clinically useful comparative-integrative psychoanalysis. The more we adopt and work with this dialectical approach, the more the pluralism problem becomes the pluralism opportunity. Under the umbrella of comparative-integrative psychoanalysis, everyone can find a better place to belong, discuss, and grow.

Beyond psychoanalysis

While some psychoanalysts might prefer to only see patients who free associate five times a week on the couch, most analysts do at least a considerable amount of less frequent, often face-to-face treatments, for various reasons. Even when they are conducting long-term, intensive psychoanalysis, James Grotstein (personal communication) stated that there are inevitably necessary moments of psychotherapy within these more formal analyses.

Several studies have shown that all psychotherapies, including psychoanalysis, are helpful to most patients. Not surprisingly for some, but embarrassingly for others, these studies have often found little or no difference between various approaches. Saul Rosenzweig's (1936) seminal article inaugurated the psychotherapy field's lasting interest in this topic. He suggested that common factors across psychotherapies were so pervasive that there would be only small differences in the outcomes of different forms of treatment. Luborsky, Singer, and Luborsky (1975) examined about 100 comparative treatment studies and found that Rosenzweig's hypothesis was essentially right. Lester Luborsky, and then others, began to characterize such small differences with Rosenzweig's quotation from *Alice in Wonderland*: "Everybody has won, so all shall have prizes." That happy conclusion had been the "Dodo bird's verdict" after judging a race in Lewis Carroll's famous (1865) book. The "Dodo bird verdict" has since become common in this discourse in which researchers continue writing articles for or against the existence of, or the meaning of, that trend (e.g., Luborsky, Rosenthal, Diguer, et al., 2002).

For these and other important contributions in psychotherapy research, Luborsky received numerous awards, including the Gold Medal for Lifetime Achievement in the Applications of Psychology by the American Psychological Association, the Sigourney Award for Distinguished Contributions to the Field of Psychoanalysis, and the Award for Distinguished Psychoanalytic Theory and Research by the American Psychoanalytic Association.

For those who regard psychoanalysis as one of the psychotherapies, what are, or should be, the relationships between these diverse approaches to understanding and treating psychological suffering? Like the differing perspectives within psychoanalysis, relationships between analysis and other psychotherapies have often been intensely conflicted. To some extent, such battles may be almost inevitable as established theses and new antitheses engage in vigorous debate. Innovative approaches may devalue and strive to replace more traditional perspectives as they attempt to make a viable space for themselves. A traditional orientation, in turn, may derogate and hope to destroy these newcomers. "Upstarts will not replace us."

In time, cooler heads may begin to prevail in these evolving debates. Some clinicians may begin asking under what circumstances an approach, or multiple approaches, may be useful for particular patients. Under what conditions might a practitioner of one perspective include insights and practices (parameters) from other approaches? Some groups, such as the Society for Exploration of Psychotherapy Integration (SEPI) (that includes many psychoanalysts), are very interested in these dialogues. Such organizations provide some balance to the increasing specialization that characterizes many clinicians who tend to talk mostly, or even exclusively, to members of their relatively narrow groups. Organizations like SEPI can help to provide a comparative-integrative tent large enough to create a mutually beneficial home for psychoanalysis and other psychotherapies. Such groups will not replace psychoanalysis or any other group. They can, however, offer an enriching counterpoint to the proceedings of the more specialized organizations.

References

Carroll, L. (1865). *Alice in wonderland*. Auckland: Floating Press.

Fairbairn, W. R. D. (1952). *Psychoanalytic studies of the personality*. London: Tavistock.

Freud, S. (1953). The interpretation of dreams. In J. Strachey (Ed. & Trans.), *Standard edition of the complete psychological works of Sigmund Freud* (Vols. 4/5, pp. 1–625). London: Hogarth. Originally published 1900.

Luborsky, L., Singer, B., & Luborsky, L. (1975). Comparative studies of psychotherapies: is it true that "everyone has won and all must have prizes"? *Archives of General Psychiatry, 32,* 995–1008.

Luborsky L., Rosenthal R., Diguer L., Andrusyna, T. P., Berman, J. S., Levitt, J. T., Seligman, D. A., & Krause, E. D. (2002). The Dodo bird verdict is alive and well—mostly. *Clinical Psychology: Science and Practice, 9*(1), 2–12. (Commentaries [pp. 13–34]: D. L. Chambless; B. J. Rounsaville & K. M. Carrol; S. Messer & J. Wampold; K. J. Schneider; D. F. Klein; L. E. Beutler.)

Mitchell, S., & Black, M. (1995). *Freud and beyond: a history of modern psychoanalytic thought.* New York: Basic Books.

Rapaport, D. (1967). A historical survey of psychoanalytic ego psychology. In M. M. Gill (Ed.), *The collected papers of David Rapaport* (pp. 745–757). New York: Basic Books. Originally published 1959.

Rosenzweig, S. (1936). Some implicit common factors in diverse methods of psycho-therapy. *American Journal of Orthopsychiatry, 6,* 412–415.

Schafer, R. (1976). *A new language for psychoanalysis.* New Haven & London: Yale University Press.

Schafer, R. (1983). *The analytic attitude.* London: Hogarth.

Schafer, R. (1990). The search for common ground. *International Journal of Psycho-Analysis, 71,* 49–52.

Schafer, R. (1994). Commentary: traditional Freudian and Kleinian Freudian analysis. *Psychoanalytic Inquiry, 14,* 462–475.

Schafer, R. (1997). *The contemporary Kleinians of London.* Madison: International Universities Press.

Willock, B. (2007). *Comparative-integrative psychoanalysis.* Hillsdale: Analytic Press.

21 Belonging and choosing not to belong to a psychoanalytic society

John Sloane

"I don't want to belong to any club that will have me as a member"
– Groucho Marx Quoted in Johnson (1949)

To belong or not to belong? That was the question I was faced with, finally, in relation to the Psychoanalytic Society where I had done my training. It had been my professional home in Toronto, the city in which I was born, then lost my father as a boy of ten. I have written about that formative experience before—ad nauseam, some might feel—but such is the legacy of parental loss in childhood; a timeless longing to know and be known and belong to a world that feels right and makes sense. Father hunger (Herzog, 2001). Mother hunger. Other hunger. Hunger for some kind of "moral third" (Benjamin, 2018).

I have presented several papers rooted in personal experience to the Joint International Conference of Psychoanalytic Societies: the loneliness of the analyst and its alleviation through faith in "O" (the ineffable, the unknowable in Bion, 1965); the failure to become a training analyst and what I learned from it; the passion of Christ/the passion of Humanity; and knowing oneself and being known as a wounded, wounding healer (Sloane, 2012; 2014a; 2014b; 2016). Presenting those papers gave me a profound sense of belonging that eased my otherwise timeless, underlying alienation, shame and guilt—all of which helped me realize, a few years ago, that it was time to leave my professional home. Events transpired to make it clear that I no longer *wanted* to belong to that "club," even though it still wanted me as a member. It did *not* want me to challenge its authority, so reminiscent of my father's. Neither could be openly questioned, objected to or differed with without being "fired" for lack of allegiance.

That most recent part of my story was painful but very effective as a liberating enactment. So when Brent Willock asked me if I planned to present on the topic of belonging, it got me thinking. Feeling, too. Not only did I feel touched and grateful for his friendly, fatherly interest and faith that I might have something to say on the subject, but also a surge of belonging to this open-minded group that keeps coming up with topics that touch my own experience. It has also been honest and respectful when my papers did not meet its criteria for inclusion in books to which not all could belong.

Although conscious self-disclosure is of debatable value to the analytic process, there is no question that it can be helpful in supervision and collegial dialogue. There is also growing appreciation of the value of acknowledging the analyst's subjectivity, as it stimulates and reflects that of our patients—and the institutions to which we belong.

I hope that what I have to say about the topic might not only be of clinical interest but useful in shedding light on the ways we co-create the institutions we belong to or depart from. All institutions make decisions, sometimes quite painful ones to all concerned, about who qualifies for membership—or not. So, too, do individuals looking for a community. In this age of inter-subjectivity, the personal is professional as well as political—and a third is a third is a Third unless it is dead or moribund, as it appears to be in this age of self-supremacy (Benjamin, 2018; Gerson, 2009; Shaw, 2014). What I have in mind by the word "Third" is an amalgam of what is variously described in the literature as co-created by two persons between or around them—or as "given" by pre-existing, shared principles in the cultural surround. It is what holds the two together and makes it possible for two separate subjectivities to hold the tension of difference between the two and prevents them from collapsing into "doer and done-to" (Benjamin, 2018).

Some of you are familiar with my previous papers and may experience some of this as repetitive. Others will need some background to understand where I'm coming from and what I'm trying to get at. Both may wonder about the usefulness of self-disclosure—but I hope you can keep an open mind to variations on repeating themes that can lead to understanding of self and other from different points of view in ever-changing contexts.

When I was a boy of ten, my father died of brain cancer. All I knew at the time was that he was becoming increasingly irrational, irascible, unreachable and punitive to a point where I had finally had enough. I may also have sensed his relative weakness, and I took advantage of that to let him have it after he said something that triggered an all-out destructive explosion in me—enabling me to speak with an authority articulate enough to get through to him about how he had abused his authority over me.

He was visibly shaken, silent and the light went out of his eyes. Not long after that, he died. It was not exactly an Oedipal victory, as one analyst interpreted it, although it did leave me feeling responsible for having killed him and for filling the void of my mother's unhappiness. More importantly, it was a profound loss of a man who might have been a good enough father had he been able to survive my destructiveness, understand where it was coming from and acknowledge what he was doing that evoked it. Like Winnicott (1969), Benjamin (2018) stresses that step as essential to inter-subjective repair and to the co-creation of reality and a moral third. Suffice it to say that I was left feeling doubly traumatized, not only by the way he had treated me, but especially by my own eruption that I thought had destroyed someone I loved and needed far more than I knew. Suddenly, I was far more powerful than I wanted to be—but not powerful enough to bring him back. I had become a destroyer of worlds, guilty and terrified of a catastrophic repetition should I be less than careful how and to whom I expressed myself, and haunted by nightmares of nuclear holocaust.

I retained, however, a deep longing for benevolent omnipotence to re-find and repair an Other who might survive my destructive omnipotence and lead the way toward a reliable, shared reality. I no longer trusted my own authority, nor that of any man with an all-knowing attitude. I took all authorities with a grain of salt, including Freud—as well as those who rejected him with such certainty. My search led through medicine, psychiatry, psychoanalysis and religion as well as fatherhood, following my marriage to a woman whose instinctive authority I trusted more than my own.

In my office, I tend to trust my patients—or what Bion (1965) called "O," the truth that emerges between us when we are able to not know, as Keats suggested with his notion of "negative capability" (Keats, 1966)—even to the point of short-circuiting my own being, knowing and doing by falling asleep. I tend to "die" in the countertransference in the absence of an emotional connection that I feel unable to grasp or confront. At those moments, I am unable to find words for something essential to a vital connection between us. In that state of not knowing and not being able to do, I am not only shamefully lacking but psychically dead. My brain stops functioning, my body becomes paralyzed and I lose consciousness, falling into what feels like a black hole (Eshel, 1998; Tustin, 1988). I have written about that experience (Sloane, 2013), along with the ways I have learned to work with it by accepting responsibility for the effect it has on my patients, some of whom become openly angry and sometimes "fire" me for abandoning or failing to be there for them. With openly aggressive or contemptuous patients, I stay alert—and am inclined to see their point of view, empathically immersing if not losing myself in it, surrendering to it (Ghent, 1990) in order to help them find words for it and acknowledging my fault—sometimes *to a fault*. That is something I was unable or unwilling to do as a boy for my ailing father. I gradually reached a point where I was confident enough that I knew what I was doing, even in those faulty states, to apply to become a training analyst and join the ranks of those who teach, supervise and analyze candidates.

To cut a long story short, the consultants who examined my work thought it was good enough to recommend my acceptance as a training analyst. The Institute committees, however, were not convinced. They decided I had a character flaw, a "lack of ego-mastery with insufficient access to my aggression, the capacity to elaborate it in fantasy, and defenses against knowing." There was certainly truth in those interpretations, which I have continued to think about ever since—but whether that rendered me less trustworthy than those who erred in the direction of all-knowing authority is moot. I had already returned to analysis several years earlier in an attempt to understand and resolve my countertransference symptom—and ended up accepting the fact that my vulnerability and disability were a part of me that could neither be fixed nor hidden in order to belong. Margaret Crastnopol (2017) has written a very useful paper on exactly that experience, "Acknowledging the Achilles Heel: On the Micro-traumatic Impact of a Person's Actual Flaws, Deficits and Vulnerabilities."

The fact is, I do not belong in the company of those whose authority is considered categorically superior to that of ordinary members. I'm not sure anyone does! But whether it was rejection on their part or failure on mine, the result of that enactment was a traumatic rupture of essential relatedness, with disillusionment and breakdown of "moral thirdness" (Benjamin, 2018) reinforcing a profound, boundless feeling of not belonging—or homelessness. Others voiced anger on my behalf—which helped to validate my own.

On some level, though, it was also a relief. I was not at all sure that I did belong or would feel comfortable "at the top." Besides, I was already well on my way to a relational view of mutual authenticity and conditional authority, subject to feedback and limited by the fact that the Unconscious is alive and well in all of us. Its emergence requires a relatively non-judgmental atmosphere of ongoing inquiry at all levels of a non-linear dynamic system that facilitates useful, ongoing re-formulation.

I did, however, continue to belong—if not cling—to the Toronto Psychoanalytic Society, and by objecting face to face with several training analysts who had voted against me but were important to me as friends, those relationships, at least, were salvaged. They were willing to listen and accept responsibility for their part in my trauma, making it possible to remain "at home." It also helped to write about it for presentation to the Canadian Psychoanalytic Society, which functioned as a moral Third by listening—respectfully and thoughtfully. Several years later, I presented an updated version to a conference in Edinburgh. Not only did people listen, they responded with animated, enthusiastic discussion. Some identified with my experience, while others had good reason to identify with the Institute with which they were in full agreement—a description of which was included in the published version (Sloane, 2014b). That, too, was a rather dramatic enactment that bolstered my courage to present the paper to my home Society, confident that I could handle whatever aggressive interpretation or judgment I might encounter—or experience within myself.

The Scientific Program Committee, however, decided it was "too personal and not scientific enough." For me, that was the last straw. I no longer wanted to belong to an institution that was not willing to listen to honest feedback about its use of authority and its effects on members of the community. I was not willing to accept its final judgment of what is or is not psychoanalytic or scientific. As someone said when he stepped up to the lectern and placed a gun on it before delivering his paper, "This is for the first person who says, 'This is not psychoanalysis!'" (i.e., "You do not belong").

Whose gun was it, anyway? In any case, I pulled the trigger and resigned from the Society, which also forfeited my membership in the Canadian and International Psychoanalytic Societies. Many colleagues urged me to stay. My voice, they said, was valuable to them—as theirs was to me. The training, mentorship, companionship and recognition I had enjoyed in the past was not something I wanted to lose—which is why I had hung on so long after it was decided that I did not belong in the upper chamber, the inner circle. I could accept that, but not the refusal to listen to and consider my views about the impact of policies designed to protect psychoanalysis, as they conceived of it, and their own positions of power. Psychoanalysis, as a discipline, functions as a Moral Third that Benjamin notes is essential to conflict resolution between "doer and done-to" (Benjamin, 2018)—but it can also function as an "Anti-analytic Third," to borrow Straker's (2006) term, a toxic, judgmental atmosphere that models a mode of relating that is inconsistent with the spirit of analysis.

In my view, psychoanalysis is not the exclusive possession of a chosen few, any more than "O" is, but a multidimensional, open-ended relational process that goes well beyond the walls of our offices and institutes (Bion, 1965). The identity of the analyst as an all-knowing authority on the Unconscious, their own and that of others, is obsolete, if not oxymoronic. We must recognize "the patient as therapist to his analyst," as Harold Searles put it (1979), and the field as one co-created by all concerned.

As the Sufi poet Rumi put it, "Out beyond ideas of wrongdoing and rightdoing, there is a field. I'll meet you there" (Rumi, 2004). In our field, where "ideas, language, even the phrase each other" (Rumi, 2004) often make no sense, we do, however, keep on trying to find words to make sense of our experience of the world and our place in it.

As it happened, the senior training analyst on the committee that made that fateful decision was also a friend of mine, someone my wife and I see regularly as part of a movie group. Once again, I decided to object to him, personally—partly in order to continue belonging to that small group, if not to the Society itself. He listened respectfully—and interpreted my motive for wanting to present the paper as revenge. Once again, I could not deny that there was truth in his view, just not the whole truth. It would definitely give me pleasure to get through to those who had caused me pain and to cause them enough pain to call attention to their part in what leads some "ordinary analysts" to avoid meetings or give up their membership—even their identity as analysts (Leonoff, 2000). As a fellow human being, he is entitled to his opinion. While those who are not with us are against us in some circumstances, that may mean they have something to teach us—and we, them. In any case, I no longer wanted to belong or pay dues to an organization that has a fixed, hierarchical authority structure, deaf to those who differ from it. For me, it was time to leave home without actually killing a man who represented my father. He and I have remained friends and occasional adversaries, both members of the larger psychoanalytic community, both teachers in other programs where we are free to agree and disagree.

In this field, is it not our "strange and dangerous habit," as Loewald (1981, p. 22) once quoted the French poet Valéry as saying, "of wanting to begin at the beginning" in order to make sense of a pre-verbal realm—including its earliest forms of oneness and annihilation? Oneness—or belonging—is inevitably disrupted by primal trauma or enactments of it, an event that both Jessica Benjamin and Mike Eigen (Benjamin, 2018; Eigen, 1993; 2011) refer to as catastrophe or total tragedy. We try to find words for it if we can, on the way toward twoness, threeness and beyond—a larger inclusiveness and essential sense of belonging to the human race. So in the space I have left, let me touch on a few other authors who speak to these experiences.

Many speak of the inescapable subjectivity and vulnerability of the analyst, clinically in relation to the subjectivity of our analysands and theoretically in our aspirations toward objectivity and recognition as having something of value to offer the field and its application to the world at large. We try to say what we see to be true of human nature, biologically, psychologically, socially, even spiritually, while remaining open to falsification (Kuhn, 1962) from other points of view. Ours is a scientific spirit, if not method—not one of infallible final authority. Absolute authority extinguishes the spirit—and inflames mutually exclusive, polarized camps of traumatized and traumatizing narcissism (Shaw, 2014). As I once wrote in a poem, protesting the arms race between the superpowers in 1989,

> Split images of Heav'n on earth
>> Attributed to men
> Each from himself, and he from her,
>> The righteous We, from them.

The notion of the Third is very useful and closely akin to Winnicott's transitional space (Winnicott, 1953/1971), where ambiguity and uncertainty are not only tolerated but facilitate creative play. If we can "stand in the spaces," light gets in to where the "Shadow of the Tsunami" (Bromberg, 2011) otherwise prevails in the aftermath of boundless trauma and timeless loss. In that dark place, all things come at us at once, from inside and out, conflicting and up for grabs as to who's doing what to whom (Benjamin, 2018). Ferenzci (1988), of course, was the first to experiment with "mutual analysis," and Searles was ahead of his time in recognizing the uncanny ability of seemingly psychotic patients to zero in on the unconscious of their analyst and drive him crazy in order to re-shape him in a form they can use (Searles, 1959; 1979). Analysis, it seems, is an ongoing process of mutual regression and progression, disintegration and reintegration, ebb and flow of feelings that matter—in search of words (Eigen, 2007). Feelings fall into repeating patterns that Eigen calls "constant conjunctions" of good and bad self-states on the way toward transformations of basic trust (Erikson, 1950), or "faith in O"; that which is, but is not yet known (Bion, 1965; Eigen, 2011). The "ownerless O," as someone in an online discussion of Eigen's work put it, emerges of its own accord if we can let go of certainty even in the face of life-or-death circumstances and bear the shame and vulnerability of not knowing and not being able to do what we or our patients urgently wish we could. In other words, we learn to live with the loss of infantile omniscience and omnipotence, mourn it and get over it in the service of those who need to get back in touch with their *own* all-knowing, all-powerful authority before letting it go in recognition of the Other. "Hullo, Object," as Winnicott said at that pivotal moment of truth when all had felt lost, only to be re-found (Winnicott, 1969). "Hullo, Subject" might be better, according to Jessica Benjamin, whose notions of inter-subjectivity, recognition, acknowledgement of fault and rhythmic or moral thirds are also very useful (Benjamin, 2018).

Margaret Crastnopol, as I mentioned, examines the effect of what she calls "Achilles Heels" (Crastnopol, 2017); actual flaws, weaknesses or deficiencies in what Hartmann considered ego-apparatuses of primary autonomy (Hartmann, 1958), or neurophysiological "givens." Such deficits, or points on a normal bell curve, as Sam Izenberg suggested in his unpublished paper on "psychopathology as a pathologizing construct" (Izenberg, 2018), enter into the complex, non-linear dynamic systems of mutual influence, not only internally but externally in the consensual reality we co-create and discover with others (Sullivan, 1953). Crastnopol draws attention to the shame that goes with those aspects of our selves that cannot be changed. They are integral parts of who we are, parts of who we become in relation to others, parts of us that impinge on or fall short of what others consider essential, if not sacred, depending on how we make sense of them with the help of others who understand or reject us in the light of what feels necessary to them. Learning disabilities and attention deficits are compounded, ironically, by inattention or non-recognition—and by too-narrowly focused attention or insistence on "fixing them." This, I think, is what Bion had in mind when he wrote about the risks of preconceptions based on memory and desire (Bion, 1967). Instead of focusing on what's psychopathological or "wrong," what's missing can be approached with non-judgmental openness and curiosity, leading to understanding, acceptance and incorporation of those elements as parts of the self that need help to grow on the one hand or have effects for which we can take responsibility on the other, not only with our patients but with our colleagues and families.

"Attention must be paid," as Linda said in *Death of a Salesman* (Miller, 1996, p. 40). Without it, we cease to exist.

A sense of belonging, as I have come to it, involves having a voice that is heard and responded to by other voices, sometimes attuned, sometimes discordant or openly opposed. Those voices provide a variety of selfobject functions; idealizable, mirroring, kinship and adversarial (Kohut, 1977; Wolf, 1980). Acknowledgment of one's own and others' inevitably occurring empathic failures allows for repair—and for inter-subjective encounters with separate selves who share common ground and common values or "ultimate concern" (Tillich, 1957)—approached from different angles, using different names for "That which is," the great "I am." Belonging is being part of something larger and more reliable than oneself, something in which one plays a part in the co-creation of the climate we live in. The analytic process that serves that end is not only interminable but boundless—well beyond the walls of our consulting rooms and even our collegial discussions, working its way toward a human community that is open to question and correction through free speech, free association, dis-association, and respect for differences. We still have a long way to go, but it is possible to have faith in the process of which we're all a part.

References

Benjamin, J. (2018). *Beyond doer and done to: recognition theory, intersubjectivity and the third*. New York: Routledge.

Bion, W. R. (1965). *Transformations: change from learning to growth*. New York: Basic Books.

Bion, W. R. (1967). Notes on memory and desire. *The Psychoanalytic Forum, 2*(3), 271–280.

Bromberg, P. M. (2011). *The shadow of the tsunami and the growth of the relational mind.* New York: Routledge.

Crastnopol, M. (2017). Acknowledging the Achilles heel: on the micro-traumatic impact of a person's actual flaws, deficits and vulnerabilities. *Contemporary Psychoanalysis, 53*(3), 317–345.

Eigen, M. (1993). *The psychotic core.* London: Karnac

Eigen, M. (2007). *Feeling matters.* London: Karnac.

Eigen, M. (2011). *Faith and transformation.* London: Karnac.

Erikson, E. H. (1950). *Childhood and society.* New York: W. W. Norton.

Eshel, O. (1998). "Black holes," deadness, and existing analytically. *International Journal of Psycho-Analysis, 79*, 1115–1130.

Ferenczi, S. (1988). *The clinical diary of Sándor Ferenczi* (J. Dupont, Ed., M. J. Balint & N. Z. Jackson, Trans.). Cambridge, MA: Harvard University Press. Originally published 1932.

Gerson, S. (2009). When the third is dead: memory, mourning and witnessing in the after-math of the Holocaust. *International Journal of Psychoanalysis, 90*, 1341–1357.

Ghent, E. (1990). Masochism, submission, surrender. *Contemporary Psychoanalysis, 26*, 108–136.

Hartmann, H. (1958). *Ego psychology and the problem of adaptation.* New York: International Universities Press.

Herzog, J. (2001). *Father hunger.* New York: Routledge.

Izenberg, O. S. (2018, January 20). Psychopathology: a pathologizing concept. Paper presented to the Toronto Institute for Contemporary Psychoanalysis.

Johnson, E. (1949, October 20). In Hollywood. *Dunkirk Evening Observer*, 22.

Keats, J. (1966). *The selected poetry of Keats.* New York: New American Library.

Kohut, H. (1977). *The restoration of the self.* New York: International Universities Press.

Kuhn, T. S. (1962). *The structure of scientific revolutions.* Chicago: University of Chicago Press.

Leonoff, A. (2000). Psychoanalytic identity. *Canadian Journal of Psychoanalysis, 9*, 243–263.

Loewald, H. W. (1981). Regression: some general considerations. *Psychoanalytic Quarterly, 50*, 22–43.

Miller, A. (1996). *Death of a salesman.* Harmondsworth: Penguin Books.

Rumi, M. J. (2004). *The essential Rumi* (new expanded edition) (C. Barks, Trans.). New York: Harper One Press.

Searles, H. F. (1959). The effort to drive the other person crazy: an element in the aeti-ology and psychotherapy of schizophrenia. *British Journal of Medical Psychology, 32*, 1–18.

Searles, H. F. (1979). The patient as therapist to his analyst (1975). By H. F. Searles (Ed.), *Countertransference and related subjects: selected papers.* New York: International Universities Press.

Shaw, D. (2014). *Traumatic narcissism: relational systems of subjugation.* New York: Routledge/Taylor & Francis.

Sloane, J. A. (2012). The loneliness of the analyst and its alleviation through faith in "O". In B. Willock, L. C. Bohm, & R. C. Curtis (Eds.), *Loneliness and longing: conscious and unconscious aspects* (pp. 197–209). New York: Routledge.

Sloane, J. A. (2013). Sleep, death and re-birth: a relational perspective on sleep in the countertransference. *Contemporary Psychoanalysis, 49*(4), 509–535.

Sloane, J. A. (2014a). The passion of Christ: the passion of humanity. Paper presented at the Joint International Conference, Florence, Italy.

Sloane, J. A. (2014b). Reflections on the failure to become a training analyst. In B. Willock, L. C. Bohm, & R. C. Curtis (Eds.), *Understanding and coping with failure: psychoanalytic perspectives*. New York: Routledge.

Sloane, J. A. (2016). On knowing and being known as a wounded healer. Paper presented at the Joint International Conference of Psychoanalytic Societies, Reykjavic, Iceland.

Straker, G. (2006). The anti-analytic third. *Psychoanalytic Review*, 93(5), 729–753.

Sullivan, H. S. (1953). *The interpersonal theory of psychiatry*. New York: W. W. Norton.

Tillich, P. (1957). *Dynamics of faith*. New York: Harper and Row.

Tustin, F. (1988). The "black hole": a significant element in autism. *Free Associations*, 1, 35–50.

Winnicott, D. W. (1971). Transitional objects and transitional phenomena. In D. W. Winnicott (Ed.), Playing and reality (pp. 1–25). London: Tavistock. Originally published 1953.

Winnicott, D. W. (1969). The use of an object. *International Journal of Psycho-Analysis*, 50, 711–716.

Wolf, E. S. (1980). On the developmental line of selfobject relations. In A. Goldberg (Ed.), *Advances in self psychology* (pp. 117–130). New York: International Universities Press.

Part 7

Conclusions

22 Reflections, discussion, and conclusions

From primary attachment to an individual to belonging to a greater whole

Rebecca Coleman Curtis

The need to belong took on a new meaning during the isolation imposed by the coronavirus. The extent to which we rely on contact, especially physically, with others for our psychological well-being became more apparent. The emphasis on belonging leads to a new, long-overdue focus in psychoanalysis. Psychoanalytic theory, since its inception, has been focused largely on individuals, in spite of Freud's concerns with civilization and the dynamics of groups. This deficit has continued in contemporary relational psychoanalysis, although culture itself did receive considerable attention from one of its forebears, interpersonal psychoanalysis. The importance of belonging to and not belonging in certain groups would benefit from further study by psychoanalysts and other scholars.

The current volume contributes to the corrective turn in our psychoanalytic imagination by looking at this theme. Some psychoanalysts have noted that loneliness was not a theme in Freud's work (cf. Willock, Bohm, & Curtis, 2011), as people were usually surrounded by others and belonged to groups as a natural part of their lives. Not belonging appears to have become more of a problem in the Western world as mobility, living further apart even in cities, and the use of technology have increased. Although relational psychoanalysis has maintained that having relationships is a primary motive, it has not specified the importance of a sense of belonging to groups. The need to belong was hypothesized as a primary motive, however, by psychologists Baumeister and Leary (1995), with extensive empirical evidence supporting this hypothesis. Further work by Baumeister and colleagues (Verhagen, Lodder, & Baumeister, 2018) showed that it is *unmet* belongingness needs, not *high* belongingness needs, that lead to adverse effects.

Acceptance of the importance of the attachment theory of John Bowlby (1973) has become prevalent in both the psychoanalytic and empirical research literatures. A secure attachment to a caretaking figure early in life is known to affect a wide variety of phenomena, including the recognition of emotions (Steel, Steel, & Croft, 2008), the occurrence of mental disorders (Mikulincer & Shaver, 2012), and identification with groups (Crisp, Ferrow, Rosenthal, et al., 2009). As noted previously, relational/interpersonal psychoanalysis has posited that the desire to have relationships is fundamental among human motivations, distinguishing itself from the Freudian psychoanalytic focus on sexual instincts. This volume takes attachment a step further. It is not just a strong attachment to one figure from whom a person benefits but an attachment to more people as well. Belonging to a group probably conveys some sort of secure base that simply having a friend or many friends, but friends who are not part of a group, does not. In the preceding chapters, we see experiential accounts of the need to belong to families, community and professional groups, nation states, and to a sense of a larger whole.

This is not to undervalue the importance of one relationship. We see in the chapter on the film *Lost in Translation* how even one close relationship can help out immensely when a person is at bay. The power of one close relationship is known to psychoanalysts and to individuals in dire circumstances who had one person—a neighbor, a religious figure, a teacher, or a coach, perhaps—who cared and gave a person an experience that may be unfamiliar.

Of course, not belonging to certain groups can also be an advantage. The advantages of not belonging are discussed by Kaufmann regarding the psychologies of two of her patients. And, along with needs to belong and not to belong, there can also be a desire for a space in between belonging and not belonging, discussed by Flax and White. The struggles that are manifest at times in the pulls and pushes of belonging are described by Borg and Berry in their work with colleagues on a writing project and Cherow-O'Leary and Sloane in their departures from one group and sense of belonging in another.

The issue of belonging in a family is taken up by Renée Cherow-O'Leary. For whatever reasons, Jewish herself, she felt more of a sense of belonging with the family of her new Irish Catholic husband than she did with her first husband's Jewish relatives. The theme of belonging or not as a couple is continued in the chapter by Dryer, who discusses what helps couples to "uncouple." This post-break-up relationship is especially important when there are children involved. She suggests that couples need to find a space outside right and wrong. To have a good "uncoupling," she notes that couples need to listen attentively, make good eye contact, not interrupt, think about "Who am I to you?" and engage in emotional regulation. As shown by Baumeister and Wotman (1994), the guilt-ridden experience of the rejecter can be as difficult as the experience of the rejected one. Not belonging where one previously belonged can be a devastating situation whether it is in a country, a group, or a couple.

Apart from the discussions of not-belonging, we have found a moving description of actually belonging by psychoanalyst Robert Langan. Such experiences no doubt lead to confidence of being accepted in the future. Teirney and Baumeister (2019) argued that it takes at least four good experiences to counteract one bad one. A bad experience may be being criticized by a parent, friend, or teacher. So how many experiences, how much intensity of goodness does it take to overcome serious traumas from war, abuse, threats to life, and bullying, for example? Certainly, more than twelve hours of cognitive behavioral therapy, desensitization, or a daily medication is going to be required. The experiences of the boys in Langan's scout group was one of many good experiences to counteract bad ones in their past or future lives.

The word *heimlich* in German, used by Langan, "can also be used to define something that is secret, concealed, unknown, or threatening," according to

Dictionary.com, and also to mean "private," which is related to the idea of homely. In this context, it is interesting to note that many fraternities (and sororities) have secret rituals and handshakes. Certainly, psychoanalytic organizations themselves have what one author has called a "shibboleth" (Schachter, 2002); that is, a secret password providing entry into their club. The members undoubtedly get a sense of belonging, in most cases, to an exclusive club. Such rituals, like initiation ceremonies (cf. Aronson & Mills, 1959), can increase liking for a group. Just how exclusive the club needs to be is the subject of Willock's chapter on psychoanalysts themselves. Most people seem to prefer a secure home group from which they then seek out the larger world.

A sense of belonging similar to that of Langan's scout group was felt in the early days of the kibbutzim, Yadin reports. In the beginning, a kibbutz was a communal settlement in Israel in which all wealth was held in common and profits were reinvested in the settlement. This feeling of family gradually eroded in the one he experienced as the economy moved from one based on agriculture to one based on industry, and capitalism, with its inherent competition, took over. These chapters bring up the topic into which the volume does delve, as to the extent to which a sense of belonging is dependent upon cooperation, as opposed to competition, and the extent to which a sense of belonging may depend on knowledge of an outgroup.

Believing there is a fair principle of the distribution of resources seems intimately linked to a sense of belonging. In a family, resources are usually distributed according to a principle of need, as they probably were in the early kibbutz. A number of studies now show that people in more unequal societies are much less likely to feel they can trust each other (Sorkin, 2013). Violence—usually measured by homicide rates—increases in more unequal societies in the US (Hagan & Peterson, 1995). People in less equal communities in the US become less willing to help each other and are less likely to belong to voluntary groups and associations or to participate in local activities (Uslaner & Brown, 2005).

Having a national identity—feeling part of a nation-state—is the subject of chapters on immigration and terrorism. These are major topics in our political discourses today. Although the chapters here do not describe any of the most wrenching, heart-torn stories we have heard, they do convey how the analysts' own experiences interweave with those of patients in the chapters by Ross, Avitzur, and Lian. The analyst is certainly no "blank screen" when listening. As mentioned previously, the difficulty breaking old relationships has been documented (Baumeister & Leary, 1995), and we can all imagine the stress of entering a new culture, especially when not even fluent in the language. We do not even address in this volume the difficulties inherent in inter-racial and international adoptions.

Terrorism is another topic dominant in our consciousnesses these days. We are fortunate to have a chapter by the prominent Egyptian scholar Emad Aysha describing the desire to be part of a larger whole of radical terrorists who feel insecure in the face of modernity and the failure of their own nation states to address it adequately. Cerfolio puts terrorism in the context of humiliation and loneliness. Certainly, belonging to a religion fulfills the need to belong for many.

The insecurity, humiliation, and loneliness of these terrorists is beyond that of most religious followers.

Potential benefits of belonging to a greater whole

In his chapter, Besner points out how a number of psychoanalytic concepts are similar to Buddhist ones. As the author indicates, this overlap has increasingly been a topic for psychoanalysts. Weber notes that the word *shunyata* or *sunyata* in Buddhism is composed of *shunya*, meaning "empty," and *ta*, meaning "belonging to," although it frequently gets translated misleadingly as emptiness. The realization of *shunyata* is wisdom, the door to enlightenment. Everything exists because everything else does, Weber tells us. Bubbles pop when we try to catch them. She quotes the Buddhist scholar Mu Soeng (2010), describing a scientist looking through an electron microscope to come upon the particles of existence: "As we move closer to the nucleus, it too begins to dissolve. It too is nothing more than an oscillating field, waves of rhythm. Inside the nucleus are other organized fields: protons, neutron, even smaller 'particles.' Each of these, upon our approach, also dissolve into pure rhythm" (pp. 38–39). Similar to the physicist David Bohm, who found that it was not possible to understand individual particles without understanding the whole:

> as with consciousness, each moment has a certain explicate order, and in addition it enfolds all the others, though in its own way. So the relationship of each moment in the whole to all the others is implied by its total content: the way in which it "holds" all the others enfolded within it.
>
> (1980, p. 80)

"Shunyata is seen not as a negation of existence but rather as the undifferentiation out of which all apparent entities, distinction, and dualities arise" (*Shunyata in Mahayan Buddhism*, 2016).There are echoes in this statement of the physicists Bohm and Hiley's (1975) idea that we are all connected: "We have reversed the usual classical notion that the independent 'elementary parts' of the world are the fundamental reality ... Rather, we say the inseparable quantum interconnectedness of the whole universe is the fundamental reality" (p. 102).

The view of reality and its connectedness in physics is similar to that of the psychoanalyst Winnicott, who famously stated, "There is no such thing as a baby, only a nursing couple" (1964, p. 88). The dominant Western view of the self, however, has been criticized in recent years not only as individualistic but as "hyperindividualistic" (Ivanhoe, Flanagan, Harrison, et al., 2018). Indeed, in their introduction to *The Oneness Hypothesis*, Ivanhoe and colleagues argue that social, political, economic, and ethical theories of the self as found in the works of Freud (1949), Nozick (1974), O'Neill (1993), and Rawls (1999) conceive of the self as pursuing self-centered calculations and planning and entering into "agreements and contracts with others in an effort to maximize its own self-interests." It is regarded as not only the best way to be but *the way people are*, in spite of having been shown to be poor at predicting how people behave (Sen, 1977) and in tracking their own best interests (Haybron, 2008). They pose in opposition to the Western view of the self the Buddhist one, also similar to the ones in Daoism, Confucianism, and Platonism—the view that a separate and enduring self is a delusion and the cause of human suffering. These traditions all suggest that belonging to a larger whole is the nature of reality, that the world is a grand interconnected whole. Allured's chapter in the current volume, in line with this thinking, suggests that our larger whole includes not only all people but the whole Earth as well.

Of course, H. S. Sullivan (1950) had long ago regarded personality in the psychological sense as an illusion and posited that the only observations of interest were those in interactions with others. Sullivan (1953) also described the vital role of peer relationships and their necessity for forming a sense of belonging. The early interpersonalists saw the similarities between psychoanalysis and Buddhism, as evidenced, for example, by the citation of Suzuki's (1938) work by Karen Horney (1945) in *Our Inner Conflicts*. Erich Fromm, another interpersonalist, traveled to Japan in order to explore the subject and wrote about this topic (Fromm & Suzuki, 1963). Once we begin to think of ourselves as belonging to a greater whole, we wonder if we are thinking of the "oceanic feeling" to which Freud objected. Although the idea of an oceanic feeling still remains a controversial one within psychoanalysis, an oceanic feeling may be similar in some respects to a sense of belonging to a greater whole, or it may be a state beyond that for meditators, especially those who are advanced in such practices.

For Freud, the oceanic feeling was "something like the restoration of limitless narcissism" (1946, p. 12) or the relic of infantile feelings of being at one with the mother, a residue of the mother-infant bond. His dismissal of this feeling, perhaps partially to distance himself from Jung, has been critiqued by many (Ackerman, 2017; Cooper, 2002; Epstein, 1990; Erikson, 1958/1962; 1959/1980; Simmonds, 2006; Werman, 1977; 1986). Romain Rolland, the first to raise the issue of the oceanic feeling with Freud in letters and conversation, stated that this feeling was a subjective experience independent of all religious dogma, a sensation "without perceptible limits" (cited in Fisher, 1976, p. 21). Silverman, Lachmann, and Milich (1982) pursued the search for oneness experimentally (subliminally), finding that a sense of oneness could enhance adaptation if a sense of self could be preserved. Oneness fantasies were also re-examined from a developmental research perspective by psychoanalysts Lachmann and Beebe (1989), who noted that flexibility between feelings of oneness and a separate sense of self is what is beneficial.

Ackerman (2017) concluded a review of the critiques and comparisons of the oceanic feeling with the following comments:

> Patients need to oscillate between immersion and self-assertion, dreaminess and goal-directed activity, in order to establish a relationship with their oceanic otherness that will provide a growing self-awareness. Psychoanalysis rests on this razor's edge, where patients are invited to fall into the oceanic, but the goal is to allow this immersion to deepen and enrich the individual's

consciousness, dipping into the oceanic without sinking entirely into its ego-less depths.

(p. 30)

The sense of belonging to a group or groups is perhaps far removed from the sense of belonging to a greater whole discussed as a spiritual or oceanic feeling, but this sort of sense may be a continuum. Such a topic is beyond the purview of the present volume.

Concluding comments

Because the issues of identity and belonging are so important, they have often been topics of the world's best writers, who often describe their experiences better than psychoanalysts do. The author Claire Messud, for example, in an interview with Lucy McKeon (December 7, 2019), stated:

> Earliest among my thematic preoccupations, and fundamental for me, is displacement and belonging. ... *The Woman Upstairs* is about a different sort of not-belonging. For much of my life, we seemed to be moving toward an openness—call it globalism or cosmopolitanism, words latterly imbued with darker connotations—toward a world in which all people might eventually "belong." Now, the pendulum has swung in the other direction, and we are living, alas, in a time of tribalisms, of division and walls and borders; a time in which questions of displacement and not-belonging are more relevant than ever.

And Ishiguro (2000), in *When We Were Orphans*, states that people need to feel they belong, or otherwise, civilization might just collapse (pp. 79–80). So feeling part of a greater whole yet belonging to a particular group appears to be part of the human experience.

Desmond Tutu put forth a position on this subject regarding *ubuntu*, meaning something like humanity's capacity for forgiveness:

> A person with ubuntu is open and available to others, affirming of others, does not feel threatened that others are able and good, for he or she has a proper self-assurance that comes from knowing that he or she belongs in a greater whole and is diminished when others are humiliated or diminished, when others are tortured or oppressed.

(Tutu, 1999, p. 31)

And Walt Whitman (1855/2010), thinking of himself and beyond, wrote, "For every atom belonging to me as good belongs to you. I loafe and invite my soul" (p. 15).

Hopefully, the current volume will add to our understanding of how an unwanted sense of not-belonging can be alleviated and how a sense of belonging can be achieved and maintained so that we feel less threatened by others. Hopefully, these contributions will also help people change their views from those of "hyperindividualistic" selves to those of selves sharing a place in a much wider universe.

References

Ackerman, S. (2017). Exploring Freud's resistance to the oceanic feeling. *Journal of the American Psychoanalytic Association, 65*(1), 9–31.

Aronson, E., & Mills, J. (1959). The effect of severity of initiation on liking for a group. *Journal of Abnormal and Social Psychology, 59*(2), 177–181.

Baumeister, R. F., & Leary, M. R. (1995). The need to belong: desire for interpersonal attachments as a fundamental human motivation. *Psychological Bulletin, 117*(3), 497–529.

Baumeister, R. F., & Wotman, S. R. (1994). *Breaking hearts: the two sides of unrequited love*. New York: Guilford.

Bohm, D. (1980). *Wholeness and the implicate order*. London: Routledge & Kegan Paul.

Bohm, D., & Hiley, N. (1975). On the intuitive understanding of nonlocality as implied by quantum theory. *Foundations of Physics, 5*, 93–109.

Bowlby, J. (1973). *Attachment and loss* (Vol. 2). New York: Basic Books.

Cooper, P. C. (2002). The enigma of the oceanic feeling: revisioning the psychoanalytic theory of mysticism. *Psychoanalytic Review, 89*(20), 286–290.

Crisp, R. J., Ferrow, C. V., Rosenthal, H. E. S., Walsh, J., Bissett, J., & Penn, N. M. K. (2009). Interpersonal attachment predicts identification with groups. *Journal of Experimental Social Psychology, 45*, 115–122.

Epstein, M. (1990). Beyond the oceanic feelings: psychoanalytic study of Buddhist meditation. *International Review of Psycho-Analysis, 17*, 159–165.

Erikson, E. H. (1962). *Young man Luther: a study in psychoanalysis and history*. New York: Norton. Originally published 1958.

Erikson, E. H. (1980). *Identity and the life cycle*. New York: Norton. Originally published 1959.

Fisher, D. L. (1976). Sigmund Freud and Romain Rolland: the terrestrial animal and his great oceanic friend. *American Imago, 33*, 1–59.

Freud, S. (1946). *Civilization and its discontents* (J. Riviere, Trans.). London: Hogarth Press. Originally published 1930.

Freud, S. (1949). *The ego and the id*. London: Hogarth Press. Originally published 1923.

Fromm, E., & Suzuki, D. T. (1963). *Zen Buddhism and psychoanalysis*. New York: Grove Press.

Gilbert, D. (2005). *Stumbling on happiness*. New York: Random House.

Hagan, J., & Peterson, R. D. (Eds.). (1995). *Crime and inequality*. Stanford: Stanford University Press.

Haybron, D. M. (2008). *The pursuit of unhappiness: the elusive psychological well-being*. Oxford: Oxford University Press.

Horney, K. (1945). *Our inner conflicts*. New York: Norton.

Ishiguro, K. (2000). *When we were orphans*. New York: Knopf.

Ivanhoe, P. J., Flanagan, O., Harrison, V., Sarkissian, H., & Schwitzgebel, E. (Eds.). (2018). *The oneness hypothesis*. New York: Columbia University Press.

Kahneman, D., Diener, E., & Schwarz, N. (Eds.). (1999). *Well-being: the foundations of hedonic psychology*. New York: Russell Sage Foundation.

Kovel, J. (1991). *History and spirit: an inquiry into the philosophy of liberation*. Boston: Beacon Press.

Lachmann, F. M., & Beebe, B. (1989). Oneness fantasies revisited. *Psychoanalytic Psychology*, 6(2), 137–149.

Markus, H. R., & Kitayama, S. (1991). Culture and the self: implications for cognition, emotion, and motivation. *Psychological Review*, 98(2), 224–253.

Marcus, R. F., & Sanders-Reio, J. (2001). The influence of attachment on school completion. *School Psychology Quarterly*, 16(4), 427–444.

McKeon, L. (2019, December 7). Claire Messud on displacement, belonging, art, and family. *New York Review of Books*, Newsletter.

Mikulincer, M., & Shaver, P. K. (2012). An attachment perspective on psychopathology. *World Psychiatry*, 11, 11–15.

Nozick, R. (1974). *Anarchy, state and utopia*. New York: Basic Books.

O'Neill, J. (1993). *Ecology, policy, and politics: human well-being and the natural world*. London: Routledge.

Parsons, W. B. (1999). *The enigma of the oceanic feeling: revisioning the psychoanalytic of mysticism*. New York: Oxford University Press.

Rawls, J. (1999). *A theory of justice* (rev. ed.). Cambridge, MA: Harvard University Press.

Roland, A. (1988). *In search of self in India and Japan*. Princeton: Princeton University Press.

Schachter, J. (2002). *Transference: shibboleth or albatross?* Hillsdale: Analytic Press.

Sen, A. K. (1977). Rational fools: a critique of the behavioral foundations of economic theory. *Philosophy and Public Affairs*, 6(4), 317–344.

Shunyata in Mahayan Buddhism. (2016, May 15). Retrieved from www.moradnazari.com

Silverman, L., Lachmann, F. M., & Milich, R. (1982). *The search for oneness*. New York: International Universities Press.

Simmonds, J. F. (2006). The oceanic feelings and a sea change: historical challenges to reductionist attitudes to religion and spiritualism from within psychoanalysis. *Psychoanalytic Psychology*, 23(1), 128–142.

Soeng, M. (2010). *The heart of the universe: exploring the Heart Sutra*. Somerville: Wisdom.

Sorkin, A. D. (2013, December 4). Economic inequality: a matter of trust. *New Yorker*, Newsletter.

Steele, H., Steele, M., & Croft, C. (2008). Early attachment predicts emotion recognition at 6 and 11 years old. *Attachment and Human Development*, 10(4), 379–393.

Sullivan, H. S. (1950). The illusion of personal individuality. *Psychiatry*, 13, 317–332.

Sullivan, H. S. (1953). *The interpersonal theory of psychiatry*. New York: W. W. Norton.

Suzuki, D. T. (1938). *Zen Buddhism and its influence on Japanese culture*. Kyoto: Eastern Buddhist Society.

Tierney, J., & Baumeister, R. F. (2019). *The power of bad: how the negativity effect rules us and how we can rule it*. New York: Penguin Random House.

Tutu, D. (1999). *No future without forgiveness*. New York: Random House.

Uslaner, E. M., & Brown, M. (2005). Inequality, trust, and civic engagement. *American Politics Research*, 33, 868–894.

Verhagen, M., Lodder, G. M. A., & Baumeister, R. (2018). Unmet belongingness needs but not high belongingness needs alone predict adverse well-being: a response surface modeling approach. *Journal of Personality*, 86, 498–507.

Werman, D. S. (1977). Sigmund Freud and Romain Rolland. *International Review of Psycho-Analysis*, 4, 225–242.

Werman, D. S. (1986). On the nature of the oceanic experience. *Journal of the American Psychoanalytic Association*, 34, 123–139.

Whitman, W. (2010). *Song of myself and other poems by Walt Whitman* (R. Hass, Introduction). Berkeley: Electronic Source. Originally published 1855.

Willock, B., Bohm, L. C., & Curtis, R. C. (Eds). (2011). *Loneliness and longing: conscious and unconscious aspects*. New York: Routledge.

Winnicott, D. W. (1964). *The child, the family and the outside world*. Harmondsworth: Penguin Books.

Index

For Product Safety Concerns and Information please contact our EU
representative GPSR@taylorandfrancis.com
Taylor & Francis Verlag GmbH, Kaufingerstraße 24, 80331 München, Germany

9 780367 671969